Achieving Economic Development in the Era of Globalization

Despite some significant gains in promoting economic growth and improving living conditions globally over the past five decades, many regions of the world still remain plagued by economic underdevelopment, with large numbers of people trapped in grinding poverty and hopelessness. At the turn of the new millennium, in an unprecedented display of international commitment to improve the lives of an estimated 2.7 to three billion people who live on under $2 per day, the 189 members of the United Nations issued the ambitious Millennium Declaration at the Millennium Summit in September 2000. The world leaders directed the UN to produce a "roadmap" for achieving the Declaration's goal by 2015. The result was the formulation of eight Millennium Development Goals (MDGs) and its 18 specific and quantitative targets for progress in areas such as halving by 2015 the proportion of people living in absolute poverty in 1990, including an improvement in education, health and the environment. While the MDGs are admirable, it has been suggested that the Declaration's architects do not provide sufficient guidelines or a coherent roadmap as to how these goals are to be achieved.

This book fills this gap by drawing on the lessons of some six decades of development experiences. It illuminates that the theoretical insights and accumulated empirical knowledge of development have much to offer the various stakeholders as they embark once again to promote economic development. Sharma highlights the fact that we now have a better understanding of what works and why, and concludes that, with less than a decade left to achieve the goals, it is time to utilize this knowledge to help translate the bold vision of the MDGs into action.

The book is relevant to subject areas such as economic development, globalization, international political economy and development studies, among many others.

Shalendra D. Sharma is Professor in the Department of Politics at the University of San Francisco. He is the author of *The Asian Financial Crisis: Crisis, Reform and Recovery* and *Democracy and Development in India*, which won the Choice Outstanding Academic Title for 1999.

Routledge studies in development economics

Achieving Economic Development in the Era of Globalization

Shalendra D. Sharma

Routledge
Taylor & Francis Group

LONDON AND NEW YORK

First published 2008
by Routledge
2 Park Square, Milton Park, Abingdon, Oxon OX14 4RN

Simultaneously published in the USA and Canada
by Routledge
711 Third Ave, New York, NY 10017

Routledge is an imprint of the Taylor & Francis Group, an informa business

© 2008 Shalendra D. Sharma

Typeset in Times by Wearset Ltd, Boldon, Tyne and Wear

British Library Cataloguing in Publication Data
A catalogue record for this book is available from the British Library

Library of Congress Cataloging in Publication Data
A catalog record for this book has been requested

First issued in paperback in 2013

ISBN13: 978-0-415-74846-9 (pbk)
ISBN13: 978-0-415-77180-1 (hbk)
ISBN13: 978-0-203-93781-5 (ebk)

Contents

Acknowledgments

This project has incurred debts of gratitude too numerous to fully express. Nevertheless, I would like to thank a number of colleagues who graciously took time from their busy schedules to comment on whole or parts of the manuscript, and those who provided support and encouragement through discussions, debates and occasionally covering for my classes. These friends and colleagues have made an indelible impression on this study and helped to make it better.

A good portion of the book was written during my sabbatical (2006–2007) while I was a visiting professor in the Department of Political Science at Leiden University, The Netherlands. The collegial and vibrant intellectual environment at Leiden was most conducive to the writing of this book. At Leiden I would like to thank my colleagues: Andy Andeweg, Jan Erk, Madeleine Hosli, Tanya Aalberts, Huib Pellikaan, Ruud Koole, Hans Vollaard, Marius de Geus, Paul Nieuwenburg, Kees Brants, Richard Sherman, Oda Crannenburg, Jan Beyers, Maria Spirova, Imke Harbers, Gerardo Scherlis, Bal Gopal Shreshta and Evangelos Venetis. At the University of San Francisco I wish to express my appreciation to Hartmut Fischer, Andrew Heinze, Roberta Johnson, Laleh Shahideh, Vamsee Juluri, Alberto Andretta, Nancy Campagna, Jay Gonzales, Horacio Camblong, Tetteh Kofi, Richard Kozicki, Michael Lehmann, Man Lui-Lau, Jacques Artus, Elliot Neaman, Tony Fels, Pavo Lutomski, Ellen Herda, Patrick Murphy, Michael Stanfield, Steve Roddy, John Nelson, Charles N'Cho, Vicky Siu, Michael Torre, John Veitch, Bruce Wydick, Bryan Whaley, Brian Weiner, Annick Wibben, Stephen Zunes, and former Dean, Stanley Nel, and current Dean, Jennifer Turpin. Special thanks to Zaheer Baber at the University of Toronto, and to my dedicated research assistants: Kiran Torani, Harpreet Sawhney, Rohit Kapuria, Gaurav Rana, Leon Smith, and Alyssa V. Ruiz de Esparza for their help over the years. I would also like to acknowledge Mandira Puri, Venu Bhakhri, and Laura Grace for their assistance. For proficient administrative assistance and support I thank Cheryl Czekala, Anna Matusik, and Kimberly Garrett, and at Leiden, Mariska Roos, Marianne Boere, and Danielle van Gaalen-Lovink. Also at Leiden I am deeply indebted to Bart Bosman of the International Tax Centre. I would also like to acknowledge the support friends and colleagues at the IMF and the World Bank have graciously given me over the years. My good gym friends, retired attorneys Yuri Walsh and Winston

Yuen, provided constant encouragement amidst heavy lifting. Heartfelt thanks to Ruby Tsang and Ken Cheung for their generosity and friendship. Ken's superb computer expertise helped us a great deal. None of these individuals bear any responsibility for the flaws in my analysis, albeit they deserve much of the credit for that which proves useful.

Thanks also to Robert Langham, Terry Clague, and Sarah Hastings at Routledge for their professionalism and patience, and for shepherding the manuscript into a book. My profound thanks also to our large extended family for the support and encouragement they have given me over the years. My greatest debt, however, is to my wife Vivian and our son Krishan. They have seen this book's long journey from the beginning to end. Despite our many travels and my many weeks of absences from home, they never wavered once in their support and let me work on the book. It is safe to say that without their support and love this book would never have been written. I dedicate this book to them.

1   Introduction

The distinguished British historian E.H. Carr (1961) once observed that history is not a single, well-defined narrative but a terrain of contestation between competing and evolving interpretations whose influence is as much shaped by time and place as by any given set of facts. Thus, it is not surprising that the past and its legacies are constantly being reassessed or, to use the more familiar term, "revised" by successive generations of scholars. Perhaps nowhere has this been more the case than in the broad interdisciplinary field of "economic development." This quintessentially American project embarked with unabashed optimism in the immediate post-war period has preoccupied some of the most gifted minds in economics, political science, sociology, and other disciplines for the better part of six decades.

Reflecting the hubris of the decolonization era, these first-generation scholars (often condescendingly lumped as "modernization theorists") believed that a bright new dawn awaited the newly emancipated nations. Trusting modernity exigencies and consumed by the enthusiasm and buoyancy of the times, they boldly predicted it would be simply a matter of time before the "newly emerging nations" overcame the legacies of colonialism and laid the foundations of a just political and economic order (Gilman 2003; Packenham 1973; Rosen 1985). Many of the era's luminaries, including Paul Rosenstein-Rodan, Arthur Lewis, Nicholas Kaldor, Walt Rostow, Simon Kuznets, Joan Robinson, Jan Tinbergen, Gunnar Myrdal, Karl Deutsch, Gabriel Almond, David Apter, and Edward Shils among others, were convinced that their particular ideas, growth models, theories and policies, if judiciously applied, would propel the new nations towards self-generating economic abundance and stable representative government (Tignor 2005). With missionary zeal some members of this legendary "epistemic community" of development professionals dutifully offered their services and advice to presidents, prime ministers, dictators, and anyone else who cared to listen on how to rapidly transform traditional and economically poor societies into modern prosperous ones.

However, by the mid-1960s, optimism gave way to disillusionment as the failure of the new nations to generate sustained economic growth and the inability of the fragile political systems to mediate dissent and conflict became evident. Rather, this combustible mix not only produced economic stagnation, but also pushed once promising experiments in nation-building towards authoritarianism and other forms of tyranny and despotism. The "modernization paradigm" quickly fell out of vogue as it came under sustained attacks from all quarters, in particular from the proponents of "dependency theory." The *dependistas* accused modernization for its ahistoricity and willful eurocentrism, and how their blinkered and anachronistic worldview led them astray and prevented them from seeing the continuing exploitative effects of neo-colonial domination on the newly emerging nations.[1] However, dependency, in particular the radical variant (which was heavy on critique and light on viable alternatives), peaked remarkably quickly, to be superseded by an austere neoliberalism in the early 1980s.[2] Pointing to the robust linkage between free markets and East Asia's economic success, neoliberalism, with its emphasis on international openness, free markets and limits on the role of the state, in one broad sweep summarily dismissed earlier paradigms. In particular, neoliberals went to great lengths to discredit the intellectual foundations of "development economics," especially the post-war "Keynesian consensus" which had long preached the virtues of state-led development.[3]

However, even as shifting intellectual fads came and went, the reality on the ground remained as intractable as ever. Indeed, the record of the past several decades of development experience ruefully described by William Easterly (2001) as the era of "the elusive quest for growth" is littered with the skeletons of a veritable array of extravagant models and grandiose plans and programs once seductively proffered as the panacea to the problems of poverty, inequality, and economic backwardness. Despite the dedicated efforts of many, not to mention the incalculable cost in treasure, the results have been conspicuously disappointing – a few successes in a landscape full of many heart-wrenching failures.

Clearly humbled by the failure to achieve the long-predicted economic "take-off," the current (and more chastened) generation of scholars are more circumspect and cautious. Unlike their predecessors, few now dare to propose a single, universal set of models and prescriptions, offering instead more tentative, if not more tempered, analysis. As never before, each theory, method, practice, presupposition, outcome and policy lesson of development comes under the microscope – every minute detail doggedly (and sometimes acrimoniously) scrutinized, exhaustively analyzed, and constantly revised. Although caution has produced a deep ambivalence, a sort of timid intellectual relativism regarding development, it has also made us better appreciate the "paradox of development" with all its nuances, ambiguities, contingencies and multidimensional complexities. The irony is that we now know far more about the political economy of development (at least, with much greater certainty) than we care to admit.

No doubt, what constitutes development and how best to achieve it will remain as passionately contested as ever. This is inevitable as economic development, like all human endeavors, is clearly an immutable process of trials, tests and experimentations across time and space. Nevertheless, certain tangible "truths" can be gleaned from the lessons of over six decades of varied and contrasting development experiences, including the ideas, insights, and intuitions of an entire generation of experts buried in a vast body of research and scholarship. Cumulatively, they offer invaluable clues regarding how development works, why some things work better than others and how it can be made to work even better. This rich and precocious repository of knowledge and practical information can serve as a "best practices" manual and potentially help the various stakeholders in development avoid not only the more egregious failures, but also the less obvious but no less wrenching ones. It is coincidental, yet propitious, as the international community embarks again on yet another ambitious development agenda under the guise of the Millennium Development Goals (MDG); it is imperative to revisit the lessons of the past to draw some tangible lessons that may help in translating the MDGs' bold vision into action, and thereby help alleviate some of the world's most inexorable problems.

The following pages discusses some of the more exigent lessons the development ledger has bequeathed us, in particular how the international community can work together to effectively translate and implement the MDGs. This is a rare opportunity, for seldom we have seen such an unprecedented display of international commitment to improve the lives of an estimated 2.7 to three billion people who live on under $2 per day.[4] Ever since the 189 members of the United Nations issued the Millennium Declaration at the Millennium Summit in September 2000, the race has been on to meet head-on some of the most intractable problems facing the world. At that Summit, the world leaders directed the UN to produce a "roadmap" for achieving the Declaration's goal by 2015. The result was the formulation of eight Millennium Development Goals and 18 specific and quantitative targets for progress in areas such as halving by 2015 the proportion of people living in absolute poverty in 1990, including improving education, health, social services, and the environment.

Despite "developments"-checkered history, the international community's subtle confidence in the MDGs reaffirms hope and the promise of a better future for the world's teeming masses. After all, there is nothing natural or inevitable in existing patterns of development and inequality. They are products of human actions, and therefore can be mitigated through determined and more prescient policy choices. Although there are no guarantees that the fruits of development will mature quickly enough, or the rewards be commensurate with the laborious toil and sacrifice that is undeniably required, and while future efforts will continue to suffer the vicissitudes and transgressions to which all human endeavors are subject – despite all this, development that enhances the dignity and well-being of all is not only a moral imperative, it is also possible. The negative externalities associated with poverty, disease and hopelessness such as conflict, violence and terrorism, among other ills, are simply too costly to ignore. Arguably, we are at a historic juncture where the moral imperatives to promote sound economic and political development and the security imperatives converge as never before. Indeed, what is at stake with the MDGs is the opportunity for hundreds of millions of people to escape grinding poverty, preventable and treatable diseases, and illiteracy, and in so doing boost prospects for long-term global security and peace. However, with only a decade remaining, progress towards the MDGs has been slower and more uneven across regions than originally envisaged (Bouillon *et al.* 2005). Clearly, the disadvantaged can hardly be expected to patiently wait forever for the charitable benevolence of the privileged, or like "trickle-down" before it, hope that the rising tide will lift all boats. Meeting the MDGs is both an achievable and an urgent task, and even if only a part of the MDGs' targets are met it will improve the lives of the world's poor immeasurably (Wolfensohn 2005). It is with these enormously important concerns in mind, as well as the tantalizing possibilities, that this book is written.

Finally, a few words on pedagogy. Over the past several years numerous technical briefs, analytical reports, policy papers, government-commissioned reports, journal articles and books have been written on almost all aspects of development. The purpose of this book is not so much to present new research, but to systematically elucidate the seemingly incongruent set of ideas and insights from a burgeoning body of scholarship, and to provide an intimately integrative and reflective analytical narrative of important "lessons" regarding what works in development and how these ideas and strategies can be practically utilized to resolve contemporaneous development challenges. Since my intended readership goes beyond the specialized research community in economics, political science, international relations and development studies, to include most social scientists, policymakers, and the informed general public, I have deliberately tried to avoid formal models, mathematical equations, and econometric tables, including the esoteric jargon and dichotomized abstractions of particular disciplines.

The six core chapters in this book are organized around thematic issues. Chapter 2 provides a broad overview and interpretation of some of the fundamental lessons learned from over six decades of development experience, highlighting what has worked and why, as well as the gaps, ambiguities and discrepancies that continue to limit our understanding of economic development. Moreover, it provides a broad assessment of economic globalization – in particular, its evolution and ever-shifting manifestations, the impact and implications of its spreading and far-flung networks of commerce and social intercourse on both the international and domestic economies, its structural and programmatic limitations and possibilities, and how developing countries can better navigate their way through an evermore enmeshed, integrated and interconnected world.

Chapters 3 to 7 bring some of the issues discussed in Chapter 2 into sharper focus. Chapter 3 examines the complex relationship between democracy, good governance and economic development, exploring conditions that can both impede and foster good governance. It illustrates how the institutional deficit that characterizes so many developing and transitional countries – weak and arbitrary governance, poor protection of civil liberties, inadequate regulatory and legal framework to guarantee property rights, enforce contracts and reduce the transaction costs – deprive these countries of needed productive investment and economic growth. Therefore, improving the quality of governance is essential for economic development. Yet, what is good governance? What types of policies and institutions have the most positive and measurable effects on improving governance? What kinds of institutional arrangements are associated with economic growth and poverty reduction? How best to promote and sustain good governance, especially in the world's poorest countries? Drawing on recent research, this chapter will show how democratic governance influences economic growth. Specifically, secure private property rights that give incentives to individuals to be productive, institutionalization of the rule of law, especially constraints against executives, and electoral mechanisms that give citizens the ability to evict the "rascals" are essential to promoting growth. Moreover, democratization and decentralization without simultaneous strengthening of property rights and the rule of law may not always lead to effective democratic governance or sustained economic growth.

Chapter 4 discusses the relationship between rural development and poverty alleviation. Since the vast majority of the people living in extreme poverty depend either directly or indirectly on agriculture for their livelihood, sustained growth in agricultural production and productivity is one of the most important ways to alleviate poverty and hunger and to achieve the MDGs. Because of the inherent "urban bias" embedded in most development strategies, the chapter deliberately begins by belaboring the obvious: since the vast majority of the world's poor depend directly or indirectly on agriculture for their livelihood, the key to reducing global poverty and the proliferation of urban sprawl is rapid acceleration of agricultural and rural development. However, for this to happen the pace of rural and agricultural development must be greatly accelerated. Public investments in rural services and infrastructure, the application of modern science and technology, and the use of new biotechnologies – the so-called "second-generation green revolution" – will be critical to boost and sustain agricultural growth, meet the food demands of a growing human population and reduce global poverty.

While the wealthy OECD countries provide about $50 billion per year in official development assistance to poor countries, there is a more effective way the rich nations can provide long-term assistance to poor countries: trade liberalization. Chapter 5 focuses on global trade, highlighting the importance of reviving and successfully completing the Doha Round of trade negotiations. The chapter begins with a discussion of the reasons behind the stalled trade talks – including the series of events that led to the failure of the Cancun Ministerial Meetings in September 2003 and to the eventual "collapse" at Geneva in June 2006, where the Doha Round was suspended. It also highlights the economic implications of the failure, as well as the necessary trade-offs member governments of the WTO need to make to revive the Doha Round. The chapter underscores that the Doha Round's commitment to multilateral, reciprocal and non-discriminatory trade liberalization offers the best single chance for the international community to achieve the development promise of trade and progress towards the MDGs. Specifically, to realize the potential of Doha, the OECD countries must take the lead by further opening their markets to the developing countries in agriculture, textiles and apparel. However, since agriculture could account for some two-thirds of the potential gains from trade liberalization, meaningful reduction in agricultural protection may be the single greatest contribution that OECD countries can make to the Doha Round. Similarly, the middle-income countries must also do their part and reduce barriers in their protected agricultural markets, besides bringing down their relatively high tariffs in manufactures. Since trade restrictions are much higher in developing countries, further liberalization, especially by the middle-income developing countries, is essential. Finally, the international community through multilateral institutions can help developing countries, particularly the least-developed countries (LDCs), to adjust to trade liberalization and enhance their capacity to take advantage of the more open global markets.

Chapter 6 reviews the conflicting "truths," "half-truths" and myths about foreign aid – a topic long an arena of partisan debates, and one that gained notoriety when in the midst of the tsunami disaster in 2005, the UN Undersecretary-General for Humanitarian Affairs, Jan Egeland, suggested that the world's richest nations are "stingy" when it comes to giving development assistance. This chapter cuts through the furor and acrimony that often characterizes discussions about foreign aid by dispassionately examining the various claims for and against aid. In particular, it critically reviews the recent Sachs–Easterly debate on foreign aid, as well as challenging the commonly held perception that OECD countries already give too much aid or that "aid does not work." Rather, drawing on a broad range of comparative cases, including recent cross-country evidence, this chapter shows that the impact of aid is far more intricate and subtle, and that well-targeted aid can have a positive impact on economic development.

Since aid and debt are intrinsically linked, for aid to be effective it needs to be better aligned with debt relief. Chapter 7 illustrates how the high levels of external debt pose a serious constraint on the ability of many poor countries to pursue sustainable economic development and reduce poverty. It reviews the efficacy of various debt-relief strategies, most notably the World Bank and the IMF's Heavily Indebted Poor Countries (HIPC) Initiative, in reducing the debt burden of some of the world's poorest nations, as well as the recent G-8 agreement to an unprecedented 100 percent debt cancellation for some of the world's most heavily indebted poor countries. The chapter argues that while both initiatives are a positive step towards debt relief and sustainability, the 100 percent debt cancellation should be extended, especially to the heavily indebted poor countries in sub-Saharan Africa. To realize the full potential of debt relief, donor countries will have to be more generous and the recipient countries need to undertake deeper structural reforms. The conclusion – or more appropriately "the postscript," as development is a continuing and salient process – reflects on the continuing challenges the international community faces in achieving the MDGs.

2 Promoting development
What works?

In September 2000, at the historic Millennium Summit, the 189 member-states of the United Nations (including the heads of state of 147 countries present at the Summit) unanimously adopted a document known as the "UN Millennium Declaration." Under this document they pledged to work towards a world in which sustainable economic development, the eradication of chronic poverty, and the promotion of peace and social justice would receive the highest priority. After consultations with a number of international organizations within the UN system, as well as the International Monetary Fund (IMF), the World Bank, and the Organization for Economic Cooperation and Development (OECD), the UN General Assembly recognized seven "Millennium Development Goals" (MDGs) as an integral component of Millennium Declaration (see Table 2.1).

In December 2000, UN Secretary-General Kofi Annan was authorized by the General Assembly to prepare a "roadmap" of how to achieve the goals laid out in the Millennium Declaration. After extensive deliberations, Annan's office issued a "consensual roadmap" in September 2001. Drawing on the broadly agreed-to seven goals, the roadmap also proposed an additional "eighth goal." Felicitously termed "a global partnership for development," the eighth goal, while it does not have time-bound and quantitative targets, comprehensively outlined the "mutual responsibilities and obligations" of the UN member-states. In December 2001, the UN General Assembly formally adopted resolution 5695 approving the eighth goal. At the UN's inaugural International Conference on Financing for Development in Monterrey, Mexico, in March 2002, some 50 heads of state and over 200 ministers (including leaders from the private sector and NGOs), from both the developed and developing countries, agreed on a new compact that stressed mutual responsibilities in the quest for the MDGs.[1] The "Monterrey Compact" called on the developing countries to deepen their economic reform programs and improve governance, and for the wealthy countries to step up their support by providing more financial assistance and access to their markets.

In accepting the eight MDGs, each country made commitments to an ambitious time-bound and measurable program of development "goals" and "targets" by the year 2015. Specifically, as Table 2.1 illustrates, the eight goals (each corresponding to a key development aim in one dimension of human welfare), are

Table 2.1 Millennium development goals: goals and targets

Goal One: *Eradicate extreme hunger and poverty*
 Target 1: Halve between 1990 and 2015 the proportion of people living in extreme poverty (or the proportion of people whose income is less than $1 a day).
 Target 2: Halve between 1990 and 2015 the proportion of people who suffer from hunger.

Goal Two: *Achieve universal primary education*
 Target 3: Ensure that by 2015 children everywhere complete primary schooling.

Goal Three: *Promote gender equality and empower women*
 Target 4: Eliminate gender disparity in primary and secondary education, preferably by 2005, and in all levels of education no later than 2015.

Goal Four: *Reduce child mortality*
 Target 5: Between 1990 and 2015 reduce by two-thirds under-five child mortality rate.

Goal Five: *Improve maternal health*
 Target 6: Reduce the maternal mortality ratio by three-quarters between 1990 and 2015.

Goal Six: *Combat HIV/AIDS, malaria and other diseases*
 Target 7: Have halted by 2015 and begun to reverse the spread of HIV/AIDS.
 Target 8: Have halted and begun to reverse the incidence of malaria and other major diseases by 2015.

Goal Seven: *Ensure environmental sustainability*
 Target 9: Implement national strategies for sustainable development by 2005 by integrating the principles of sustainable development into country policies and programs, so as to reverse the loss of environmental resources by 2015.
 Target 10: Halve by 2015 the proportion of people without sustainable access to safe drinking-water.
 Target 11: Have achieved by 2020 a significant improvement in the lives of at least 100 million slum-dwellers.

Goal Eight: *Develop a global partnership for development*
 Target 12: Develop further an open, rule-based, predictable, non-discriminatory trading and financial system.
 Target 13: Address the special needs of the least developed countries via tariff- and quota-free access for exports, enhanced program of debt relief, including the cancellation of official bilateral debt, and more generous official development assistance for countries committed to poverty reduction.
 Target 14: Address the special needs of land-locked countries and small island developing states through the Program of Action for the Sustainable Development of Small Island Developing States.
 Target 15: Deal comprehensively with the debt problems of developing countries through national and international measures in order to make debt sustainable in the long term.
 Target 16: In cooperation with developing countries, develop and implement strategies for decent and productive work for youth.
 Target 17: In cooperation with pharmaceutical companies, provide access to affordable essential drugs in developing countries.
 Target 18: In cooperation with the private sector, make available the benefits of new technologies, especially information and communications technologies.

Source: *UN Millennium Project 2005.*

backed by 18 specific targets designed to quantify the broad goals in a measurable manner. In addition, there are some 48 indicators, each of which is associated with a specific target. These are meant to be monitoring variables whose evolution can be evaluated to verify progress toward the goals. The UN "country teams" are to assist countries integrate the MDGs into their national development frameworks and tailor the MDGs to national circumstances by building them into national development strategies and policies, including incorporating them in budgets and ministries' priorities. The goals are also to be integrated into assistance frameworks and programs. For the more than 70 of the world's poorest countries, this means that the MDGs must be integrated in their main strategic tool – the nationally owned poverty reduction strategy – which relates to national budgets, development activities and other assistance frameworks. Finally, each year, the secretary-general's office is to prepare a "monitoring report" for the UN General Assembly on progress achieved towards implementing the Millennium Declaration, based on data on the 48 selected indicators, aggregated at global and regional levels.[2]

The challenge

While the MDGs have been applauded for their bold and ambitious vision, there is also much skepticism. The concern is that, good intentions notwithstanding, by creating unrealistic expectations (as meeting many of the goals is simply beyond the reach of most countries) the initiative is setting itself for failure. Since the MDGs architects provide insufficient guidelines or a coherent roadmap as how these goals are to be achieved, the fear is not only that the MDG will become the latest casualty in a long list of unrealized UN-sponsored programs, but that failure could also lead to resignation and the pernicious "development fatigue." Indeed, such concerns are not misplaced, as official action to follow through on their promises has long belied public pronouncements.[3] If the past is any guide, intense activity on the development front is generally followed by long periods of benign ambivalence as the uncomfortable truths about development become visible and stakeholders – especially the rich countries – lose heart and interest. Seemingly cognizant of this, even the most indefatigable proponents of the MDGs – who are quick to assure that the MDGs are different from earlier efforts in that they are mutually reinforcing and that the MDGs have established specific and quantifiable yardsticks for measuring results – recognize that achieving the Millennium Development Goals will not be easy.[4]

At a minimum, translating the MDGs' bold vision into action will require both an unprecedented international cooperation and national commitment – what Jeffrey Sachs (2003) has called "a shared stewardship between rich and poor."[5] This is paramount if the widening gap (between the 16 percent of the global population who live in the most affluent countries and control 81 percent of total global income and the 84 percent who share the remaining 19 percent) is to be ameliorated (World Bank 2003a: 235). However, there is no guarantee that the international consensus on the MDGs will hold. If anything, the discordant history of North–South relations is replete with examples of how competing agendas and interests can undermine the best of intentions. Moreover, since the major responsibility for implementing the MDGs lies with national governments, many developing countries (both low-income and middle-income[6]) are hardly up to the task. The implicit assumption that these countries in short order will substantially improve their domestic governance, adopt policies that promote economic growth with equity, and demonstrate a determined commitment to the MDGs through expeditious implementation is, to say the least, overly optimistic. This is especially true for the 40 or so low-income or LDCs (the least-developed countries) who face the sobering task of simultaneously building their political-institutional capacities while generating sustained levels of economic growth in order to meet their commitments.

By way of preamble, it is important to reiterate that behind the cold statistics of the estimated 2.7 to three billion individuals who currently live on less than $2 per person per day are real human beings. For them, the lack of progress on the MDGs will have immediate and tragic consequences. It will mean that every week in the developing world, some 200,000 children under the age of five will continue to die of preventable diseases, and 115 million children will not be attending school. It will also mean that in sub-Saharan Africa alone, two million people will die of AIDS in 2007. Suffice it to note, even if the MDGs met only a part of their targets, this would improve the lives of the world's poor immeasurably. Clearly, we have the resources and know-how to alleviate human suffering. The task now is implementation – to translate the MDGs' vision into action.

The lessons: what works

The famous Kuznets hypothesis (1955, 1963) claimed that economic growth and inequality are related in an inverted U-shaped curve. That is, in the early stages of economic development, income distribution tends to worsen and does not improve until countries reach "middle-income" status. The implications of the Kuznets hypothesis were unambiguous: since in the early stages economic growth leads to more inequality, then poverty will take many years, if not decades, to decline. Heavily influenced by Kuznets' works, Chenery and his co-authors (1974: iii), confidently declared, "it is now clear that more than a decade of rapid growth in underdeveloped countries has been of little or no benefit to perhaps a third of their population." Similarly, Adelman and Morris (1973: 189–93), argued that

> development is accompanied by an absolute as well as a relative decline in the average income of the very poor.... The frightening implication is that hundreds of millions of desperately poor people ... have been hurt rather than helped by economic development.

However, as it turned out, the Kuznets hypothesis proved to be fatally flawed.[7] To the contrary, if decades of development experience have made anything irrefutably clear it is that the most powerful force for the reduction of poverty is sustained economic growth.[8] It also means that there is no trade-off between policies that foster economic growth and poverty reduction – rather, the higher the level of asset inequality, the lower the gains of growth to the poor (Solimano *et al.* 2000). Overall, the evidence unequivocally shows that countries which have been most successful in reducing poverty are those that have grown the fastest, whereas those that have stagnated have seen increases in their poverty levels. The reason for this is simple: in the poorest countries with high levels of *absolute poverty*,[9] even if current incomes were redistributed without reducing the total national income, most people would still be poor as there is simply not enough income to go around. Therefore, the poor generally benefit from rising aggregate incomes and suffer from economic contractions. During the 1990s, it was estimated that the "growth elasticity of poverty" (or how much poverty will decline in percentage terms with a given percentage rise in economic growth) was between –2.0 and –3.0 (Adams 2003; Ravallion and Chen 1997). This meant that a 10 percent increase in economic growth (however measured) would result in a 20–30 percent decrease in poverty (however measured). However, new estimates by Bhalla (2002) suggest that the earlier growth elasticities of poverty are too low, and that the "correct" growth elasticity of poverty is around –5.0.[10] In other words, in a large selection of developing countries in which roughly half of the population lives in poverty, a 10 percent increase in economic growth will reduce the percentage of the poor to about 25 percent, rather than to between 35 and 40 percent as estimated earlier.[11]

The experiences of sub-Saharan Africa, China and India are illustrative. Artadi and Sala-i-Martin (2003) note that while the rest of the world's economy grew at an annual rate of 2 percent from 1960 to 2002, the growth rate in Africa has been dismal. From 1974 through the mid-1990s, growth was negative, reaching –1.5 percent in 1990–1994. As a consequence, hundreds of millions of people in Africa have become poorer: one-half of the African continent lives below the poverty line. In sub-Saharan Africa, per capita GDP is now less than it was in 1974 – having declined by over 11 percent. In 1970, one in ten poor people in the world lived in Africa. However, by 2000 the number was closer to one in two. This translates into 360 million people in 2000, compared to 140 million in 1975. Tragically, much of Africa today is caught in a vicious "poverty trap" – a condition which makes a poor country simply too impoverished to achieve sustained economic growth (Sachs 2005). On the other hand, the number of rural poor in China was reduced from 250 million in 1978 to about 26.4 million in 2001 mainly due to the high annual growth of GDP which averaged 9.5 percent between the start of the reforms in 1979 and 2001. This enabled per capita GDP to increase almost six times over the same period (Stern 2002: 109–43; also Bhalla 2002).

However one interprets the data, what clearly emerges is that the rapid economic growth of China and India (both of which account for about one-third of the world's population) has contributed significantly to global poverty reduction (Bhalla 2002; Goldin and Reinert 2006; Prestowitz 2005). Danny Quah (2002) estimates that the number of people who lived on less than $2 a day declined in China from a range of 37–54 percent in 1980 to 14–17 percent in 1992, while in India it declined from 48–62 percent in 1980 to 12–19 percent in 1992. Although the population increased in China from 981 million in 1980 to 1.1 billion in 1992, and in India from 687 million in 1980 to 884 million in 1992, the number of poor people declined in China from 360–530 million in 1980 to 158–192 million in 1992, and in India from 326–426 million in 1980 to 110–166 million in 1992. Indeed, Kraay (2004) and Dollar and Kraay's (2002) study underscores that China and India are not exceptional cases. Their study based on the examination of household survey data from 80 countries over the past four decades shows that the average real income per capita of a country's poorest quintile (defined as the bottom one-fifth of income distribution) moved practic-ally one-to-one with the average real income per capita of the country's whole population. Specifically, they find that when inequality is on the rise, poor households benefit less from economic growth than wealthier ones. In fact, average incomes of the poorest fifth of society rise proportionally with per capita income, indicating that inequality does not systematically increase with growth. The authors note that since few countries show significant trends in income inequality, on average economic growth has been the main driving force of poverty reduction in developing countries. Not surprisingly, Dollar and Collier (2001) and Dollar and Kraay (2002) conclude that "since the share of income going to the poor does not change *on average* with growth, the poor benefit from growth." This means that "growth is pro-poor."[12] A good example in the 1990s is Vietnam – which experienced rapid per capita GDP growth of 6 percent per year with no significant change in the distribution of income. This distribution-ally neutral growth led to tremendous improvements in the material well-being of poor Vietnamese. Dollar and Kraay (2002) confirm that the income of the poor increases with overall economic growth. This implies proportional benefits of growth for the poor as well as the non-poor. It also implies that growth regardless of its nature is good for the poor (Besley and Cord 2006). The message cannot be clearer: unless countries accelerate economic growth they will fall short of achieving the targets set forth in the MDGs. (See Table 2.2.)

Second, as Hollis Chenery and his co-authors (1974) pointed out long ago, more skilled workers with more human capital contribute to increased produc-tivity and growth. Endogenous growth theory now confirms that rapid economic growth is not only compatible with, but is likely to be enhanced by policies that improve the quality of human capital through access to primary and secondary education, health care and other basic social services.[13] Education and health are examples of what economists call "positive externalities" because the positive effects of doing something for some people spill over to benefit others. For example, education is an important mechanism for human capital formation, and human capital can promote growth through different channels. Education deter-mines the rate of technological innovation or absorption and exerts a counter-vailing effect on the diminishing returns to factors of production such as capital. In a particularly illustrative study Young (1995) notes that the increase in the

Table 2.2 Number of people living on less than $1 per day (in millions)

Region	1990	2000	2015 (estimate)
East Asia and Pacific	470	261	44
– China	361	204	41
– Rest of East Asia and Pacific	110	57	3
Europe and Central Asia	6	20	6
Latin America and the Caribbean	48	56	46
Middle East and North Africa	5	8	4
South Asia	466	432	268
Sub-Saharan Africa	241	323	366
Total	1,237	1,100	734
Excluding China	877	896	692

Source: *Global Economic Prospects 2004.*

number of years of schooling played a central role in the rapid growth of the East Asian newly industrializing countries (NICs). Similarly, Ravallion and Datt (2002) show from an analysis of household survey data across 15 Indian states over 1960–1994 that non-farm growth is less effective in reducing poverty in states with poorer initial conditions in terms of rural development, human resources and land distribution. They found that nearly two-thirds of the difference between the elasticity of headcount poverty index to non-farm output for Bihar and Kerala is attributable to the latter's substantially higher initial literacy rate.[14] Therefore, a well-educated labor force can help boost productivity, contributing to wider economic growth and distribution.

Moreover, education empowers the poor and disadvantaged in society to escape poverty through their own efforts. That is, it enables them to counter "irreversibilities" and poverty traps. Specifically, since getting out of poverty is much more difficult than falling into it because of a potentially irreversible loss of wealth, health or opportunity, a child or youth who did not have access to education, or who dropped out of school and could not go back, becomes a victim of irreversibility. Similarly, in a poverty trap, regardless of the growth rate, the poor are not able to pull themselves out of poverty because they lack basic skills or opportunities to participate in economic activity. In fact, Attanasio and Szekely (2001) and Lele (2005) identify education as a critically important asset for the poor and unequal access to education as a key cause of the unequal distribution of income in Latin America.[15] Therefore, improvements in human capital through education are critical if poor people and countries are to take advantage of the opportunities created by market reforms and the expansion of the information technology.[16]

Greater access to health care can greatly affect GDP per capita growth as healthy workers are more productive (for example, with businesses suffering less absenteeism) than workers who are otherwise comparable but for their health. Moreover, rising longevity opens up new incentives to save – an incentive that can have dramatic effects on national saving rates.[17] Better health care also creates a better quality of life by bringing positive spillover effects for both the recipients of the care and their families. Positive externalities also arise in the context of gender-specific development and poverty alleviation programs (Correia and Bannon 2006). It is well recognized that women's lack of education, health care, and economic and social opportunities (both absolute and relative to men) inhibits economic growth. Since women bear a disproportionate burden of poverty, better education for women is often associated with declines in fertility rates and better education, nutrition and health of their children.[18] For example, a recent study by Stotsky (2006) shows that gender-based differences in behavior are systematic and widespread and can influence macroeconomic variables such as aggregate consumption, savings and investments (also see Agarwal 1994; Boserup 1970). Gender influences consumption, as women tend to devote a larger share of household resources to meeting the household's basic requirements and to foster their children's well-being.

Thus, positive externalities can add up to a virtuous circle of economic growth and improving living standards – or what Nobel-laureate Amartya Sen (1983, 1999) has referred to as the "enhancement of human capabilities." To Sen, growth is simply an *instrumental* variable – as a means to an end – and the end is clearly the elimination of poverty and the empowerment of the poor. Thus, as Sen aptly notes, development cannot be viewed simply in narrow economic terms as the growth of aggregates such as income per capita. Rather, for development to be meaningful it must enhance individuals' abilities to shape their own lives. It must take into account all aspects of an individual's well-being – physical and economic security, as well as their ability to exercise their civil rights and political freedoms. Policies and programs that lessen disparities in incomes and assets, build human capital via access to education and health care and provide safety nets for the vulnerable and the poor are critical to achieving such broad-based human and economic development.

Third, contrary to anti-globalization claims, globalization offers both challenges and opportunities. While a multifaceted and disparate phenomenon such as "globalization" is hard to define, I use the term broadly as the process through which an ever-expanding free flow of ideas, people, goods, services and capital leads to further integration of economies and societies worldwide.[19] While the world has experienced successive waves (albeit not in a linear fashion) of what we now call "globalization," the latest phase, which began in the early 1980s with the unprecedented advances in information technology, has made the world a much smaller place. What distinguishes this latest phase from the earlier "partial" ones is the rapid incorporation of most of the developing and post-communist countries – the so-called "new globalizers" – into the global economy (Keohane 2002; Deardorff and Stern 2002). This process has been driven largely by the dramatic cross-border trade and capital and investment flows. International *trade* has seen a 16-fold expansion over the past 50 years, and foreign direct investment (FDI) and capital flows which totaled around $160 billion in 1991 soared to over $1.1 trillion in 2000 and accelerated to $2 trillion in 2005 (World Bank 2002, 2006), while the flows of capital across borders – including debt, portfolio equity, and direct investment-based financing – topped $6 trillion in 2005. These huge volumes of funds can move instantaneously across countries at the touch of a computer key. Today, almost all national economies are integrated into a single global marketplace through trade, finance, production networks and a dense web of international treaties and institutions.

The speed and intensity of global integration has provoked fierce debates about the consequences, implications and future trajectory of globalization. For political-economists the issues range from globalization's impact on the nation-state to questions of whether global economic integration promotes growth and reduces poverty, including whether it "lifts all boats" – meaning whether all countries benefit equally from globalization. Clearly, answers to these deceptively simple questions remain unresolved, not only because globalization is a multifaceted and evolving process, but also because the composite nature of globalization defies definitive answers. Nevertheless, parsing through an already prodigious and growing body of research and scholarship allows us to make general observations about some questions and more definitive conclusion about some others.

Regarding the first question: ever since the signing of the Treaty of Westphalia in 1648, the nation-state has been the dominant political and economic force in the world. However, a large body of scholarship claims that the preeminent position of the state can no longer be taken for granted in this era of globalization. Susan Strange (1996: 4) observed some time back that

> the impersonal forces of world markets ... are now more powerful than the states to whom ultimate political authority over society and economy is supposed to belong ... the declining authority of states is reflected in a growing diffusion of authority to other institutions and associations, and to local and regional bodies.

Others have echoed similar prognosis, arguing that globalization undercuts state sovereignty, greatly reducing its ability to regulate and govern domestic and international affairs. For example, Rosecrance (1999) claims a "virtual state" is replacing the real one, while others see the vacuum left by the shrinking state filled by a web of non-state actors, including multinationals, NGOs and an array of transnational activist networks (Friedman 1999; Griffin 2003; Keck and Sikkink 1998; Ohmae 1995).

As is well known, there are always limits to the reach of the state, however potent its hegemony (Scott 1998; Shue 1988). Nevertheless, there is evidence of a "hollowing out" of the state because, among other factors, globalization has made territorial borders – many which were only provisionally settled – even more porous. Increasingly, contemporary borders do not always correspond to the ever-changing economic, political and socio-cultural spaces on the ground. However, even as social, cultural and political identities and citizens' allegiances have multiplied, political boundaries have remained fixed in many settings. As will be discussed in Chapter 3, some states have responded to these

challenges by either involuntarily retreating from the sociopolitical and economic arena or by devolving power to sub-national and regional authorities. Still
others have attempted to maintain the status quo through various stratagems,
including coercion, compromise and accommodation. No doubt, as globalization
further deepens, the idea of a shared political community vis-à-vis the nation-
state will be fiercely tested as peoples and communities forge deeper common
discourses and alliances across societies, cultures and states. What strategic
choices nation-states will make, and how they will resolve these and newer challenges, remains to be seen.

However, this does not mean that nation-states have lost their salience and are
becoming irrelevant. As Weiss (2003, 1998), among others, has noted, the pur-
ported decline of the state has been greatly exaggerated (Skocpol 1995, 1979). To
the contrary, states have tremendous resilience and remarkable abilities of self-
perpetuation and a strategic retreat from excessive activism may only strengthen
the state. To Weiss, globalization has proven to be "enabling" for state authorities, rather than simply constraining. Clearly, the state has hardly disappeared.
The fact is that the number of nation-states has increased from 96 in 1960 to 193
in 2006, and states are still the most influential actors in the international system.
From providing public goods, resolving collective-action problems, maintaining
law and order, and forging new social contracts with their citizens, to managing
markets (as markets are neither autonomous nor self-regulating), the state
remains an indispensable institution. Indeed, reminiscent of Karl Polyani (1944),
who argued in his classic, *The Great Transformation*, that markets are con-
structed through the use of public authority, Gilpin (2000) argues that markets are
neither autonomous nor self-regulating. Rather, an open world economy marked
by free trade and capital mobility can be managed most effectively by rules-based
regimes undergirded by the state's sovereign power. Without this discipline, the
global order will only fragment towards antagonistic blocs.

Moreover, "national interest" remains as pervasive as ever because, as Cohen
(2006) notes, the "new closeness between nations" is still more virtual than real.
In his insightful book, *All Politics is Global*, Drezner (2006) convincingly challenges the claim that globalization has diluted the power of national governments to regulate their own economies. He argues that despite the pervasive
power of globalization, states – in particular the great powers (defined as governments that oversee large internal markets) – still dominate international regulatory regimes, and the regulatory goals of states are driven by their domestic
interests. States, especially powerful states like the United States and the European Union, remain key players in writing global regulations and will continue
to remain so given the size of their internal economic markets and vested interests. Levy (2006: 2–3) beautifully captures this Janus-faced nature of the
contemporary state by noting that while the place of the state is changing, "that
change should not be equated with eclipse." Rather,

> the contemporary context of globalization and liberalization has spelled not
> the erosion of state activism but rather the redeployment of state initiatives

on behalf of new missions. State authorities have shifted from a market-steering orientation ... to a market-supporting orientation in the present period. Market support is not synonymous with state withdrawal, however. On the contrary, the move toward the market has generated a raft of new state missions.

The unprecedented spread of *economic globalization* (broadly defined as the movement across international borders of goods and factors of production) signifies the triumph of market economies over socialist or centrally planned ones. It confirms that a well-functioning market economy adhering broadly to the principles of the "Washington Consensus" are superior – indeed, indispensable in this era of globalization.[20] The evidence is uncontestable: countries around the globe have now embraced the market system underscores that there are no viable alternatives to free markets (Cohen 2006; Feenstra 2004; Frieden *et al.* 2006; Larsson 2001; Panagariya 2004; Wolf 2005). However, to function effectively markets require transparent rules and institutions (McMillan 2002). As will be discussed in Chapter 3, a market economy embedded with strong institutions and operating in a free democratic society is demonstrably the most effective form of economic organization. As John Kay (2004:, 5), writes in his insightful book, *The Truth about Markets*,

if the strength of the market economy were encapsulated in a single phrase, it would be disciplined pluralism – the process of perpetual experiment in market economies, in which most experiments fail and are terminated, but the few that succeed are quickly initiated.

Thus, experimentation and reform are not a one-time process that governments undertake and then put behind them. As market economies evolve, the economic framework undergoes constant adjustment, to reflect the changes that are always taking place. Kay notes that the genius of markets "is that they are not depended on the genius of any individual." Rather, market systems facilitate internal reforms which, in turn, enable economic activity to function in ways that significantly improve the prospects for economic growth. In contrast, under central planning or in autocratically managed systems, where a "single voice" usually articulates the "right answer," such systems are bound to eventually fail.[21]

Fourth, while international trade poses both benefits and risks, the benefits outweigh the risks. Economic theory going back two centuries to Adam Smith and David Ricardo, and more recently to the Heckscher–Ohlin–Samuelson model of trade, has long claimed that the free movement of goods and factors of production (capital and labor) operating in a well-integrated world economy provides the greatest potential for maximizing human welfare (Dollar and Collier 2001; Legrain 2004). Economic integration and free trade provide economies of scale for countries too small to achieve them domestically and stimulate economic growth through the diffusion of new technology and competitive pressures; these reduce the monopoly power of domestic firms, which are forced to innovate (Berdell 2002). Moreover, global trade liberalization boosts the demand for exports of goods that intensively use unskilled labor – and as a consequence boost unskilled wages relative to skilled wages and capital earnings. Indeed, Robert Flanagan (2006) in his book *Globalization and Labor Conditions* compellingly challenges the contention that globalization worsens the conditions of labor by creating a "race to the bottom." Basing his argument on analyses of three decades of data from many countries, Flanagan concludes that the three economic dimensions of globalization – expanding foreign trade, foreign direct investment, and international migration – are strongly associated with better working conditions (higher wages and fewer hours of work) and improved workers' rights (reduced child labor and greater freedom of association).

The expansion of international trade in the twentieth century has contributed to unparalleled economic growth. Global per capita GDP has increased almost five-fold – although this growth has not been uniform. The strongest expansion came during the second half of the century, a period of rapid global trade expansion (Bordo *et al.* 1999; Prasad *et al.*, 2003). No doubt, the tremendous expansion in global prosperity in the second half of the twentieth century was possible in the context of broad-based multilateral trade liberalization within a framework of reciprocity and rules (Bhagwati 2002; 2004; Panagariya 2004). Again, the evidence is unambiguous: countries that have entered export markets through trade and intensified their links with the global economy have tended to grow faster than those that have not. As Mayda and Rodrik (2001: 1) note, "the consensus among mainstream economists on the desirability of free trade remains almost universal."

Two influential articles, one by Sachs and Warner (1995) and the other by Dollar and Kraay (2004), persuasively demonstrate that countries that are open to international trade experience unconditional convergence to the income levels of the rich countries. Specifically, Sachs and Warner construct a 0–1 dummy of openness for 79 countries that takes a 0 if any one of the following five conditions holds over the period 1970–1989: average tariff rates are over 40 percent on capital goods and intermediates; non-tariff barriers cover 40 percent or more of imports of capital goods and intermediates; the country operates under a socialist economic system; there is a state monopoly of the country's major exports; and the black-market premium on its official exchange rate exceeded 20 percent in the 1980s or 1990s. A value of 0 is viewed as indicating a closed economy, while a value of 1 indicates an open economy. Controlling for such variables as the investment rate, government spending as a fraction of GDP, secondary and primary schooling, the number of revolutions and coups, the authors find their openness index to be positively related to the growth rate of per capita GDP in a statistically significant sense. Dollar and Kraay (2004) explore the relationship between trade, growth and poverty by studying the experiences of "post-1980 globalizers" – or a "group of 24 developing countries that have significantly opened up to international trade." To make their case even stronger, they excluded the high-performing East Asian economies (South Korea, Hong

Kong, Taiwan and Singapore) and Chile. Their study provides strong evidence that increased trade has strongly encouraged growth and poverty reduction in these countries. Specifically, they found that per capita GDP growth in the post-1980 globalizers increased from 1.4 percent a year in the 1960s and 2.9 percent a year in the 1970s to 3.5 percent in the 1980s and 5.0 percent in the 1990s. On the other hand, the non-globalizing developing countries saw their annual growth rates falling from a high of 3.3 percent during the 1970s to only 1.4 percent during the 1990s. Berg and Krueger (2003) also show that an increase in openness is an important contributor to growth, and that trade-led growth does not worsen the income distribution. Rather, trade openness would likely reduce poverty through its impact on growth (also see Bhagwati 2002, 2004; Irwin 2002), while Ben-David and Loewy (1998) show that trade liberalization can facilitate the diffusion of knowledge and move the steady-state income of lower income economies to a higher level.

These findings have been corroborated in the exhaustive World Bank (2002) study, *Globalization, Growth and Poverty: Building an Inclusive World Economy*. The study provides strong evidence that economic globalization can serve as a positive force in promoting development. The study distinguishes "newly globalizing" countries (also called "more globalized") from "nonglobal-izing" or "less globalized" countries. It measures globalizing by changes in the ratio of trade to GDP over 1977–1997. Ranking developing countries by the amount of change, it calls the top third the "more globalized countries" and the bottom two-thirds the "less-globalized countries." Drawing on the experiences of the 24 more globalized developing countries which increased their integration into the world economy over two decades, the study shows that these countries achieved higher growth in incomes, no increase in inequality, longer life expectancy and decline in poverty levels. The 24 countries, home to some 3 billion people, enjoyed an average 5 percent growth rate in income per capita in the 1990s compared to 2 percent in rich countries. Many of these countries, including China and India, have adopted domestic policies and institutions that have enabled their citizens to take advantage of global markets – thereby sharply increasing the share of trade in their GDP, besides increasing incomes and redu-cing poverty. On the other hand, countries (and regions within nation-states) that have not integrated successfully into the global economy – particularly those in sub-Saharan Africa, the Middle East, and the former Soviet Union (home to some 2 billion people) – have been left behind. These countries have seen their ratio of trade to GDP either remain flat or actually decline. On average, these economies have contracted and poverty levels have risen – in some cases sharply. Thus, for many of these countries, especially the LDCs, the problem is not that they are being impoverished by globalization, but rather that they are being excluded from it (Lindert and Williamson 2003; Larsson 2001).

Two important studies underscore this. Sala-i-Martin's (2002) innovative study which constructs a world income distribution by aggregating individual country distributions concludes that both global poverty (measured by poverty rates as well as absolute headcounts) and income inequality declined significantly from 1970 to 1998. Using income data covering 97 countries, Sala-i-Martin estimates five income shares for each country from 1970 to 1998. He then integrates the individual country data to form a single picture of global income distribution. He further incorporates 28 additional countries for which there are no individual income share data available, bringing the total in his sample to 125 countries making about 88 percent of the global population in 1998. Based on this, the author finds that on a global level, the number of people living in extreme poverty (income of less than $1 per day at 1985 prices) and poverty (less than $2 per day) declined sharply during the period under study. That is, in 1970 about 40 percent of the global population lived under the $2 poverty line, while about one-sixth lived under the $1 poverty line. This trend remained largely unchanged in the 1980s, but "things changed dramatically in the 1990s" when China, India, and Indonesia began growing rapidly. By 1998, less than 20 percent of the world's population was under the $2 mark, and less than 7 percent under the $1 level. Similarly, Hanson's (2005) study on globalization and poverty in Mexico is instructive. He finds that in the 1990s, income growth fared poorly in parts of Mexico that experienced little of the effects of globalization when compared to the so-called "high exposure" states in the north. He finds that average labor earnings decreased by 10 percent for "low-exposure" states, relative to high-exposure states where export-oriented industries are located. Hanson (2005: 5) notes that "this is further evidence that during Mexico's globalization decade, individuals born in states with high exposure to globalization have done relatively well in terms of their labor earnings."

Yet, even the staunchest advocates of economic globalization realize that it is no magic bullet. In his bestseller, *The World is Flat: A Brief History of the Twenty-First Century*, *New York Times* columnist Thomas Friedman lucidly argues that to reap the benefits of globalization, countries must strengthen their macroeconomic management and create a positive climate for private sector activity. He advises the governments of advanced economies to stay ahead of the competition by investing in education and by constantly upgrading workforce skills (as the short-run costs of globalization fall disproportionately on low-skilled workers) rather than by erecting protectionist barriers. Sometimes it may also mean providing assistance to the "losers" from trade liberalization. For example, recognizing that the gains of the "winners" exceed the losses of the "losers" from trade liberalization, the US Congress has institutionalized the Trade Adjustment Assistance as a means of compensating the losers. This includes financial assistance, job retraining and improvements in human capital via education and skills training. To Friedman, emerging market economies and poor developing countries should also eschew protection and engage in "retail" or micro-level reforms because removing the numerous and petty legal and institutional impediments to doing business will spur productivity and growth.

However, *financial globalization* poses greater risks and challenges to both the transitional and developing countries (Tornell *et al.* 2004). Financial globalization refers to the worldwide phenomenon of capital flows across national borders and the integration of a country's domestic financial system with international financial markets and institutions. During the past two decades, financial markets around the world have become increasingly interconnected via capital account liberalization[22] and the creation and widespread use of a range of new financial instruments such as short-term portfolio capital, bank and corporate bonds, stocks, equities, private and government securities, mutual funds, pension funds, hedge-funds and derivatives, including a variety of instruments offered through the proprietary trading of banks and international securities houses (Hausler 2002). Perhaps the most dramatic has been the sharp rise (in terms of both absolute levels and the share of total inflows) of short-term portfolio capital flows in the form of short-term interbank loans (which can be readily withdrawn), commercial bank debt, tradable bonds, and equity shares. As noted earlier, all these have produced a huge volume of internationally mobile pool of capital and liquidity – dramatically changing the structure of national and international capital markets.

Macroeconomic theory informs that both rich and poor economies can accrue significant benefits by fully integrating and participating in the global economy. By opening their economies to cross-border capital inflows, countries can improve financing opportunities through a more diversified and competitive financial and credit system, diversify risk, deepen their financial sector and gain greater market access (Prasad *et al.*, 2003; Williamson 2005). Specifically, free capital movements contribute to efficient allocation of capital and provide opportunities for both foreign investors and domestic residents. For lenders, the advantages include increased portfolio diversification and higher returns from more productive foreign projects. Similarly, borrowers can gain in several ways. They can obtain resources to finance cyclical downturns and balance of payments disequilibria, thus allowing them to smooth out consumption. Emerging economies can augment savings available from domestic sources and finance projects with higher social returns. When combined with the liberalization of entry for foreign banks and brokerages, an open capital account can support reform and competition in the financial sector. Portfolio capital flows consisting of international placements of tradable bonds, issues of equities in international markets, and purchases by foreigners of stocks and money market instruments (in particular, securities and mutual funds) can greatly benefit emerging economies by fostering financial integration and improving the returns on investments through knowledge/skills spillover, enhanced competition, and market efficiency effects. Further, by reducing the scope for discretionary policy at home, openness to international capital markets can impose fiscal and monetary discipline on domestic policymakers. Finally, the efficiency gains from the reallocation of capital from industrial to developing countries can improve living standards by mobilizing global savings to finance investments in countries where the marginal productivity of investments is relatively high (Bekaert *et al.* 2001).

Yet, research also shows that there are risks associated with the free flow of capital – especially short-term speculative capital. For example, Demirguc-Kunt and Detragiache (1998) find that financial liberalization has a statistically significant effect on the probability of a banking crisis. If anything, the financial crises of the 1990s taught us that the phenomenal expansion of cross-border financial flows can make even seemingly stable economies vulnerable to shocks and financial collapse (Agenor 2004; Burtless *et al.*, 1998; Obstfeld and Taylor 2005; Williamson 2005). Indeed, the Asian financial crisis of 1997–1998 starkly demonstrated that even "model" emerging market economies can succumb to the vagaries of international capital markets with disastrous implications. In Asia, massive capital outflows during the crisis led to wide currency fluctuations and a liquidity crisis that sharply reduced output and employment, with highly negative socioeconomic and political impact (Sharma 2003).

This is because the benefits of free-flowing capital can be offset by various capital market imperfections (such as herding, panics and boom-bust cycles), often caused by a lack of information (Obstfeld 1998; Obstfeld and Taylor 2005). Compounding this, capital inflows can encourage countries to overspend. Access to world capital markets makes it easier for governments to borrow – often excessively and on a short-term basis. The accumulation of short-term debt in foreign currencies makes such countries more vulnerable to changes in investor sentiment. Cumulatively, the conditions of domestic and global market imperfections coupled with the fluctuating nature of capital flows tend to intensify a country's sensitivities to financial shocks – with the potential to affect a country's macroeconomic stability. Unimpeded capital inflows can lead to real exchange-rate appreciation and current account deficits, and force authorities to engage in sterilization operations in an attempt to retain control of the money supply. In addition, sudden outflows can disrupt domestic financial markets, forcing authorities to choose between higher interest rates and a depreciation of the exchange rate. The balance of payments and banking crises that often accompany sudden stops in inflows have not only resulted in severe recessions in emerging markets, but have also imposed large losses on investors and lenders. In fact, in the recent wave of financial crises, whether in Mexico, Russia or East Asia, much of the turbulence was caused, at least initially, by over-exposure to foreign currency denominated short-term debts. Thus, the Janus-faced nature of capital flows has the capacity to both improve and destabilize an economy.

Countries are particularly vulnerable to such shocks if they do not have the right financial infrastructure in place, or do not maintain macroeconomic discipline. For example, reckless domestic macroeconomic policies that lead to large fiscal deficits and excessive borrowing can trigger unpredictable cycles of speculative capital outflows and higher interest rates with serious negative consequences. What can countries do if they want to benefit from a more open capital account yet minimize the cost associated with volatility? Research shows that appropriate sequencing of trade reforms and capital account liberalization (that is, capital account liberalization should follow, not precede, the liberalization of trade), is essential. This is because the massive inflows of capital that generally follow the freeing of the capital account could cause a large appreciation of the real exchange rate, leading to large import surges that could destabilize domestic industries and the balance of payments. Thus, unlike trade in goods and services, free flows of capital across borders can cause bubbles and crashes.

However, specific economic policies can mitigate these risks and greatly reduce the costs associated with volatility. It is important to recognize that it is not just the aggregate amount of capital inflows, but also their nature and composition that eventually determine the quality of a country's experiences with financial globalization. For example, overall volatility may be reduced by shifting the composition of capital flows from loans to equity, and within equity from portfolio investments to FDI. This is because FDI tends to be more stable than bank lending or portfolio flows. Also, private firms in many emerging markets should be discouraged from issuing foreign currency denominated debt since currency mismatches aggravate crises. Equally important, emerging market economies should avoid overvalued exchange rates to avoid potential currency mismatches, and even use capital controls during periods of large-scale capital outflows. Indeed, when distinguished economists like Jagdish Bhagwati (2002, 2000), Paul Krugman (1998, 1999), Dani Rodrik (1997, 1999), and Joseph Stiglitz (2002), among others, call for better "management" of globalization, among other things, they advise against full convertibility on the capital account for developing countries – with Bhagwati observing that "the optimal speed at which a country liberalizes is not necessarily the fastest."[23] Eichengreen (2000: 1105) is more blunt, stating,

> this means not freeing capital flows before substantial progress has been made in liberalizing domestic financial markets and strengthening financial supervision. It means liberalizing foreign direct investment first, access to stock and bond markets second, and offshore bank funding last. It means putting in place exchange rate, monetary and fiscal policies that do not destabilize the capital account.

Yet, all the authors also agree that while such risks offer reasons to proceed with financial liberalization carefully, they are not reasons for turning away from it altogether. That is, developing countries can reap significant advantages from opening up to the outside world. Therefore, the solution is not to retreat into autarky and economic isolationism. Rather, developing and transitional countries must build and strengthen the supporting institutions, particularly the legal, regulatory and administrative frameworks to effectively participate and benefit from the opportunities afforded by the global economy. This case is made most compellingly in Frederic Mishkin's (2006) aptly titled book, *The Next Globalization: How Disadvantaged Nations Can Harness Their Financial Systems to Get Rich*. Mishkin argues that economic development requires a well-functioning financial market, which in turn requires extensive links to world capital markets. Well-regulated and well-supervised financial markets are very important for ensuring that capital inflows are channeled to productive uses. To achieve this, countries must implement good regulatory and prudential policies,

have low corruption and a favorable economic environment with strong funda-
mentals. Such countries are successful in attracting more foreign direct investment and other forms of more long-term capital investments. In contrast,
countries which are perceived by investors as lacking in transparency, and/or as
having weak policies, tend to rely more on "hot money" such as short-term bank
loans, and less on foreign direct investment – thereby making them more prone
to financial instability. Last, but not least, as Prasad and coauthors (2003) show,
once financial integration crosses a certain threshold, the positive effects of
international capital flows (cheaper access to capital, transfer of new technology,
development of the banking system) begin to cancel out the negative effects.

Finally, to further underscore a point made earlier, globalization does not
reduce national sovereignty in economic policymaking. Rather, it creates strong
incentives for nation-states to cooperate with each other to pursue sound economic policies for the common good. Cooperation is essential if governments
are to more effectively manage a complex range of economic activities that has
both domestic and international ramifications. As the former United States
Treasury Secretary Robert Rubin (1998) noted in the midst of the Asian financial crisis: "the task before the global community is to construct a new international financial architecture that is as modern as the markets." Among the key
goals of the work on the international financial architecture is to develop standards and codes that are based on internationally accepted principles that can be
implemented in many different national settings. Suffice it to note, government
policies largely determine the freedom and efficiency with which markets function, or do not function, across national borders. Governments must provide the
institutional and policy framework that allows market economies to reap the
benefits of globalization. Clearly, nation-states are indispensable actors.

Fifth, there is now virtual scholarly unanimity that good institutions matter.
Institutions are the rules, organizations, and social norms that facilitate
coordination of human action. Institutions can be both formal and informal.
Formal institutions include legal regulations and laws, while informal institutions are not legally codified. These include the norms, values, conventions and
the "social capital" that are often embedded in societies. Because institutions
govern behavior, they are social assets (or liabilities when bad or weak). In the
economic realm, institutions that support market transactions perform three
functions: smoothing information asymmetries (that is, ensuring that all market
participants have access to reliable information), defining and enforcing property
rights and contracts, and regulating competition. Barro (2000: 209) notes that
"differences in institutions across countries have proved empirically to be
among the most important determinants of differences in rates of economic
growth and investment." Research is increasingly pointing to institutional
factors being more important than differences in capital labor ratios and factor
accumulation in explaining cross-country differences in income per capita. For
example, Easterly and Levine (1997) point out that the conventional factors of
growth (labor, physical and human capital accumulation) do not fully explain
Africa's experience. Rather, they argue, many African countries possess very

weak public and private institutional frameworks – and sub-Saharan Africa has experienced the slowest economic growth of any region in the world.

The quality of institutions and the efficacy of political administration are central to development, as the institutional capacity necessary to carry out the most basic functions in a society have much to do with success or failure in economic development. Without good institutions, growth will be difficult to achieve on a sustained basis because vibrant institutions are the underpinnings of market economies.[24] Institutions that enhance the functioning of markets are those that provide secure private property rights protected by the rule of law, impartial enforcement of contracts through an independent judiciary and appropriate government regulations to foster market competition. Moreover, effective corporate governance and a transparent financial system help smooth information asymmetries to ensure that all market participants have access to reliable information. This allows for more prudent savings and investment decisions, better aligns economic incentives with social costs and benefits, and helps make the economy less vulnerable to domestic and external market instability. The late Mancur Olson (1996: 22) once noted that poor countries have failed to realize "many of the largest gains from specialization and trade" because they lack "the institutions that enforce contracts impartially, and so they lose most of the gains from these transactions."

A particularly probing study by Easterly (2000) which examines the connection between ethnic conflict and economic development argues that the quality of institutions is a key factor in the equation (also Posner 2005). Specifically, high-quality institutions, such as rule of law, bureaucratic quality, freedom from government expropriation, including freedom from government repudiation of contracts, mitigate the adverse economic consequences of ethnic fractionalization. In countries with sufficiently good institutions, ethnic diversity does not lower growth or worsen economic policies. High-quality institutions also lessen war casualties on national territory and lessen the probability of genocide for a given amount of ethnic fractionalization. However, ethnic diversity has a more adverse effect on economic policy and growth when institutions are poor.[25] Poor institutions have an even more adverse effect on growth and policy when ethnic diversity is high. In countries with sufficiently good institutions, ethnic diversity does not lower growth or worsen economic policies. Good institutions also lower the risk of wars and genocides that might otherwise result from ethnic fractionalization. The lesson which follows is that ethnically diverse nations that wish peace and prosperity must build good institutions. Thus, for many developing countries, strengthening and building institutions that provide dependable property rights (against both state expropriation and predation by private agents) manage conflict, maintain law and order, and align economic incentives with social costs and benefits are the foundations of long-term economic growth.

Sixth, positive long-term economic performance and good governance is highly correlated. The building and strengthening of institutions will require good governance. The basis of good governance (that is, representative and responsive government) is a well-functioning democratic political system with an engaged and vibrant civil society. Although the paradigm shift towards neoliberalism in the early 1980s saw a justified effort to reduce the stifling role of the erstwhile interventionist state and broaden the role of markets, it is now recognized that a minimalist state tends to further enervate the already acute problems of governance. Rather, a *democratic state* that is market-conforming rather than predisposed towards excessive intervention and regulation can play a positive role in economic development. Thus, the received wisdom which alleges an incongruity between the state and the market, including the claim that democracies are incapable of enacting market reforms, have proven to be misplaced. These issues are addressed in detail in Chapter 3.

Seventh, since markets are imperfect, correcting market failure may justify welfare-improving state interventions. Moreover, a responsive and accountable state is critical to ensure the provision of public goods which have positive externalities such as health care and education as well as correcting negative externalities such as income inequalities. This is because economic growth does not always produce a vertical flow of income from the rich to the poor – and despite the fact that the poor may benefit from growth and poverty rates may actually decline, "the proportional benefits of growth going to the poor will always be less" (Kakwani and Pernia 2000: 2). Thus, although, economic growth reduces poverty, growth alone does not always eliminate entrenched or absolute poverty, nor is the rate of decline in poverty always commensurate with the rate of growth of aggregate income. As Kanbur and Squire (2000: 193) note, in "many countries over long periods of time, inequality has been surprisingly persistent, and where inequality has changed rapidly, it has increased." Evidence shows that a given amount of growth can translate into different amounts of poverty reductions in different countries and regions. Therefore, despite sustained economic growth, income inequality (both among and within nations) can also increase. Growth can occur nationally, but poor regions may experience less growth or may benefit less in terms of poverty reduction as a result of a given national rate of growth. For example, Ravallion and Chen (2004) show that while the incidence of extreme poverty in China fell dramatically over 1980–2001, progress was uneven over time and across provinces. Rural areas accounted for the bulk of the gains to the poor, though migration to urban areas helped. Provinces starting with relatively high inequality saw slower progress against poverty, due both to lower growth and a lower growth elasticity of poverty reduction. Chen and Wang (2001) note that China's inland provinces lag far behind coastal regions – with national poverty rates ranging from 43 percent in Guizhou to negligible levels in the coastal province of Guangdong. Similarly, in India's poorest states, such as Bihar and Orissa, almost half the population live below the national poverty line, compared with less than 10 percent in the richer states such as the Punjab and Haryana (Deaton 2003; Sharma 2003a). In regions of high inequality such as Latin America and Africa, one can observe significant growth in real incomes while many still remain in absolute poverty.

The key policy issue is how to improve the poverty reduction elasticity of growth, and specifically, how to ensure that economic growth has a significant broad-based impact on poverty reduction. To the advocates of "pro-poor growth" national governments must adopt a "strategy that is deliberately biased in favor of the poor" (Kakwani and Pernia 2000: 3). Specifically, to narrow the gap, governments need to pursue well-targeted public policies and safety-net programs to ensure that the broad cross-section of society benefits from the fruits of economic growth. Since it is well known that the education fees and the opportunity costs of educating children, rather than putting them to work to earn money or help at home or on the farm, can be prohibitive, the public sector, for example, in its expenditure policies can subsidize the provision of basic social services (such as education and health) which contribute not only to the current welfare of society but also to the accumulation of human capital in the more vulnerable sectors so that they have the potential to escape poverty. Since children of low- and (sometimes) middle-income households are particularly vulnerable to income variability because these families often respond to a decline in the earnings of the main breadwinner by increasing the employment of other family members (including pulling children out of school), specifically targeted programs designed to improve the human capital of the poor, such as the PROGRESA in Mexico, Bolsa Escola in Brazil, Chile Joven in Chile and the Red de Proteccion Social (RPS) in Nicaragua can make a huge difference in bettering the lives of the poor.

Both PROGRESA and RPS provide cash transfers and nutritional supplements to families in extreme poverty in the rural areas. However, these funds are conditional on children's school attendance rates of at least 85 percent, as well as regular visits to health clinics for check-ups and follow-ups. The cash transfer is given to the mother, who also has to attend a series of courses on health practices. Bolsa Escola provides scholarship funds (held in a special account) for disadvantaged children that can only be accessed after the beneficiary completes a schooling cycle. Chile Joven is also a cash-transfer program provided to young adults as a training incentive (Attanasio and Szekely 2001).

Research shows that these safety-net programs work, protecting vulnerable households from destitution in the short term as well as offering long-term routes out of poverty. An evaluation of Nicaragua's PRS program underscores this. Started in 2000 to assist children living in extreme poverty in the countryside, the PRS provides a cash transfer to families, conditional on their children attending school and regularly visiting health clinics. A detailed evaluation of 1,500 households surveyed three times between 2000 and 2002, as well as during extended stays in several villages, revealed that PRS improved the nutrition and education of approximately 10,000 of the country's poorest families. More specifically, the evaluation found substantial increases in family purchasing power – up to 40 percent for the extremely poor, a reduction of five percentage points in the incidence of children under five who are stunted, a nearly 20 percentage-point rise in enrolment rates for primary school children, and a 50 percent reduction in child labor (IFPRI 2005). In fact, research has long shown that even basic welfare-enhancing programs can make a huge positive difference in the lives of the poor (Streeten 1986). For example, school feeding programs that provide a mid-morning snack consisting of fortified wheat biscuits (at a cost of 6 US cents per packet), containing 300 kilo-calories and 75 percent of the recommended daily allowance of vitamins and minerals, can sharply increase children's nutritional status, raise school enrollment, improve retention rates, and reduce health problems. Overall, well-targeted safety-net programs can help alleviate the short-term economic fluctuations that can have long-term consequences for children vulnerable to poverty, thereby limiting their education and further increasing their vulnerability to poverty in the future. In addition to such well-targeted transfer programs, public works schemes, food subsidies and food-for-work programs can also supplement incomes, particularly for the unemployed – augmenting, directly or indirectly, consumption of the most vulnerable groups in society.

Eighth, good governance and institutions are only one part of a strategy for promoting development. If the vast majority of people in developing countries are to reap the benefits of market-based growth, they need to be able to participate in markets. That is, markets must be accessible to them. However, since most poor people do not have "collaterizable wealth" (i.e. funds or property that can be used as collateral), they cannot effectively participate in markets. This problem is further compounded by imperfect and underdeveloped capital markets which impede many people's ability to save, borrow, and invest. As a result many potentially viable projects are not financed, and the poor remain trapped in poverty. There seem to be two complementary ways to remedy this problem. First, as Hernando De Soto (2000) argues in his bestseller, *The Mystery of Capital*, giving poor entrepreneurs legal title to the assets they already hold will unleash this "dead capital" which can be used as collateral for loans to fund new businesses. Second, since poverty combined with slow economic growth in the formal sector has forced a large part of the developing world's population into self-employment and informal activities, providing access to micro-credit to the many potential entrepreneurs who lack usable collateral (as done so effectively by the Grameen Bank in Bangladesh) will help both business and employment growth (Yunus 1999). That is, the use of non-collateralized loans will allow for the delivery of critical short-term working capital to micro-entrepreneurs and poor households.[26]

Research shows that microfinance fills the gap left by banks – which in most developing countries serve anywhere from 5 to 20 percent of the population. By 2002 more than 1,000 microfinance programs around the world had reached about 30 million borrowers, lending about $3.5 billion, with an average loan size of $280 (World Bank 2004d: 120). Yet, according to the World Bank (2004a), over 500 million poor people around world who run profitable micro-enterprises often cite credit as the primary constraint to business growth. In the poorest countries, these activities constitute a significant part of the private sector generating jobs and resources for services crucial to poverty reduction, especially for women.[27] But despite the rapid growth of microfinance institutions over the past decade, fewer than 5 percent of micro-entrepreneurs have access to formal financial services and instead must use less reliable informal sources (Ledgerwood and White 2006). In other words, "an estimated 400–500 million people world-wide do not have access to financial services other than informal moneylenders" (IMF 2005: 72).

Yet, by itself, microfinance is unlikely to be big enough to reach all potential borrowers. Moreover, microfinance services are not always cheap as microfinance institutions tend to face relatively high overhead costs vis-à-vis the value of their loans and deposits. These costs and related risk-factors often force microfinance institutions to charge relatively high interest rates on loans, besides offering rather low yields on deposits. Not surprisingly, many microfinance institutions continue to remain in business because they are subsidized either directly through grants or indirectly through soft terms on donor loans. Such subsidization comes at the risk of relaxing budgetary discipline in the microfinance industry and creating unfair competition with traditional financial institutions, preventing them from expanding their outreach – especially to the "core poor" (Weiss and Montgomery 2005). Studies also indicate that only 1 percent of existing microfinance institutions worldwide are financially stable. The few financially self-sustainable microfinance institutions tend to be larger, spreading fixed costs and achieving greater efficiency, although those striving to become commercially viable do not tend to target the poor (IMF 2005: 73).

For microfinance to achieve its full potential it is crucial to integrate the many quasi-formal microfinance institutions (in particular, the small and highly subsidized ones) with the formal financial and banking system. Contrary to the common impression, this will not undermine microfinance institutions or the country's formal banking system. Rather, evidence shows that well-managed microfinance institutions often outperform mainstream commercial banks in portfolio quality, and in some countries microfinance institutions tend to be more profitable than commercial banks. For example, in 1992 ProDem, a microfinance NGO, became BancoSol, the first commercial bank in Latin America dedicated to microfinance. The transformation enabled the expansion from 14,300 clients to 70,000 within five years of commercialization, and by 1998 BancoSol was the most profitable licensed bank in Bolivia (World Bank 2004d: 120). Similarly, as Littlefield and Rosenberg (2004: 38) note,

> In turbulent times, microfinance has been shown to be a more stable business than commercial banking. During Indonesia's 1997 crisis, for example, commercial bank portfolios deteriorated, but the loan repayment among Bank Rakyat Indonesia's 26 million micro-clients barely declined. And, during the recent Bolivian banking crisis, MFI's [microfinance institutions] portfolios suffered but remained substantially healthier than commercial bank portfolios.

Thus, integrating microfinance with financially sound financial and banking institutions would "deepen" the scale and scope of microfinance institutions and enable them to extend their reach beyond the rural and urban poor to other groups who may not be classified as poor, but who are generally excluded from the services of both the formal banking system and microfinance institutions. This is particularly important as privatization of state banks often results in the closure of rural and semi-urban branches, reducing the net flow of credit to poor farmers and small entrepreneurs. Experience shows that providing opportunities for poor people to generate income themselves will go a long way in reducing poverty. Thus, supporting micro-enterprises not only has the potential to raise the living standards of poor people: they also provide jobs and contribute to GDP and economic growth. Given the fact that well-managed microfinance institutions have proven to be commercially viable, creating and expanding such services to the entrepreneurial poor will help increase household income, reduce unemployment, create demand for many other goods and services, and help deepen the financial sector.

The role of the North

As the MDGs aptly note, a determined inclusive global partnership of the North and South is necessary to achieve progress across all dimensions of development. However, as Chapters 5, 6 and 7 will show, although the challenges are formidable, much can be achieved if the rich Northern countries take the lead role in this partnership. There are several ways by which the rich OECD countries can assist the South, especially the LDCs.

New Institutionalism theories have long argued that global institutions, especially the Bretton Woods sisters – the IMF, the World Bank, and the GATT/WTO – serve a positive role because they help to facilitate multilateral cooperation in an anarchic world. These institutions not only constrain the behavior and imperatives of the most powerful countries, but also help through the lowering of transaction costs and the provision of assistance and information to weaker states. As Robert Keohane (1984: 97) noted some time back, international institutions "facilitate agreements by raising the anticipated costs of violating others' property rights, by altering transaction costs through clustering of issues, and by providing reliable information to members." International institutions "are relatively efficient institutions, compared to the alternative of having a myriad of unrelated agreements, since their principles, rules, and institutions create linkages among issues that give actors incentives to reach mutually beneficial agreements." Of course, these institutions have not always lived up to their expectations, with numerous studies questioning their role and efficacy, besides providing prescriptions for making them work better, or eliminating them altogether. Nevertheless, these institutions are here to stay, and making them more attentive to the needs of the developing nations, in particular the LDCs, can help in bridging the North–South gap. If the World Bank and the IMF can be made more transparent and accountable by giving developing nations greater say or "ownership" over policy decisions, the WTO system which tries to balance countries' gains and losses via reciprocity is currently attempting to address the concerns of developing nations in international trade. The successful completion of the Doha Round of trade negotiations will signal not only the utility of global institutions, but also the North's commitment to partnership and multilateralism.

Therefore, ninth: trade and market access facilitated by the WTO is critical for developing countries. This theme will be addressed in Chapter 5, including the mix of forces that led to the collapse of the Doha Round of trade negotiations under the WTO in June 2006. Special emphasis will be placed on why the removal of trade barriers, in particular agricultural subsidies in the industrialized world, remains an agonizingly intractable issue. According to the World Bank's Agriculture and Rural Development Department report (Cleaver 2004), of a total OECD agriculture subsidy of $315 billion per year from 2000 to 2002, $26 billion was in the form of budgetary transfers to consumers through food stamps, and $54 billion on account of support for general services such as research and development (R&D), extension services, and other support services to OECD farmers. But the biggest chunk of subsidies – $235 billion – was constituted as direct government payments to farmers – $89 billion – and an indirect consumer-financed component of $146 billion through import barriers and tariffs.[28] The report notes that

> of the total farm support estimate of $315 billion, $104 billion was accounted for by the European Union, $94 billion by the US, and $60 billion by Japan. The annual per farmer subsidy worked out to $23,000 in Japan, $19,000 in the US, and $16,000 in the EU, while averaging $11,000 for the OECD countries as a whole.

Overall, agricultural subsidies and high tariffs add up to roughly seven times what rich countries spend on development aid.

In doling out such huge subsidies, the OECD countries not only distort world trade in agricultural products but also contribute to huge income losses for developing-country farmers. Moreover, these subsidies not only result in higher taxes and higher prices for the citizens in rich countries, they also hurt consumers, especially the poor in developing countries. More than three-quarters of the world's poor live in rural areas, depending on agriculture or activities related to the agricultural sector for their livelihood. Thus, agricultural sector reforms, in particular global trade liberalization, is crucial in giving them opportunities for better lives. However, the OECD's protectionist policies in agriculture lock many low- and middle-income countries out of rich-country consumer markets and their massive agricultural subsidies destabilize and depress world prices for commodities. This contributes to worldwide overproduction and dumping that usually floods global markets, and only serves to undermine incentives for local production, besides destroying livelihoods and impoverishing millions of farm communities in many developing countries. In fact, by bringing down their trade barriers and making the WTO Doha Development Agenda a reality, the rich nations can contribute significantly to the needs of the developing world.

Chapter 5 will show that while the world's trading system is far more liberal than it was 40 years ago, it still discriminates against poor countries, partly because they work in sectors such as agriculture that are most affected by industrial-country tariffs and subsidies. Indeed, trade barriers tend to be highest on labor-intensive goods and services in which developing countries have a comparative advantage. Poor-country exports are locked out by high tariffs (concentrated not only on agricultural products but also on textiles and clothing) and by tariff escalation – whereby the tariff increases the moment a commodity is processed. Also, while the Uruguay Round of multilateral negotiations did away with agricultural quotas, it left in their place "tariff-rate quotas" that kick in at prohibitive tariff rates once threshold import volumes are reached. All this makes it exceedingly difficult for developing countries, especially the least-developed nations, to develop and move away from being dependent on the export of raw commodities.

Chapter 5 will also argue that the completion of the Doha Round is a shared responsibility and will require commitments from both the North and South. The OECD countries have obligations to provide market access and reduce trade-distorting subsidies. Put bluntly, the developed countries need to lead by example by delivering on areas in which developing countries have a comparative advantage on a nondiscriminatory basis. In particular, they should aim for a complete elimination of tariffs on manufactured products, complete elimination of export subsidies and complete decoupling of agricultural subsidies from production, including the reduction of agricultural tariffs. The liberalization of trade is particularly important in agriculture, where average protection in the OECD countries is more than seven times as high as in manufacturing. However, developing countries must also play their part as they have the most to gain from a Doha agreement. Some of these gains will come from trade liberalization by and among the developing countries themselves. While middle-income countries generally have lower and less distorting protection in agriculture, they have high average tariffs in all sectors, and are more restrictive in services. As South–South trade increases in importance, this protection not only undermines low-income trading partners but also tends to undercut middle-income countries' productivity growth. Latin American exporters, for example, face average tariffs in Latin America that are seven times higher than those faced in industrial countries, and in manufactures 60 percent of total tariff payments by East Asian exporters are paid to other developing countries (World Bank 2004a: 19). Developing countries clearly have much to gain from their own liberalization. Finally, while low-income countries would benefit from non-discriminatory market access to every market in products where they have a comparative advantage, rather than special preferences in some markets and exemptions from rules, they will also benefit by removing their own trade barriers. Indeed, the long-term viability of the global trading system is dependent on an effective mechanism that allows countries to integrate more fully and benefit from increased international trade – vital for economic growth and poverty alleviation.

Tenth: well-targeted aid can greatly help in meeting the MDGs. Recent cross-country evidence shows that official development assistance (ODA) or foreign aid has a strong positive effect on a country's economic performance if the country has undertaken certain policy and structural reforms. Evidence also shows that private investors can be slow to respond when low-income countries improve their investment climate and social services. It is precisely at this stage that aid can have a great impact on growth and poverty reduction. Thus, if the OECD nations were to increase their foreign aid budgets only modestly, it would go a long way in assisting the LDCs. While the aid target set by the United Nations states that high-income countries should deliver 0.7 of 1 percent of GNP in aid, only one or two high-income countries meet this target. The fact is that ODA is on a downward trend. It fell in 2000 to 0.22 of 1 percent of the rich countries' GNP – down from more than 0.4 of 1 percent in the 1960s and slightly more than 0.3 of 1 percent in the 1970s and 1980s. Today, development assistance is at one of its lowest levels at 0.22 percent of GDP compared with 0.5 percent 30 years ago.[29] Chapter 6 demystifies some of the issues surrounding foreign aid and suggests ways in which it can be made more effective in achieving development objectives, especially in supporting economic growth.

Eleventh: since aid and debt are intrinsically linked, for aid to be effective it needs to be better aligned with debt relief. The harsh reality is that the excessive debt burdens in many poor countries pose formidable challenges for these countries to meet their development objectives. Between 1990 and 2001, external debt as a percentage of gross national income rose from 88.1 percent to 100.3 percent in the "severely indebted" countries. In 2001, the LDCs were spending almost 3 percent of GDP on servicing debt (World Bank 2002a). The growing problem of "debt overhang" does not only undermine urgently needed progress on policy reforms: besides discouraging private investment, lenders may be forced to allocate scarce concessional resources to keep high debtor countries afloat, often at the expense of other deserving countries. While the primary responsibility for achieving debt sustainability lies with debtor countries themselves – in particular, they must keep new borrowing in step with their ability to repay, and adopt policies that increase their resilience to exogenous shocks – the donors and creditors also have a responsibility. Chapter 7 examines both the effectiveness and the limits of the various debt-relief strategies, including the World Bank and the IMF "Heavily Indebted Poor Countries (HIPC) Initiative." It argues that while long-term debt sustainability will depend on sustained economic growth, and while debt relief programs such as the HIPC Initiative can greatly help, the rich nations can and should do much more to help. At a minimum, debt relief should not come out of the shrinking pie of foreign aid, but should be part of the larger development strategy.

3 Good governance and economic development

How important is good governance for economic growth? Can economic growth be sustained without good governance? The answer is best captured in the oft-cited aphorism that good governance promotes growth and that growth further improves governance. Mauro (2004: 1) notes "a consensus seems to have emerged that corruption and other aspects of poor governance and weak institutions have substantial, adverse effects on economic growth." Hall and Jones (1999: 84, 95), who found large productivity differences across countries, conclude:

> our hypothesis is that differences in capital accumulation, productivity, and therefore output per worker are fundamentally related to differences in *social infrastructure* across countries. In fact [our] central hypothesis ... is that the primary, fundamental determinant of a country's long-run economic performance is its social infrastructure. By social infrastructure we mean the institutions and government policies that provide the incentives for individuals and firms in an economy.

There are extensive econometric studies that show strong correlation between long-term economic performance and good governance. For example, Acemoglu *et al.* (2001), Dollar and Kraay (2003), Kaufmann and Kraay (2003), Landes (1998) and Rodrik *et al.* (2004), among others, argue that the quality of governance fundamentally determines long-run developmental outcomes. Kaufmann and Kraay (2003) draw on a large World Bank dataset designed to measure (1) the link between governance and development, and (2) countries' monitoring of their performance. They track the quality of governance from 1996 to 2003 in some 200 countries.[1] The quality of governance is divided into six categories aimed at capturing how governments are selected, monitored, and replaced; a government's capacity to formulate and implement sound policies; and the respect of citizens and the state for the institutions that govern them. The six measured indicators include: (1) voice and accountability; (2) political stability and lack of violence; (3) government effectiveness; (4) regulatory quality; (5) rule of law; and (6) control of corruption. The authors conclude that good governance is not only critical to development but is the single most important factor in determining whether a country has the capacity to use resources effectively to promote economic growth and reduce poverty. Similarly, research by Roll and Talbott (2003) shows that government institutions and policies explain most of the variation across nations in economic development – with secure property rights, business transparency, political rights, civil liberties and stable rule of law as significant factors accounting for development success.

Not surprisingly, the importance of good governance has now become an article of faith, with donors and lenders increasingly basing their aid and loans on the condition that policies that ensure good governance are adopted (World Bank 2005, 2002, 2000b). But what is good governance? Since creating the political and social framework conducive to economic growth is often the greatest challenge many countries face, what types of policies and institutions have the most positive and measurable effects on improving governance? As a corollary, what kinds of institutional arrangements are associated with growth and poverty reduction? How best to promote and sustain good governance, especially in the world's poorest countries? These and related issues are discussed in the following sections.

What is good governance?

Broadly speaking, the term "governance" encompasses all aspects of the way a country is governed. Good governance has several characteristics. It is participatory, consensus-oriented, accountable, transparent, responsive, effective, efficient, equitable, and inclusive, and follows the rule of law. At a minimum, good governance requires fair legal frameworks that are enforced impartially by an independent judiciary, and decisions and its enforcement are transparent or carried out in a manner that follows established rules and regulations. Since accountability cannot be enforced without transparency and the rule of law, accountability is a key requirement of good governance. Not only governmental institutions but also private sector and civil society organizations must be accountable to the public and to their institutional stakeholders.[2] Moreover, given that a society's well-being depends on ensuring that all its members feel that they have a stake in it, good governance requires that institutions serve all stakeholders fairly.

How to achieve good governance

The UN Millennium Project (2005), the UNDP's (2003) *Human Development Report 2003* and the various World Bank's, *World Development Report* each list over 100 "must do" items for countries to achieve good governance. Even allowing for the considerable overlap among the various items, it is a formidable agenda – not only for the world's least developed and post-conflict countries, but also for many middle-income and transitional economies. However, the reports provide little prioritization or guidance regarding what governance items are essential and what can wait, how they should be sequenced and implemented, how much it would cost and how it will be paid for. They also suffer from flaws typical to commissioned reports: a tendency to provide "one-size-fits-all" prescriptions despite the fact that research shows that while governance reforms share commonalities, they must also be judiciously determined on a country-by-country basis – the institutional innovations tailored to local political and institutional realities with the most essential sequenced in first.

The various reports recommendations can be broadly divided into two sections: the *general* and the *substantive*. The general emphasizes "capacity development" which includes both the building of effective states (which can deliver public goods and services to the populace and ensure peace and stability), and an empowered and responsive society which can hold states accountable for their actions. The reports correctly note that poor or inadequate governance may not always be the result of venal or rapacious leadership, but may also be because the state may suffer from weak formal political institutions, and lack the resources and capacity to manage an efficient public administration. However, what is not always appreciated is that good governance cannot be had on the cheap – simply through the implementation of bureaucratic and administrative policies. Moreover, governance reforms without concomitant economic reforms are doomed to failure. Again, research shows that political-institutional reforms are more successful in settings where economic development has already started to take place (Stern 2002). This is not to imply that political development is automatically a consequence of economic development, but to underscore that institution-building and consolidation are more likely to succeed where development has already taken place, or is taking place. In fact, many of the items listed on the good governance agenda as preconditions for development are actually consequences of it. The implications are profound: institution-building and the promotion of good governance demand simultaneous commitment to economic development. Finally, measuring good governance and overall governmental performance generally requires measuring what Rotberg (2004) calls "outcomes" and not just "inputs." That is, what needs to be measured is the government's delivery of public goods and not just its budgetary provisions: its actual accomplishments and not just its good intentions.

Substantively, the reports view institution-building, democracy and political-economic decentralization as essential for good governance and economic development. While intuitively appealing, the question of precisely how each contributes to democratic institutionalization and economic development is poorly understood – and the reports' overly sanguine rhetorical statements shed little light on these issues. For example, how to devise an institutional framework that nurtures both democracy and market economies; how best to ensure that governments have sufficient power to provide security and public services while inhibiting it from predation on its own citizenry; how to ensure democratic governance, economic growth and human development become mutually reinforcing; how to ensure that the devolution and decentralization of political-economic authority do not exacerbate regional or particularistic divisions. While the reports do not provide a nuanced discussion of these issues, a growing body of research sheds useful insights into these important issues. The following sections will draw on this scholarly research to elaborate these issues.

Institutions and good governance

Nobel laureate Douglass North (2005), in his recent book, *Understanding the Process of Economic Change*, reiterates that good institutions beget good governance.[3] Institutions matter for both the long and short term because they form the incentive structure of a society and provide the underlying determinants of economic performance. Institutions are composed of both formal (constitutions, laws, and regulations) and informal rules (such as social norms, customs, and traditions) that constrain human economic behavior. Specifically, institutions set the framework of rules and incentives that affect how people, organizations, and firms utilize resources in political and economic decision-making or how they "play the game." According to North, when incentives encourage individuals to be productive, economic activity and growth take place. However, when they encourage unproductive or predatory behavior, economies stagnate.

While informal interpersonal exchanges and social networks can serve the needs of traditional societies, modern economies (given their specialization and complex division of labor) require formalized political, judicial and economic rules. In providing specific rules of the game, political and economic institutions create the conditions that enable the functioning of a modern economy. That is, formal institutions, by securing property rights, establishing a polity and judicial system and flexible laws that allow a range of organizational structures, creates an economic environment that induces increasing productivity. To North, institutions are "growth-enhancing" because they reduce uncertainty and transaction costs.[4] Thus, North's paradigm is often labeled as the "new institutionalism" because it has at its core a set of ideas derived from the analysis of "transaction costs" – that is, costs that result from the imperfect character of real-world institutions and that have to be surmounted in order for economic activity to occur.

Specifically, the institutional framework affects growth because it is integral to the amount spent on both the costs of transactions and the costs of transformation inherent in the production process. Transaction costs are far higher when property rights of the rule of law are absent and not enforced. In such situations private firms typically operate on a small scale and rely on extra-legal means to operate. On the other hand, an institutional environment which provides impartial third-party enforcement of agreements will promote exchange and trade because the parties know that a good or service will be delivered after it is paid for. Because institutions and the enforcement of rules largely determine the costs of transacting, good institutions can also minimize transaction costs – or costs incurred in making an economic exchange. Both political and economic institutions are necessary to sufficiently reduce transaction costs in order to make potential gains from trade realizable. North (with others) confirms that among the plethora of institutional rules seen as most critical to economic growth is the protection of private property rights.[5] This is because property rights and contract enforcement are integral to reducing uncertainty in a market because modern economies require property rights and effective, impersonal contract enforcement. On the other hand, personal ties, voluntary constraints, and ostracism are less effective in a large, complex, and impersonal economy.

North points out that every market is different, and that to work efficiently each market must find the right mix of formal and informal rules and the appropriate enforcement mechanisms. Moreover, what makes a market work well in a given period in time may not be necessarily appropriate over time, as critical elements such as technology, information costs, and political regimes can change raising transaction costs. Therefore, economic performance is not only determined by the kind and quality of institutions that support markets: economic change depends largely on "adaptive efficiency" – or the political system's effectiveness in creating institutions that are productive, stable, fair, broadly accepted, and flexible enough to be changed or replaced in response to political and economic feedback.

Democracy, development and governance

Not only are the political institutions necessary for economic development more likely to exist and function effectively under democratic rule, the adaptive efficiencies are best sustained in democracies because institution-building to promote good governance and economic development is conterminous with democracy (Dahl 2005; Jackman 1973; Lipset and Lakin 2004; Londregan and Poole 1996). It is no accident that countries that have reached the highest level of economic performance across generations are all stable democracies.[6] In fact, one of the most robust findings of some two decades of research on democratization is that durable democracy is strongly correlated with economic development[7] – albeit, as Chong (2004) argues, there is some evidence of a "political Kuznets curve" in which the immediate effect of democracy is to exacerbate inequality, while the long-run effect is to diminish it.

Today, liberal democracy justifiably enjoys near-universal appeal and is regarded as the ideal system of government. According to the "procedural minimum," liberal democracy is a form of government where citizens through open and free institutional arrangements are empowered to choose and remove leaders through competitive struggle for the people's vote.[8] According to Robert Dahl (2005), the dean of democratic studies, a true representative democratic government must be based on the principles of popular sovereignty, competitive political participation and representation, an independent judiciary, free, fair and regular elections, universal suffrage, freedom of expression and conscience, the universal right to form political associations and participate in the political community, an inclusive citizenship, and the government in power must adhere to the constitution and the rule of law.[9]

Scholars have long argued that democracies have embedded institutional advantages that support economic development.[10] According to Nobel laureate,

Amartya Sen (2001, 1999), democracies enrich individual lives through the granting of political and civil rights, and do a better job in improving the welfare of the poor (also Acemoglu and Robinson 2005; Bueno de Mesquita *et al.*, 2003). Second, it provides political incentives to rulers to respond positively to the needs and demands of the people (Lake and Baum 2001; McGuire 2006). That is, democracies are seen to be responsive to the demands and pressures from the citizenry since their right to rule is derived from popular support manifested in competitive elections – or as Robert Dahl (1971) long ago noted, governmental responsiveness to citizens' demands is built into periodically held electoral contests guaranteed by juridically protected individual rights.[11] Numerous studies corroborate this. For example, an analysis of 44 African states by Stasavage (2005) finds strong evidence that democracy helped increase government spending on education. Similarly, Avelino *et al.* (2005) find that democracy is robustly linked to higher spending on health, education, and social services. Third, the open dialogue and debates inherent in open democracies aids in the development of values and priorities, and this "constructive function" of democracy can be very important for equity and justice. Sen (1999: 152) notes that this explains, for example, the remarkable fact that in the terrible history of famines around the world,

> no substantial famine has ever occurred in any independent country with a democratic form of government and a relatively free press. Famines have occurred in ancient kingdoms and contemporary authoritarian societies, in tribal communities and in modern technocratic dictatorships, in colonial economies run by imperialists from the north and newly independent countries of the south run by despotic national leaders or by intolerant single parties. But they have never materialized in any country that is independent, that goes to elections regularly, that has opposition parties to voice criticisms, and that permits newspapers to report freely and question the wisdom of governments' policies without extensive censorship.

Fourth, it is now irrefutably clear that, contrary to earlier claims, there is no "trade-off" or "cruel choice" between democracy and development.[12] Rather, a responsive democratic state is essential for economic development. Empirical and qualitative research comparing economic growth under both democratic and authoritarian settings has found anomalies in the core assumption of the cruel-choice hypothesis. In particular, no convincing evidence supports the claim that authoritarian suppression of political and civil rights is helpful in encouraging economic development – even if development is identified simply with economic growth. Inter-country comparisons by Barro (1996), Kohli (1986), Przeworski (1995) and others have contradicted the thesis of any conflict between political freedoms and economic performance. They argue that the frequently made casual generalizations about the negative impact of democracy on economic growth are simply assumptions because the actual directional linkages are tentative and seem to depend on many other factors. Kohli (1986: 153) notes that the "developmental performance of Third World democratic regimes [India, Malaysia, Sri Lanka, Venezuela, and Costa Rica] must be judged satisfactory."

In their comprehensive study aptly titled *The Democracy Advantage: How Democracies Promote Prosperity and Peace*, Halperin *et al.* (2005) further confirm the above assessments. Their results based on a survey of over 100 rich and poor countries compellingly shows that democracies outperform (in terms of economic development) autocracies or quasi-authoritarian polities – despite the fact that several autocracies, including North Korea, Iraq, Afghanistan, and Cuba, were not included in the sample because of the lack of reliable data. Suffice it to note, the actual growth figures for autocracies would be substantially lower if the "performance" of these countries were included. The data unequivocally show that both developing-country democracies and non-democracies grew at approximately 1.5 percent of GDP per capita per year during since the 1960s, only when the high-performing East Asian economies (specifically, Taiwan, South Korea, Singapore, and Hong Kong) were included in the sample. However, when these countries are excluded, the performance of democracies is better – growing at 0.5 percent per capita per year faster than autocracies and mixed polities. Furthermore, democracies outperform autocracies in the consistency of their growth. That is, an analysis of the 80 worst economic performers of the last 40 years reveals that all but three have been autocracies. The authors note that the range of development experiences among democracies can be explained by the differing success each has with institutional development. In fact, both autocracies and democracies with more robust institutions enjoyed higher rates of economic development than countries without well-established institutions. This explains why some of the former East Asian autocracies performed better than some democracies.

Fifth, the claim that the nascent democracies in the developing world and in post-communist transition settings are ill equipped to implement needed economic reforms cannot be sustained. Specifically, it has been argued that because neo-liberal or market reforms carry with them attendant short-term pain such as rising unemployment, inflation, higher prices on state subsidized goods, falling wages and other austerity measures, political reformers find it difficult to generate popular support. Because governments, especially democratically elected ones cannot afford such popular backlashes, the reforms are usually watered down or altogether abandoned. Indeed, Adam Przeworski (1991) in his important book *Democracy and the Market* predicted that economic reforms introduced in new democracies would produce populist policies that would undermine both the economy and democracy. Other analysts have highlighted the probable coalitions against reform, arguing that vested rent-seeking beneficiaries of protectionist, state-led development strategies often mobilize through democratic channels to block reforms. On the other hand, since the beneficiaries of reform are presumed to be widely dispersed and unorganized, they cannot counter the vested interests. Again, the political implications were that reforms were likely to be unpopular and politically costly and elected politicians, including well-intentioned democratic governments, would understandably do what is politically expedient but fiscally irresponsible – delaying or altogether scuttling necessary economic reforms (Haggard and Kaufman 1995).

However, actual experience belies such pessimistic assessments. For starters, until the 1980s, most countries in Latin America and sub-Saharan Africa were governed by repressive authoritarian regimes, the majority of which proved incapable of implementing the far-reaching economic and political reforms they promised when seizing power. Arguably, it was the poor performance of these authoritarian regimes (including communist regimes in Eastern Europe) that explains the dramatic shift toward civilian governments in these regions (Huntington 1999). In fact, one of the most interesting research findings was the so-called "post-communist paradox" – that among post-communist countries, it was precisely the most democratic regimes that carried out the most comprehensive economic reforms, whereas the more authoritarian ones proved largely incapable. That is, frequent elections, unpredictable executive tenure, growing societal pressures did not prevent countries such as the Baltic states and Poland from implementing radical macroeconomic reforms, whereas the more authoritarian Belarus, Ukraine, Moldova and the regimes in the Caucasus and Central Asia not only failed to do so but, given the fact that authoritarian leaders in these countries have few checks on arbitrary power, they engaged in cronyism and corruption (Hellman 1998; Kitschelt 2003).

Moreover, research confirms that new democracies with a cohesive party system, strong executives and insulated economics ministries and central banks, as well as those operating under coalition governments with fragmented party systems (but with responsive political institutions), have demonstrated capacity to implement economic reforms (Pereira *et al.*, 1993; Bates and Krueger 1993; Haggard and Kaufman 1995). Beginning in the 1980s, a number of democratic regimes, including fragile and "uninstitutionalized" new democracies in a number of developing and transition economies, have enacted far-reaching market reforms – despite the high short-term costs this imposed on powerful domestic groups, including larger segments of society. These democratic governments were able to build coalitions across social groups through targeted policy measures. For example, Roberts and Arce (1998) note that in Peru, the government, through its strategically targeted economic programs to key constituencies, especially the working poor, was able to garner popular support for market reforms – including during periods of severe economic contraction. Similarly, Kurtz (2004: 8; also see Stein *et al.* 2006) notes that in Chile and Argentina,

> a democratic government was able to push through and consolidate a package of economic liberalizations far more ambitious than those even a previous savage bureaucratic authoritarian government was unable to impose, and more extensive than those undertaken in the East Asian newly industrializing countries over the course of decades.

It is now recognized that new democracies were able to do all this because popular societal actors had the opportunity to exert pressure for reforms through lobbies, the media, networks of nongovernmental organizations, legislative representatives, the courts (to challenge the constitutionality of various laws), in addition to having greater associational autonomy from the state. This not only has allowed new democracies to pursue reforms without resorting to the draconian measures of their authoritarian predecessors, but has also allowed them to better amplify the voices of the popular sectors in policy decisions – and despite, at times, domestic and external pressures, to have a better track record in providing safety-nets to the vulnerable and those hurt most by market reforms. Not surprisingly, there is general consensus now that the implementation of the more exacting "second-generation reforms" (such as flexible labor markets, tax reform, capital account opening, banking and financial sector reforms, anticorruption measures, improved corporate governance, competent bureaucracy, and targeted poverty reforms, among others) requires political deftness and finesse that only representative democratic regimes can muster.

Sixth, many observers mistakenly assume that the establishment of a democratic regime will also lead to the swift consolidation of democratic institutions and procedures.[13] However, cross-national country experiences show that the *ancien regime* tightly bound by its own administrative and bureaucratic culture and traditions can be remarkably impervious to change (Pei 2006). Moreover, democratization does not always mean a rupture with the past suggesting that the formal democratic order can persist alongside authoritarianism, elitism, and social exclusion. Thus, the process of democratic consolidation can be long and arduous – as democracies can deepen, but can also remain partial, deteriorate or altogether break down. In their original study, O'Donnell and Schmitter (1986) point out that the pattern of transition can profoundly determine the extent of democratization. The most successful are "pacted transitions" between "softliners" in the *ancien regime* and moderates in civil society. However, where one side is more powerful than the rest, it will dictate the rules. If the powerful are autocrats (which often is the case) the pattern of transition will be autocratic. When the distribution of power between "autocrats" and "reformers" is more equal, an unstable regime is most often the outcome.[14]

Overall, almost a quarter century after the beginning of the third-wave of democratization, the quality of democracy remains poor in most settings. The reality on the ground tends to support Zakaria's (2003: 3) pessimistic assessment that while "democracy is flourishing; liberty is not." What explains this paradox and what can be done to correct it? Reminiscent of what O'Donnell (1994) earlier called "delegative democracy," and Diamond (1999, 2002) described as "hybrid regimes" where electoral democracies combine authoritarian practices, Zakaria notes that although the idea of democracy (in the sense of devolution of power to the masses) has spread rapidly, what is much less clear, however, is the extent to which democratic consolidation or the institutionalization and routinization of democratic norms and values within the political system is taking place.[15] Rather, in most settings, the result is often the emergence of what Zakaria terms "illiberal democracies" – a form of governance which deliberately combines the rhetoric of liberal democracy with illiberal rule.[16] For example, although regular, competitive multiparty elections are held qualifying the country as an "electoral" democracy, the everyday practices of the state are marked by arbitrariness and abuses. Similarly, political freedoms and civil rights may be formally recognized, but hardly observed in practice; the judiciary officially deemed independent is easily compromised and the free press harassed in numerous ways. Even in established democracies such as India, democratization has meant "opening up its politics to a much broader group of people who were previously marginalized," creating new political parties that have made India "more democratic," but "less liberal" (Zakaria 2003: 7). Thus, illiberal democracy (that is, nominally democratic government shorn of constitutional liberalism and institutional checks) is not only potentially dangerous – bringing with it the erosion of liberty, the abuse of power, ethnic divisions and conflict – "illiberal democracy has not proved to be an effective path to liberal democracy" (Zakaria 2003: 9).

Zakaria provocatively argues that the most effective way to turn developing or traditional societies into liberal democracies is by first fostering constitutional liberty rather than democracy. This is because if electoral democracy is established before a society has achieved constitutional liberty, it is likely to end up as an illiberal democracy or degenerate into authoritarianism. To Zakaria, liberty leads to democracy and democracy ends up undermining liberty. As an illustration, he argues that if free elections were held in Islamic countries, most fundamentalist parties would win and then proceed to destroy liberty – "it would be one man, one vote, one time" (Zakaria 2004: 2). To Zakaria, "liberal authoritarian regimes" like Singapore and formerly in South Korea, Taiwan, Chile, are best suited to create the constitutional liberal infrastructure from which democracy would eventually emerge. No doubt, to label authoritarian regimes that once ruled Taiwan, South Korea or Chile as "liberal" or to generalize complex country experiences is not persuasive. Moreover, as Carothers (2007: 14) points out, the "sequencing fallacy" "rests on the mistaken two-part premise: that a significant number of autocrats can and will act as generators of rule-of-law development and state-builders and that democratizing countries are inherently ill-suited for these tasks." It seems that while Zakaria's analysis is plausible, his prescriptions are not.

Arguably, constitutional liberty and democracy are not always antithetical, but could reinforce one another. It seems to me that the "restoration of balance" which Zakaria wants can best be achieved through political moderation that simultaneously builds both constitutionalism and democracy. Specifically, if illiberal tendencies are to be restrained, political moderation is necessary. However, moderation requires most critically effective democratic institutions and structures that can restrain illiberal, populist and crudely majoritarian practices. At the minimum, democratic structures such as parliaments and legislatures must represent the interests of all citizens, provide a system of checks and balances, and oversee and impose clear constitutional limits on executive authority. Such limits are necessary against the corrupting effects of power.

Also, the judicial and legal institutions must be independent of special influences, and protect political and civil rights of all citizens. They must provide equal protection to women, minorities and other subordinate groups, and fair access to judicial and administrative systems, and must be accountable to the public – including allowing citizens to seek protection of their rights and redress against government actions.

Byman (2002) notes that moderation is absolutely critical in fractious multi-ethnic and plural societies, indeed in the emerging democracies as a whole, where political competition among the various contending groups often becomes an uncompromising winner-take-all battle, with the numerically larger groups using elections and other legitimate democratic forms in pursuit of particularistic interests or to ensure their dominance – the so called "tyranny of the majority."[17] In such settings, to view "democracy" simply in terms of elections and majority rule before the institutions and norms essential for the functioning of democracy are established is misguided, and has the potential to exacerbate long-festering social feuds and cleavages to produce illiberal results. The most effective way to moderate political competition and mitigate divisions is to create meaningful disincentives to the formation of factionalized political groupings led by itinerant demagogues and popular majorities based on narrow communal, ethnic, religious or other group-based identities. To achieve this, the constitutional provisions and electoral systems must be deliberately engineered to promote the public good by encouraging genuine nationwide participation, negotiation and compromise. To this end, political parties must seek support from a cross-section of groups and communities to gain power. Here, the case of Nigeria and Indonesia is instructive: Nigeria requires political parties to include representatives of two-thirds of the country's states on their executive councils and has made it illegal for parties to use communal and chauvinist references in their names and platforms. Similarly, Indonesia requires political parties to establish offices in two-thirds of the provinces nationwide, including a significant number of members in two-thirds of the districts and municipalities within these provinces in order to compete in parliamentary elections. In both countries, the electoral system has fostered moderation, leaving demagogues and firebrands isolated. On the other hand, in Sri Lanka, the majority Sinhalese long-held monopoly on power, coupled with the maximalist demands put forth by both Sinhala and Tamil nationalists, has provoked a long and bloody civil war. Likewise, in the former Soviet Republic of Georgia, democratization resulted in civil war as the minority Abkhaz feared that their distinct culture would be threatened by the Georgian majority. Hence, they resorted to armed resistance when it became clear that the unabashedly defiant group of Georgian nationalists would win the elections. Thus, the evidence is equivocal: federal arrangements that encourage the various stakeholders to work with elected officials from rival groups and communities can help forge more durable political alliances across groups, including electoral coalitions (Byman 2002). Successful political cooperation is essential to protect group prerogatives in divided societies – thereby reducing tensions and keeping the peace.

Seventh, the assumption that economic reforms under democracies would automatically lead to simultaneous income redistribution and rising living standards has proved to be overly sanguine. Rather, as noted earlier, there is evidence of a "political Kuznets curve" in which the immediate effect of market reforms under democracy is to exacerbate inequality, while the long-run effect is to diminish it (Chong 2004). This means that market reforms under democratic auspices are necessary conditions for promoting economic growth, but not sufficient ones to reduce inequalities – at least not in the short run. Experience suggests that simultaneous improvements in state capacity and institutions, accountability, representation, and governance are important factors in achieving economic growth with greater equity. Similarly, the conventional belief that there is a direct correlation between economic development and the emergence and durability of democracy is problematic. In his seminal research, Przeworski and his coauthors (2000, 1997) have challenged the claim that economic growth leads to democracy. Rather, they compellingly point out that growth has a measurable effect on the survival rate of democracy, but not on the rate of its emergence. Specifically, they argue that statistical relationship is as follows: when per capita income is $1,000 (measured in purchasing power parity), a democracy's life expectancy is eight years. When per capita income is between $2,001 and $3,000, the life span of a democracy rises to 26 years. However, the authors note that when per capita income rises above $6,000, democracy gains permanence. Nevertheless, the authors caution that non-democracies can persist above these income thresholds – meaning that non-democracies can remain autocratic despite rising income prosperity. The experience of the People's Republic of China and Southeast Asia lucidly underscores this observation. According to Dickson (2003) in China the evidence indicates that economic entrepreneurs, major beneficiaries and party elites favor greater economic freedoms, but are not interested in democracy. Indeed, in Singapore, Malaysia and Indonesia, political elites before the Asian crisis of 1997 used to argue that greater political openness and participatory institutions would undermine economic growth and growing prosperity. In fact, maintaining economic growth became the principal justification for authoritarianism – couched under labels such as "Asian democracy" and "Asian values."

Eighth, some two decades ago Robert Jackson (1990) distinguished between *de jure* and *de facto* states. However, many *de jure* states are in effect *quasi-states* as they exist simply because other nations recognize them as legal sovereign entities despite the fact that they lack many of the attributes of a functioning government. Today, these quasi-states are often referred interchangeably as "weak," "failed," "failing," "collapsing" "fragile," "rogue" or "post-conflict states," among others. Regardless of the label, these states pose formidable problems for democratic governance, economic development and global stability as they are unable to provide effective legitimate rule or deliver essential public goods such as security, law and order, education and other essential services.[18] The World Bank (2005) has identified about 30 low-income countries as being "under stress" – although some have put the number of weak or fragile states at around 50 (Eizenstat *et al.* 2005; Rotberg 2003). In such settings of lawlessness, violence and impunity where the "state" lacks even the most basic attributes of sovereignty, the challenge is to literally transform the "state" into an effective and responsible sovereign. But, how can this be done? Countless cases of failed democratization show that democracy cannot flourish under conditions of anarchy. As Rotberg (2003: 3) notes, among a "hierarchy of political goods" nothing is "as critical as the supply of security, especially human security." Similarly, Fukuyama (2005: 87) argues for "stateness first" – pointing out that "at the core of state-building is the creation of a government that has monopoly of legitimate power and that is capable of enforcing rules throughout the state's territory." Therefore, establishing political order and security is absolutely essential. Once order is established, the key is not only to empower citizens and their independent organizations, but also to simultaneously strengthen the nascent institutions of governance and the rule of law, as well as the development of formal representative organizations such as political parties – which constitute an essential link between citizens and the formal policymaking bodies (Birdsall *et al.* 2006; Fukuyama 2006; Chesterman *et al.* 2005). In some settings it may also mean the formal state structures building partnership with a diverse range of local non-state intermediaries and rival sources of authority to provide core functions such as public security, law and order and conflict management – although such formulas should only serve as a transitional phase towards consolidation of the formal governing bodies.

Ninth, it is important to reiterate that democratic state-building cannot be had on the cheap. Given weak and failing states' inability to raise revenue on their own, state-building will require external sources of funding and logistical assistance – sometimes for extended periods. This means that the international community, especially the rich nations, must be willing to stay the course. However, as Carothers (2004, 1999) and others have argued, this does not mean that grandiose and overly-ambitious nation-building plans are the answer. Instead, the goals should be well-targeted and expectations kept realistic, and second, nation- or state-building is not a technical exercise. Rather, every society is going to build institutions that are unique to its own culture, history, traditions, ethnic makeup. Therefore, adapting to local traditions is essential. Moreover, Fukuyama's (2006, 2005, 2004) caution to democratic nation-builders that there is a difference between "state"- and "nation"-building" is worth keeping in mind. If a state is the government, a nation is that and much more, because it also includes shared memories, culture, values, language, and a common sense of identity. Clearly nation-building is much more ambitious and challenging than state-building. As Fukuyama notes, it is relatively easy to create an army or a police force, but to convince people divided by region, religion or ethnicity to live together in the same society and have common interests is much more difficult.

Therefore, democratic state- and nation-building is a two-pronged process. At a minimum, it must include creating or strengthening core government institutions such as the security apparatus, judiciaries, economic agencies, and social-welfare systems such as education and health care. As Fukuyama argues, the first phase should involve stabilizing the country by establishing law and order, rebuilding basic infrastructure, and jump-starting the economy. The second phase must begin after stability has been achieved. This should include creating self-sustaining political and economic institutions that will ultimately permit democratic governance and economic growth to take place. Perhaps the best argument for such measured state-building is that the alternatives are worse. It not only acts a bulwark against grandiose and ultimately futile and costly experiments such as Iraq, it also means that leaving fragile states to their own devices could renew civil wars and interstate conflict, making the long-term costs far heavier.

Finally, the governance deficit is not only a problem in weak and failed states. Many functioning states also face challenges to effective governance. To reverse this process and consolidate good governance and the rule of law will require building state capacity. In Linz and Stepan's (1996: 7) pithy observation, "democracy is a form of governance of a state. Thus, no modern polity can become democratically consolidated unless it is first a state." Effective state capacity means that the institutions of governance are meritocratically organized and rule-based. This will enhance the state's ability to deliver public services, maintain a degree of regulatory oversight, enforce rules and regulations and maintain social order. The experience of the East Asian newly industrializing nations vividly underscores this. East Asia's "development states" played a crucial role in growing the economy while dramatically cutting poverty levels.

Like the "top-down" authoritarian East Asian developmental states, building effective democratic states means strengthening the states' formal powers embodied in the executive and legislative branches so they are able to translate diverse partisan preferences into effective policy options – either through majority rule or through the establishment of viable coalitions. However, unlike the erstwhile East Asian states, it also means putting in place the rule of law with transparent standards, a fair electoral system that represents all stakeholders, and representative political parties that effectively convey citizen preferences. After all, markets cannot be expected to work effectively in the absence of political stability and the rule of law. Given their "adaptive efficiencies," democratic regimes are indispensable because they can create a facilitating enabling environment for the market to function, besides providing more responsive and accountable governance. Such logic goes against the core tenet of neoliberalism which alleges an incongruity between the state and the market. Although neoliberalism justifiably sought to reduce the stifling role of the interventionist state and broaden the role of markets, it is now recognized that the so-called "minimalist state" proposed by neoliberals creates its own problems by further enervating the already acute problems of governance.[19] Indeed, in their eagerness to reduce the scope of the state, policymakers in many places have inadvertently weakened the capacity of the states to do even the most basic things that all states have to do, such as enforce rules or protect property and individual rights. Therefore, if "too much state" resulted in the problem of *etatism* (that is, excessive regulation, economic mismanagement and rent-seeking behavior) "too little state" inevitably creates an institutional deficit spawning poor governance (Fukuyama 2004). Therefore, if the various statist and predatory states were part of the problem, representative democratic states can be part of the solution.

Decentralization and good governance

Concern about the arbitrary powers of central governments has led some to advocate a decentralized federal form of democratic governance.[20] Although the economic and political arguments for decentralization have conspicuously converged, there is no consensus as to what precisely "decentralization" should entail in practice. Since in most cases decentralized systems of government have three different levels of government (a national level, a regional level, and a local level), in general it implies devolution of power (which may include the transfer of either resources, responsibilities for public services, or decision-making authority) away from the central government to political and administrative jurisdictions below the center. For some, this means the transfer of authority and responsibility for public activity from the central government to "sub-national" or the provincial or state-level governments. To others, it is devolution to district, municipal and other local government – including the lowest possible rung of local government. To still others, it is devolution to quasi-independent organizations, and to ancillary local community-based self-governing organizations and NGOs.

The belief that local self-governing institutions operating within the overall framework of a democratic federal arrangement will lead inexorably to political stability and act as a catalyst to economic incentives is not new. In his celebrated *Democracy in America*, Alexis de Tocqueville (1961) argued that a vibrant and robust civil society was the foundation of early nineteenth-century America's democratic success. In Tocqueville's view, American democracy was sustained by the richness and diversity of its voluntary associations – from religious groupings to business and commercial associations. These independent and active civic associations served as an important bulwark against the negative effects of centralization by keeping in check the dictatorial tendencies of the state. In recent decades, the conspicuous failure of centralized and bureaucratic statism to deliver on either political stability or sustained economic growth, not to mention the egregious human rights record of many, created disillusionment with all forms of top-down technocratic and managerial governance and calls to roll back the state. It also led to renewed interest in decentralized forms of democratic governance.

Clearly, democracy is strengthened when its formal representative institutions are supplemented by vibrant and participatory civic associations (Clark 1991). Decentralized governance can help revitalize associational life long stifled under various forms of centralized and authoritarian rule. It can help give voice to the traditionally excluded and marginalized constituents, enhance civic pride, broaden participation and improve administrative functioning and accountability. In an important comparative study of the performance of decentralized governments in Bangladesh, the Indian state of Karnataka, Côte d'Ivoire and Ghana, Crook and Manor (1994) note that in all four cases decentralization helped to improve public accountability (for example, in Karnataka it significantly improved the attendance of school teachers), as well as the speed and quality of official response to local issues and needs. Similarly, participatory budgeting undertaken since 1989 by Brazil's Workers' Party in municipalities it controlled allowed poor residents to improve their lives. The experiment which began in Porto Alegre, a city of roughly one million residents, gradually spread throughout the 1990s until it included about 100 municipalities under the Brazilian Workers' Party control in 2000. The participatory budgeting included poorer neighborhoods (thus reversing the existing trend) and allowed residents to see that resources and spending priorities were fairly allocated, as well as monitor program implementation (Heller 2001).

Moreover, decentralization by granting more autonomy to localities and regions can strengthen nation-building by reducing conflict. Democratic federal arrangements that guarantee the rights of ethnic, religious, regional and minority groups by granting them power with respect to fundamental concerns such as education, religion, language, taxation, and law and order, can greatly reduce incentives for conflict (Lijphart 1981, 1996). Similarly, broad local participation and the representation of diverse political, ethnic, religious, and cultural constituencies in public policymaking not only give national initiatives and policies greater legitimacy, but also enhance program implementation and follow-up. Finally, decentralization by bringing government "closer to the people" can help make government more efficient and responsive to local conditions and needs (Kaufman 1996; Gurr 2000; Horowitz 1991; Tsebelis 1990). A corollary to this is that by mobilizing citizens to manage and control public programs at the local level, decentralization can help local economies become more prosperous and equitable.

For example, Ostrom (1990) and Wade (1987), argue that decentralization can help resolve collective-action problems in the management of environmental and common property resources, while Bardhan (1997: 45–6) notes that at the local level

> transaction costs are relatively low and the information problems (which cause government failures) less acute ... local information can often identify cheaper and more appropriate ways to provide public services, apart from getting a better fit for locally diverse preferences (or getting rid of uniformity constraints in service delivery that a centralized supplier is sometimes compelled to adopt).

Some studies have highlighted that decentralization can contribute to sound investment decisions. Specifically, decentralization of regulatory responsibilities can help locales adapt approaches to their conditions and preferences and facilitate the involvement of all stakeholders. Fiscal decentralization can assure local authorities that taxes raised locally will not be appropriated by the central government, giving local authorities incentives to develop their local tax base and target their spending policies (as well as the delivery of public goods) to match the needs and preferences of local residents (Oates 1972).

In fact, in their seminal paper, Montinola *et al.* (1995) argue that it was the devolution of government power and authority from the central to sub-national or local governments (the latter including provinces, prefectures, counties, townships, municipalities and villages) that has been the engine behind China's rapid economic transformation. The authors argue that the Chinese-style "fiscal federalism" was fundamentally "market-preserving federalism." By devolving regulatory authority from the central to the local governments, the interventionist role of the central government was limited because it created political checks on the central authorities. Their theory provides two possible mechanisms for aligning local government's interest with promoting markets. One is through inter-jurisdictional competition under factor and goods mobility to discipline interventionist local governments. That is, decentralized control over the economy by sub-national governments within a common market prevents the central government from interfering in markets, besides reducing its scope for rent-seeking. Another is through linking local government expenditure, with the revenue generated to ensure that the local governments face the financial consequences of their decisions. In addition, inter-governmental competition over mobile sources of revenue constraints individual sub-national governments. These served to harden budget constraints on enterprises, forcing them to restructure. Finally, some studies have shown that decentralization can permit a degree of institutional competition between centers of authority that can stimulate policy innovation and reduce the risk that governments will expropriate wealth (World Bank 2004d).

However, there is no *a priori* reason why more decentralized forms of governance will be more democratic or efficient, or will provide a close match between citizen preferences and the allocation of public resources. Comparative research is increasingly showing that, more often than not, political parties are key actors in decisions on decentralization and that they are most likely to decentralize in a specific situation. O'Neill (2005: 5) aptly notes that

> the party in power believes it cannot hold on to power that is centralized in the national government but believes it has a good chance of winning a substantial portion of decentralized power through subnational elections. Decentralization distributes power at one moment in time to the venues where a party's political allies are most likely to win in future contests. Thus, decentralization can be seen as an electoral strategy to empower political parties with reasonably long time horizons.

Indeed, recent research has compellingly argued that there is no necessary relationship between decentralization and improved democratic governance, and that we do not fully understand why some sub-national governments are effective in advancing democracy while others are not (Oxhorn *et al.* 2004). In multi-ethnic and/or divided federations, decentralization can be particularly destabilizing, especially if there is a history of unpredictable cycles of group conflict or the perception that rival groups or communities have disproportionate advantages, and where interregional and interethnic groups, including the various nationalities, engage in confrontational mobilizations in their efforts to capture central spoils (Hadenius 2003; Horowitz 1993). Competition in such settings often becomes greatly exacerbated when malcontents in the various administrative and jurisdictional units vicariously mobilize in the pursuit of parochial interests, or when political entrepreneurs politicize group cleavages to exploit the politics of grievance. Experience shows that in such environments even political movements that start as economic protests can quickly become overtly parochial and chauvinistic – with some groups and communities pursuing policies to "cleanse" pockets of rival communities.

To date, the most comprehensive study on these issues is by Brancati (2006). Using a statistical analysis of 30 democracies from 1985 to 2000, she shows that decentralization may decrease ethnic conflict and secessionism directly by bringing the government closer to the people, including increasing opportunities for citizens to participate in the government. Yet, paradoxically, decentralization may also increase ethnic conflict and secessionism indirectly by encouraging the growth of regional parties. These parties tend to increase conflict and secessionism by reinforcing ethnic and regional identities, producing legislation that favors some groups over others, and mobilizing groups to engage in ethnic conflict and secessionism. In some cases, political mobilizations under decentralized contexts have the potential to fragment, if not altogether destroy, the state's cohesion. Even in relatively homogenous societies, excessive mobilizations can quickly overwhelm the national political system. As Huntington (1968) noted long ago, instability results when newly mobilized groups frustrated by the lack of opportunities for socioeconomic mobility overload fragile and underdeveloped political institutions. Second, federal power-sharing arrangements that allow groups to have their own schools and religious institutions also magnify the salience of communal identity, making it harder to create cross-cutting ties or build a shared national identity (Kymlicka 1998). Third, lower levels of government are not necessarily "closer to the people." Rather, decentralization can entrench inequalities and transfer social conflicts to the local level. Since much associational life in the developing and transition economies follows inherited patterns rather than voluntary ones, decentralization has the potential to reinforce the traditional relationships of dominance and subordination.

Fourth, decentralization may not always be economically rational or efficient, especially when (1) key institutional and financial pillars are absent from the federal framework or when there is lack of clarity in the respective roles of each tier of government, and (2) if the central government devolves extensive expenditure responsibilities to sub-national governments while tightening control over revenue sources. This type of fiscal "centralization by decentralization" increases the political dependency of sub-national governments on the center, and weakens their accountability to the citizens who elected them (Ter-Minass-ian 1997; Wibbels 2004). Moreover, decentralization is generally associated with large and persistent government deficits when sub-national governments are simultaneously dependent on transfers and are free to borrow (Rodden 2002).

There can be a loss of economies of scale as the central government loses control over scarce financial resources, and efficiency losses because of poor local capacity. Furthermore, fiscal decentralization which involves shifting some responsibilities for expenditures and/or revenues to lower levels of government can have significant negative implications on macroeconomic stabilization. While in theory the reason for devolving the power to tax to sub-national and local governments is because it will encourage fiscal probity, practice generally shows otherwise. Empirical studies by Prud'homme (1995) and Ter-Minassian (1997), show that decentralization often results in sub-national fiscal indiscipline, besides worsening fiscal problems at the central level. It seems that when the political and economic logics of decentralization come into conflict, sub-national politicians are hardly prudent – often making important policy decisions (such as spending and delivery of public goods) to gain political advantage. Indeed, some sub-national governments have a poor track record on both revenue and expenditures, often out-spending what they collect in revenue. The massive debts accumulated by sub-national governments in India, China, Argentina, Brazil, Mexico, and elsewhere have exacerbated national deficits and undermined macroeconomic performance (Tanzi 2000).

Drawing on the experiences of over 20 countries, Ter-Minassian (1997) concludes that not only does decentralization make it more difficult to carry out the redistributive and macroeconomic management objectives of fiscal policy, but that cross-country empirical analysis shows that decentralization is associated with lower growth, higher deficits, and larger governments. Also, as Bardhan (1997: 54) points out,

> a decentralized tax system can distort the allocation of mobile factors across localities and hamper the operation of the domestic common market. Many developing countries do not have a constitutional provision akin to that in the United States preventing restraints on interstate commerce; under the circumstances, inter-jurisdictional beggar-thy-neighbor tax competition can easily lead to social inefficiency.

Since in many developing countries, the economic network of the parallel or "informal" economy operates outside the official or formal economy, decentralization can further entrench these patterns. Weak administrative and technical capacity at local levels may result in both poor service delivery and haphazard and ineffective program implementation. Since vested interests are more entrenched locally, and corruption and clientelism more prevalent there, decentralization only enables local elites to further consolidate their political and economic control (Shleifer and Vishny 1993). Moreover, in many poor countries, especially the failing or failed states, the almost complete collapse of the institutional fabric – from the institutions of law and order, public infrastructure, basic services – has left behind a political vacuum that cannot be filled by local government. In such a setting, reconstructing a functioning national state is most critical.

Thus, centralization or decentralization by itself is no panacea. Because central and local interests never exist in perfect accord, any attempt to create "local autonomy" along lines drafted in national ministries is bound to fail. Rather, an appropriate balance of centralization and decentralization is essential to the effective and efficient mediation and functioning of government. Such a balance demands good design, sound management and constant adaptation by all levels of authority. It requires that the national, sub-national and local-level governments responsibly share policy and supervisory duties – although the national authorities must initially create or maintain the "enabling conditions" that allow local units of administration to take on more responsibilities, besides strengthening local institutional capacity to assume their responsibilities. On the other hand, local politicians and decision-makers must bear the costs of their decisions and be held accountable for their promises. Finally, there must be a mechanism by which local communities can express their preferences in ways that are binding on local leaders and politicians – so there is a credible incentive for citizens to participate. Thus, there must be a system of accountability that relies on public and transparent information which enables the community to effectively monitor the performance of the local government and react appropriately to that performance, so that politicians and local officials have an incentive to be responsive. The recent effort by the Brazilian government to redesign its federal system to improve incentives for prudent fiscal behavior is instructive. The Brazilian government's bailout of states in 1997 required states to sign formal debt-restructuring contracts with the federal government which made the states responsible to bear part of the bailout costs. All new state borrowing was banned until states lowered their debt-to-revenue ratio. Interest penalties were imposed for noncompliance and states could only use constitutionally mandated transfers as collateral for the new state bonds. They were also required to provide down-payments worth 20 percent of a jurisdiction's outstanding debt stock, and had to agree to fixed payment schedule based on a jurisdiction's revenue mobilization capacity. These actions have greatly improved both the central and state government's fiscal position.

Conclusion

The "dual transition" toward democracy and free market that has swept across much of the world over the past few decades has meant that countries must simultaneously cope with the demands of economic development, political and social integration, as well as greater public demand for a more equitable distribution of the fruits of development. The ability to respond effectively to these challenges depends much on each country's institutional endowment. Building and strengthening these institutional endowments is a precondition for good governance because sustained economic development is impossible without good governance.

In turn, good governance is not only key to the promotion of human rights and protection of civil liberties, it is also highly correlated with economic development with the potential to deliver significant improvements in living standards. Although a number of countries have improved the quality of their governance, much still needs to be done. While it is the responsibility of countries themselves to improve governance, the developed world has a large stake in promoting good governance, especially in failing and post-conflict states.

4 Agricultural development for inclusive growth

According to the World Bank's *Global Monitoring Report 2004*, per capita consumption of US$1 a day represents a minimum standard of human existence in the low-income nations of Africa, Asia, Latin America and the Middle-East. Yet more than a billion people live on much less. For middle-income economies, the World Bank estimates a poverty line of US$2 as closer to the basic minimum. Overall, in 2002 an estimated 2.8 billion people (roughly half the population of the developing world), lived on less than US$2 a day. Given that the poor have very limited purchasing power, they suffer from malnutrition and debilitating diseases as they cannot meet the per capita daily caloric intake threshold of 2,350 calories that the United Nations Food and Agriculture Organization (FAO) defines as the basic minimum for an adequate diet. Moreover, the vast majority of the poor live in relative isolation in rural areas – where the basic necessities of life in terms of food availability, access to clean water, shelter and health care, and basic services such as access to education, transport, communication, and law and order are disproportionately far worse than in the urban areas.

Since the vast majority of rural poor in developing countries depend either directly or indirectly on agriculture for their livelihood, sustained growth in agricultural production and productivity is one of the most important ways to alleviate hunger and poverty.[1] However, given that much of the earth's arable land is already under the plough, where will these increases come from? Some four decades ago, Theodore W. Schultz (1964) in his seminal *Transforming Traditional Agriculture* outlined a set of specific policies to promote agricultural development. These are still relevant today.[2] Schultz cautioned against treating the agricultural economy in isolation from the rest of the economy. He reasoned that not only was the agricultural sector an integral part of the entire economy, but also the imbalance between the relative poverty and backwardness in agriculture compared with the higher productivity and the higher income levels in industry and other urban economic activities could be overcome.

Schultz's analysis of the development potential of agriculture was based on the so-called "disequilibrium approach." Specifically, he argued that it was the gap between traditional production methods, on the one hand, and the more effective modern methods, on the other, which creates the conditions necessary for a dynamic development. Using this approach, Schultz not only presented a sharp critique of developing countries' pro-industrialization or "urban-biased" policies and their neglect of agriculture, but also challenged the prevailing view (notably that of W. Arthur Lewis) by arguing that labor is efficient within traditional agriculture.[3] That is, peasants in poor countries are rational decision-makers who make the best with the resources at hand. Yet, they remain poor because most developing countries provide them with only limited technical and economic opportunities to which they could respond. To Schultz, the peasants were both "poor but efficient" and "efficient but poor." Fortunately, a "high pay off" growth in agriculture could be achieved if: (1) the capacity of the agricultural research system to provide new "location-specific" technical knowledge was enhanced; (2) the capacity of the industrial system to develop, produce and market the "green-revolution" technical inputs employed in agriculture (including a "package" of improved HYV (high-yielding varieties), seeds, fertilizer, pesticides, and herbicides) was developed; (3) market imperfections in the supply of agricultural R&D and in the diffusion of technologies were removed by the government;[4] and (4) investment was made in education to enhance the capacity of farmers to use modern inputs effectively and to adjust to market forces.[5]

Today, some four decades later, Schultz's prescriptions have been vindicated. First, those regions of the developing world that have experienced broad-based agricultural modernization, including the use of the green revolution, are relatively free from mass poverty and hunger. However, regions, in particular sub-Saharan Africa, that have experienced either anemic or no green revolution remain mired in agricultural stagnation (if not decline), poverty and destitution (Federico 2005). Indeed, currently three-quarters of Africans live in rural areas where agriculture is the single most important source of employment. Yet, Africa's agriculture is the least productive in the world, leading to some of the highest levels of rural poverty and recurring food crises (Christiaensen and Demery 2007). Second, subsequent empirical evidence has unambiguously shown that the "agriculture multiplier" is real. That is, agricultural growth is not only effective in reducing rural poverty, but it is also more effective than industrial growth in reducing urban poverty (Chambers 1983). For example, in their analysis of extensive household surveys in India over the period 1951–1991, Ravallion and Datt (1996: 19) conclude:

> Both the urban and rural poor gained from rural sector growth. By contrast, urban growth had adverse distributional effects within urban areas, which militated against the gains to the urban poor. And urban growth had no discernible effect on rural poverty.... Our investigation points clearly to the quantitative importance of the sectoral composition of economic growth to poverty reduction in India. Despite the rising urbanization of Indian poverty, it is likely to remain true for many years to come that – from the point of view of India's poor – it is the dog (the rural economy) that wags the tail (the urban sector), not the other way around. Fostering the con-

ditions for growth in the rural economy – in both primary and tertiary sectors – must thus be considered central to an effective strategy for poverty reduction in India.

Peter Timmer's (1997) study based on a sample of 35 developing countries arrives at a similar conclusion:

> a one percent growth in agricultural GDP per capita leads to a 1.61 percent increase in per capita incomes of the bottom quintile of the population in 35 developing countries. A similar one percent increase in industrial GDP increases the incomes of the poor by 1.16 percent.

While the data are not very different numerically, extrapolated over several years it represents a potentially large difference in the incomes of the poor. Currently about three-quarters of the world's poor live in rural areas (FAO 2004). For them, agriculture remains the catalyst for improving their overall economic situation. However, for this to happen, the remaining regions of the world trapped in traditional agriculture need to be modernized. As the following sections will show, public investments, the application of modern science and technology, and use of new biotechnologies or the so-called "second-generation green revolution" will be critical to boost and sustain agricultural growth.

Targeted public investments

Public investment in agriculture and rural development is a major determinant of agricultural growth and rural poverty reduction in most developing countries. However, under ISI (Import-Substitution Industrialization) there was a neglect as well as misallocation of resources in agriculture and rural development.[6] Similarly, under the recent wave of macroeconomic policy reforms, many developing countries reduced their levels of investment in rural areas – not only to agriculture, but also to critical infrastructural institutions such as those regulating or maintaining public goods, including roads, railways, communication networks, irrigation systems, extension services, storage facilities, and markets.[7] This neglect has been costly. It has not only affected productivity growth and food supplies: in some areas it has also exacerbated poverty levels and accelerated the degradation of natural resources (Grey and Sadoff 2006). In hindsight, making the necessary investments in agriculture would have been far more cost-effective than importing ever-increasing volumes of food, or becoming dependent on food aid.

Increasing public investment in agriculture and rural development will also help unleash private sector investments – which complement public investment. Specifically, investments in rural infrastructure, sound management and sustainable use of natural resources – land, water and genetic endowments – has the potential to accelerate agricultural production and productivity and improve rural livelihoods. Investment in roads (all-weather as well as feeder roads), storage facilities (including cold storage), irrigation infrastructure (coupled with effective management of water resources), and electrification is essential for reducing post-harvest losses and ensuring a better return to farmers. Investment in agro-processing industries, as well as collaboration between the producer cooperatives and the corporate agro-processing units in key producing areas, will help expand market opportunities, reduce wastage, especially of horticultural produce, increase value addition, and create off-farm employment for the landless poor and others who lack productive assets or marketable skills.

Research shows that investment in infrastructure that strengthens the economic linkages between rural and urban centers creates new opportunities in the countryside, smaller provincial towns and cities. For example, Pender *et al.* (2006) show how infrastructure made agriculture more profitable for the rural poor in the highlands of East Africa. The authors found that in areas with high agricultural potential and favorable access to urban markets, a virtuous circle is possible. Farmers can increase their production of high-value commodities and employment in non-farm activities – which inevitably contributes to higher incomes and enables farmers to invest in land-improving and productivity-enhancing technologies. On the other hand, without reliable access to markets, farmers only have a "comparative advantage" in nonperishables such as coffee or cereals. The World Bank Report (2004d: 134) also highlights a particularly illustrative example from Morocco – new roads which allowed farmers to move their goods more often and more cheaply.

> In some cases the time it took to get to rural markets fell by half. The cost of shipping a truckload of merchandise also fell by half. In the areas benefiting from the road upgrading, the land is more productive, and the volume and value of agricultural products is higher. As it became easier to ship produce quickly without damaging it, farmers shifted from low-value cereals to high-value fruits. As the price of bringing goods to the farms fell, farmers used more fertilizer. Improvements in the agricultural economy spurred the growth of other business. Off-farm employment grew twice as fast as in areas not benefiting from road improvement.

Moreover, improved roads

> made it easier for children to go to school and, by making the delivery of butane more affordable, reduced the need for women and girls to collect firewood. After the road improvements, primary school enrollment rose from 28 percent to 68 percent.

Evidence from other countries also shows that road and transportation corridors linking key agricultural regions with rural towns and secondary cities greatly stimulates growth and entrepreneurial activity in all areas (Estache and Wodon 2007). For example, improvement of roads and ports in Tanzania can help land-locked countries such as Uganda and Malawi transit their trade more efficiently

– so in some areas infrastructural reforms need to be addressed regionally. Moreover, in this era of globalization infrastructure has the potential to give some countries the edge over others. In a recent study by Fan *et al.* (2004) and IFPRI (2002), note that in sub-Saharan Africa, where some 70 percent of farmers are poorly connected to markets, high transportation costs generally account for between 30 and 60 percent of private traders' operating costs. This puts African agricultural goods at a competitive disadvantage in global markets.[8] On the other hand, in India, government spending on road construction has helped to reduce poverty. In China, roads rank third among poverty-reducing investments. In both countries, roads had a greater impact on poverty reduction and agricultural productivity than did electricity, communications, irrigation, or soil and water conservation investments. Clearly, infrastructure is a necessary component for rural development. Public investments in the construction and rehabilitation of roads and related transportation networks (preferably using labor-intensive techniques to create employment), will pay dividends.

Since the leading resource and environmental constraints faced by farmers include soil loss, erosion, nutrient-degradation, water-logging, and salinity, investments to improve the quality of land and soil resources, as well as the reclamation of degraded and fallow lands, are critical. Experience from sub-Saharan Africa shows that inexpensive "green fertilizers" made from naturally available resources such as nitrogen-fixing leguminous plants, indigenous rock phosphates in phosphorous-deficient soils, and biomass transfers of leaves and shrubs – used in combination or separately – have in many cases doubled or tripled yields for farmers. As the UN Millennium Project (2005: 69) aptly notes, sustained investment by national governments and donor agencies in "green fertilizers" is a prudent cost-effective strategy because

> distributing green fertilizers to tens of millions of African farmers will cost an estimated $100 million a year for each of the next ten years. This is only a tenth of the amount currently spent each year to deliver food aid.

Also, given the fact that much of the developing countries' cropped land is dependent on rains, optimum harvesting and conservation of rainwater through irrigation systems, and watershed development (which can be achieved with relatively inexpensive conveyance systems) in the high rainfall areas, coupled with sustainable rain-fed agricultural practices, will help reduce the risk of seasonal flooding and other vagaries of nature. In regions or areas that are heavily dependent on river or surface irrigation and/or ground water, , especially in marginal and dry-land areas, the problem of declining water quality and receding ground-water levels (as a result of over-exploitation of underground aquifers and wells), has reached alarming levels and requires immediate attention. Experience shows that in many countries, large-scale irrigation investments have generally underperformed and represent a heavy drain on government capital. Rather, evidence shows that in fragile areas, management of water resources by local communities, and the use of relatively small-scale and low-cost technologies such as individual low-lift water pumping systems and the pressured irrigation systems like drip and sprinkler, combined with traditional mulching, greatly reduces overuse and wastage.[9] Moreover, maintenance of irrigation networks, the use of drought-resistant crop varieties and sustainable agricultural practices can also help mitigate wastage and inefficiencies, besides reducing the risk of seasonal scarcity and drought. Similarly, protecting the rapidly diminishing plant and animal genetic resources is critical as it directly affects food security. The conservation of both indigenous and exogenously introduced genetic variability in crop plants and animals,[10] and, as the next section will argue, the use of bio-technologies which consume less water, are drought-resistant, pest-resistant, contain more nutrition, give higher yields and are environmentally safe, must be promoted.

Agriculture in the developing world is characterized by the dominance of smallholders (farmers with up to two hectares of land), including marginal or subsistence farmers who also constitute the bulk of private sector economic activity in many developing countries.[11] Contrary to conventional belief, smallholder agriculture has proven to be at least as efficient and productive as large farms and modern agro-industry when poor farmers have received similar support services and inputs such as seeds, fertilizer, credit, and access to markets. Thus, raising the productivity of small and marginal farms would not only improve the lives of these impoverished farmers, it would also help lower domestic food prices – indeed, stimulate the entire economy. According to the (IFPRI) International Food Policy Research Institute (2002: 5) "each 1 percent increase in agricultural productivity in Africa has been shown to reduce poverty by 0.6 percent. Stated differently, a 1 percent increase in yields can help 6 million people raise their incomes above US$1 per day."

In agrarian societies land is an indispensable resource – conferring status and privilege, providing collateral for credit markets, the key resource to accumulating wealth and the most prized asset that can be passed across generations. However, without secure property rights, farmers have little incentive to invest in the land or use and manage it prudently. Institutional reform that provides secure land and tenure rights to small and poor farmers will go a long way in unleashing their productive energies. Specifically, clearly defined laws that recognize ownership and property rights of farmers, including women's rights in land, is critical. As the IFPRI (2002: 5) study aptly notes:

> providing sustainable support to women farmers will be a critical element of any new smallholder-led development effort. Women, who supply more than 70 percent of agricultural labor in Sub-Saharan Africa, have historically been agricultural innovators and the providers of family care and nutrition. Yet agricultural researchers, extension workers and credit providers have long neglected women's needs. When women obtain the same levels of education, experience and farm inputs as men, they produce significantly higher yields in a range of farming systems. Designing gender-sensitive agricultural projects is a win–win strategy for reducing hunger in Africa.

Finally, tenancy rules that clearly recognize the rights of the tenants and share-croppers, transparent rules that allow for equitable use of common property resources, land reforms designed to consolidate fragmented land holdings and redistribute surplus and "waste lands" to the small and landless farmers, can greatly enhance security and thereby investments in land. Equally important, the creation of marketing institutions such as cooperatives and farmers' associations can greatly help farmers negotiate with market intermediaries. As Ravallion and Chen (2004) show, rural poverty rates fall most dramatically when rural producer prices are higher – implying that most of the rural poor have their net incomes directly and positively affected by food prices. Therefore, improving the terms of trade for farmers is equivalent to removing a tax on their incomes and does not actually have a direct impact on food prices for consumers.

Second-generation green revolution

Schultz's (1964: 145) claim that "the principal sources of high productivity in modern agriculture are reproducible sources. They consist of particular material inputs and of skills and other capabilities required to use such inputs successfully" was realized by the green revolution (Pearce 1980). The green revolution technology introduced in the late 1960s and early 1970s quickly increased both agricultural production and productivity. Indeed, the spectacular improvements in the yields of staple food crops such as rice, wheat, and maize helped turn heavily populated food-deficit countries in Asia and Latin America into self-sufficient producers in the space of just a few years. As Glaeser (1987: 1) aptly notes,

> the [green revolution was] introduced in several Asian countries in 1965, and, by 1970, these strains were being cultivated over an area of 10 million hectares. Within three years, Pakistan ceased to be dependent on wheat imports from the United States. Sri Lanka, Philippines and a number of Latin American countries achieved record harvests. India, which had just avoided a severe famine in 1967, produced enough grain within five years to support its population.

Specifically, in the case of India in 1965–1966 and 1966–1967, the country's total foodgrain output stood at a deficit (in terms of population growth) of 72.3 and 74.2 million tons respectively. However, with the rapid dissemination of technological innovations, foodgrain output increased to 95 million tons in 1968–1969, to 108.4 million tons in 1970–1971, to 133 million tons in 1981–1982 and to a record high of 178 million tons in 1990–1991.[12]

The green revolution not only averted a major food crisis and a potential Malthusian-type famine, it contributed much to alleviating hunger and reducing poverty. Inflation-adjusted prices of rice and wheat fell by 30–40 percent between 1970 and 1997 (World Bank 1990–1999; Evenson and Gollin 2003). In Asia, "real per capita incomes almost doubled between 1970 and 1995, and poverty declined from nearly three out of every five Asians in 1975 to less than one in three by 1995" (IFPRI 2002a: 3). Similarly, Datt and Ravallion's (1998) comprehensive study illustrates that higher crop yields reduced both the number of the rural poor and the severity of rural poverty in many parts of South Asia. On the other hand, a vast body of research has attributed the pervasive agricultural stagnation in sub-Saharan Africa to the region's failure to reap the bounty of the green-revolution technology and modern farming methods (Sachs 2005).

Unlike in much of Asia and Latin America, growth-accounting exercises show that the adoption of the green-revolution technologies in sub-Saharan Africa was not accompanied by the increased investment in infrastructure (especially roads and irrigation networks) and fertilizer use. This suggests high levels of market imperfections and associated transaction costs as a major factor. Others have highlighted the "land frontier" hypothesis, implying that as long as low-cost cropland expansion is feasible, African countries do not make the necessary investment in agricultural modernization. Still others, most notably Jeffrey Sachs and his co-authors (2004), have argued that the green-revolution technology has not been easily transferable to conditions in Africa. Since most Africans south of the Sahara live and work in the interior of the continent, the few natural waterways, unpredictable and erratic rainfall, and lack of infrastructure to manage the available water resources make it extremely difficult to successfully adopt the modern technologies. They note that the share of Africa's agricultural land that is irrigated is one-twentieth that in other developing countries, and African farmers use only 6 percent as much fertilizer per acre. Furthermore, the region's relative isolation from global markets and its poor infrastructure (and therefore, very high transport costs) make the use of the green-revolution technologies uneconomic. Suffice it to note, the near-collapse of agriculture in many parts of sub-Saharan Africa and the resultant periodic famine, perennial food shortages and higher prices on what is available, and the tragic toll on human lives, all underscore the importance of investment in agricultural and rural development.

Yet, after some three decades of unprecedented success, the green revolution has been experiencing diminishing returns.[13] With world population expected to grow to between 8 and 9 billion by 2020 and over 10 billion by 2050 (from the current 5.6 billion), there is justified concern that the world's food supply may not stay ahead of future aggregate demand.[14] To prevent such a nightmarish Malthusian scenario and the resultant conflict over scarce resources, governments, think-tanks, advocacy groups and researchers have been promoting the so-called "second green revolution" based once again on the Promethean advances in modern science – specifically agricultural biotechnology – as the solution to the world's future food deficit problems. However, unlike the green-revolution technologies, the investment and use of biotechnologies has generated heated debates (Bernauer 2003). Yet, there is much misunderstanding about the new biotechnology and its implications.[15] The following sections attempts to address several interrelated questions: What is biotechnology? What explains the controversy around it? Is it the panacea to the world's growing food needs?

What are the potential implications of this new technology on the environment and society? Is the potential contribution of GM foods (or genetically modified foods[16]) to ensuring food security large enough to outweigh the risks?

Biotechnology's promise

The father of biotechnology is Gregor Mendel, who in the 1850s bred and cross-bred pea plants to create new combinations of height, color and shape. The scientific knowledge Mendel derived about genetic inheritance eventually allowed scientists in the twentieth century to create high-yielding seeds (Kloppenburg 2004). Modern biotechnology originated in the mid-1970s with new advances in genetics, immunology, and biochemistry. Given its broad scope, coming up with precise definitions has been difficult. However Pinstrup-Andersen and Schioler (2000: 36) provide a working definition stating that "the term biotechnology covers all the techniques that use living organisms or substances from organisms to produce or alter a product, cause changes in plants or animals, or develop microorganisms for specific purposes." Biotechnology encompasses several techniques and methods, including genome mapping, gene splicing (or the transfer of one or more genes with certain prospectively useful qualities to plants, domestic animals, fish and other organisms), and molecular breeding. Based on this, the FAO (2004a: 4) defines agricultural biotechnology as encompassing

> a range of research tools scientists use to understand and manipulate the genetic make-up of organisms for use in agriculture: crops, livestock, forestry and fisheries. Biotechnology is much broader than genetic engineering and includes tissue culture, genomics and bioinformatics, marker-assisted selection, micro-propagation, cloning, artificial insemination, embryo transfers and other technologies.

Although genetic modification of crops and domesticated animals has been occurring over the millennia using tools such as selective breeding and hybridization, modern biotechnology can speed up the process enormously, incorporating new traits from virtually any species at will. Examples include implanting an Artic flounder gene that resists cold temperatures into a strawberry plant to defend against frost, or inserting soil bacteria and daffodil genes that induce vitamin A production into rice. Biotechnology's unprecedented ability to move genes within and across species, including the ability to move genes across distantly related species and potentially even between animals and plants, makes it a powerful tool for modifying nature. Indeed, biotechnology's potential seems endless.

Although, the first biotechnology-based foods entered the marketplace in 1994, by 2001 over "50 modifications involving 13 crops had been approved and produced on more than 52 million hectares in at least 14 countries" (Phillips 2003: 2). In 2004, the global area under biotech crops grew by 20 percent – with some eight million farmers in 17 countries engaged in biotech cultivation (FAO 2004). The bulk of the growing commercial applications of biotechnology are concentrated in agriculture and food processing, particularly in the development of new varieties of food plants, diagnostics for plant and animal diseases and vaccines against animal diseases, including reduced herbicide and pesticide use through the utilization of biological control agents. For example, in Mexico, cultivation of GM cotton by small producers has led to a 50 percent reduction in pesticide use, including better yields and lint quality. One of the technology's first applications included staple vegetables such as tomatoes and corn and crops such as cotton – the latter two have been bioengineered to make toxins capable of killing insect pests. For example, "Bt maize" has been genetically modified in order to make it produce a protein from the bacterium *Bacillus thuringiensis*. This protein kills the corn-borer insect, which is a major threat to maize crops. Similarly, crops such as squash, potatoes, wheat, papaya and raspberries have been successfully engineered to resist common plant diseases and to be kept much longer in storage and transport. Transgenic tomatoes and bananas have been developed with slow ripening properties.[17] Genetically modified soybeans, corn, canola and cotton have been developed with resistance to the herbicide glyphosate and are now widely used in the United States.

Moreover, biotechnology has successfully enhanced the quality of food by increasing the levels of essential amino acids and vitamins to foods traditionally lacking in those nutrients. For example, after some two decades of research, the incorporation of three genes (two from soil bacteria and one from daffodils) that produce beta-carotene and vitamin A to a rice variety (called "Golden Rice") was a major breakthrough. If used widely it has the potential to substantially increase the nutritional quality of diets and reduce visual impairment and blindness and other health troubles in millions of adults and especially children in the developing world – keeping in mind that globally about three million children of preschool age have visible eye damage owing to a vitamin A deficiency (Datta and Bouis 2000). Similarly, enhancing fruits and vegetables to contain vaccines against deadly and debilitating diseases such as hepatitis, cholera and malaria will greatly help developing countries where such infectious diseases are rampant – especially among children. Of course, the key will be the ability to grow and distribute foods containing these edible vaccines locally and at relatively low cost. And, last but not least, modifications to tissue culture, marker-assisted selection and DNA fingerprinting now allow a faster and much more targeted development of improved genotypes for crop varieties. This has enabled crops to be grown in difficult environments such as those that have irregular water supplies or poor soils, to greatly reduce post-harvest losses, and to strengthen a crop's own ability to defend itself against destructive insects, thereby reducing the need for chemical pesticides. Thus, biotechnology and genetic engineering has the potential to help increase production and productivity in agriculture, forestry and fisheries. It could lead to higher yields on marginal lands in countries that today cannot grow enough food to feed their people.

These advancements in science and technology have been hailed as the coming of a second green revolution – giving farmers a powerful tool in their struggle against the vagaries of nature and the age-old scourge of pestilence and disease. For the millions of cultivators in developing countries struggling with low yields due to droughts, disease, pests, pathogens and poor soils, biotechnology holds the promise of providing higher-yielding, disease-resistant, and more nutritious crops to reduce malnutrition and poverty and sustain the needs of the burgeoning population.

Concerns and implications

Opposition to biotechnology ranges from concerns regarding gene splicing and the patenting of living organisms on religious and ethical grounds, to fear of unexpected health and environmental consequences. However, the harshest opposition is reserved for the supposedly "unregulated" production of genetically engineered or modified foods – dubbed "Frankenfoods" by some. Critics, including NGOs such as Oxfam, Greenpeace, and Friends of the Earth, argue that there has been insufficient testing on GM foods and that the benefits and safety of such foods have not been adequately demonstrated. They point out that the potential risks of adulterated GM foods may include toxic reactions, food allergies, increased cancer risks, antibiotic resistance, and sometimes even death. Critics claim that the transfer of toxins from one life form to another and the creation of new toxins, including the transfer of allergenic compounds from one species to another, has already occurred, resulting in the sharp rise of allergic reactions throughout the world. In the case of foods, the inadvertent mixing of genetically modified and conventional corn stocks,[18] the concern that the gene marker (antibiotic resistance) used in the FlavrSavr tomato could result in consumers developing resistance to medication, and the deaths from "mad cow disease" only served to further galvanize both environmental and consumer advocacy groups against GM foods.

Critics also see a clear potential for a massive ecological disaster as a result of wholesale genetic pollution via cross-breeding and gene transfer to non-target plant and animal species. The fear is that such practices would result in the creation of new viruses and bacteria, the inevitable mutation of weeds and pests into deadly "superweeds" and "superpests" either via the accidental transfer of the herbicide resistance genes from crops to weeds, or as weeds and pests eventually develop resistance to pesticides and vaccines in the genetically engineered crops.[19] Compounding this is the concern that eventually biotechnology will greatly reduce biodiversity. That is, in their efforts to deliberately promote certain plants and species over others, biotechnology will reduce the genetic pool of plant and animal life, making the planet even more dependent on a handful of food varieties. In fact, environmental activists and NGOs have called for a complete moratorium on further development of biotechnology, while others have urged developing countries to refrain from producing GM foods because they may lose export markets in industrialized countries where consumer anxiety over genetically engineered foods remains palpable.

Despite expert reassurances from several US agencies, including the Food and Drug Administration (FDA), the Department of Agriculture, the Environmental Protection Agency (EPA) and the United States Department of Agriculture (USDA), that biotech foods on the market are safe for human consumption, the European Union (EU) has adopted a more precautionary approach to the regulation of GM foods. This has resulted in a de facto moratorium on GM crop approvals and imports of genetically modified organisms (GMOs) in Europe from 1998–2004, and the concerns about GM foods remain deep-rooted in Europe. According to Bernauer (2003), this "regulatory polarization" which has the potential to put the US and the EU on a collision course is primarily due to three main factors. First, in contrast to the United States, the EU considers genetically modified crops as "novel foods" because they contain proteins that do not exist in traditional varieties. Second, there are different pressure group dynamics in the EU and the United States. In the former, where consumers have long been concerned about GM foods, various advocacy groups were able to mount effective public campaigns against GMOs. However, in the United States, where consumers were not as concerned, pressure groups were not able to rally the public around the issue. The third is linked to different institutional structures in the two economies. In the EU, the institutional system in regard to GMO regulation is more decentralized, giving member-states greater autonomy over policy, while in the US the more centralized federal system has acted against divergent regulatory approaches.

Furthermore, much of agricultural biotechnology research has concentrated primarily on commercial agriculture and on industrialized countries' staple crops, rather than the food needs of developing countries. Investments in crops consumed by the vast majority of people in developing countries, such as cassava, millets, sorghum, sweet potatoes, yams, legumes, lentils, pigeon pea, chickpea, cowpea, traditional rice varieties and groundnuts, remain insignificant (Naylor and Falcon 2004). This is unfortunate as the resilient transgenic plant varieties have the potential to improve farm productivity and rural livelihoods. To take one example, cowpea is a low-cost vegetable protein usually cultivated by women. The stover of cowpea is used as fodder, besides enriching soil through nitrogen fixation. However, cowpea cultivation has fallen because of severe pests and diseases during the vegetative growth process. Similarly, the cassava mosaic disease, a viral infection, destroys about one-third of the harvest each year in sub-Saharan Africa – and cassava is the second most important crop in Africa.

Such neglect has led many to conclude that these biases are deliberate as the private investment in biotechnological research is oriented towards agriculture in higher-income countries where there is purchasing power for its products. Of equal concern, the development of substitutes for such major developing-country export crops such as cocoa and sugarcane could have a devastating impact on these economies. One possible reason for these trends has to do with the interests spearheading the new biotechnologies. Unlike the earlier green revolution technologies, which were developed mainly by publicly funded institutions in both developed and developing countries and philanthropic organizations such as the Ford and Rockefeller foundations, agricultural biotechnology remains largely the prerogative of multinational corporations, in particular those in the pharmaceutical and food-processing industries. At present, biotechnology applications remain concentrated among a few large corporations such as Aventis, Monsanto, AgrEvo, Syngenta, DuPont, Zeneca, and Dow. Unlike the philanthropic organizations which literally gave away the high-yielding seed varieties to developing countries, these corporations usually agree to transfer proprietary technologies at cost – some even demanding royalties up-front before making any transfer. As will be discussed later, such actions have inevitably raised concerns that property rights protection on the processes and products of biotechnology might prevent cultivators in developing countries from benefiting from the new technologies. Clearly, developing-country governments must strengthen their own capacities in biotechnology by putting the needed investments in agricultural R&D and through greater public and private sector cooperation. The latter is still in its infancy, but has great potential because, while the tools of agricultural biotechnology are in the private sector, much of the genetic material for crops is in the CGIAR (Consultative Group on International Agricultural Research) genebanks.[20] Moreover, donor aid in the form of GM research, infrastructure and training will go a long way towards capacity-building in developing countries.

Maximizing biotechnology's potential

Not surprisingly, the FAO Assistant Director-General, Louise Fresco, has warned of a "molecular divide" between the countries of the "North and the South" stating that "the gap between rich and poor farmers, between research priorities and needs, and between technology development and actual technology transfer is widening."[21] In order to narrow the North–South molecular divide so that all nations can benefit from biotechnology's potential, several challenges need to be met. But first, two caveats.

It is important to reiterate that while biotechnology (like the green revolution before it) has the potential to dramatically increase both the quality and quantity of agricultural products, it alone cannot solve the food insecurities problem facing the world's poor. As Nobel laureate Amartya Sen (1999) has reminded us, hunger and destitution are not usually due to a lack of food, but to the poor's inability to purchase food. Thus today, even in the midst of sufficient global food supplies, over one billion people go to bed hungry every night, while over two billion are either already disabled by malnutrition or at risk from micronutrient deficiencies. The case of India is illustrative. The green revolution enabled India to quickly move from a food-deficit nation in the 1960s to a food-surplus nation by the mid-1970s. Today, India is not only a major exporter of food-grains, but has over 60 million tons of food in stock (in mid-2004), against a norm of around 17 million tons considered necessary to ensure the country's food security. Yet, over 300 million Indians remain malnourished and some 200 million who live on less than US$1 a day are severely malnourished because they simply cannot afford buy enough food to keep body and soul together (George 2005; Sainath 1996). Thus, unlike in Africa, in much of Asia the problem of hunger and malnutrition is largely a problem of income distribution and purchasing power rather than food supplies.

Second, there is substantial variation among developing countries in terms of their capacity to develop and use products from biotechnologies. Some countries such as China and India, with their large pool of scientific talent, established R&D sectors, and vibrant information technology and pharmaceutical industries, already have thriving biotech industries and are well positioned to benefit from its many applications. The case of India is illustrative (Dhar 2003; Scoones 2006). In 1986, the Indian government established a separate Department of Biotechnology (DBT) under the Ministry of Science and Technology to give a new impetus to the development of modern biotechnology. The DBT has the mandate to promote biotechnology throughout the country by collecting and disseminating relevant information, developing biosafety guidelines, and promoting biotech education and R&D by fostering university and industry interaction, establishing biotech research institutes, and approving proposed biotech projects. A recent national budget provides significant increases for R&D spending on biotechnology, and beginning in 2001 biotech firms enjoyed a 150 percent tax deduction for R&D industrial parks. This has resulted in the proliferation of biotech parks like the Marine Biotech Park in Chennai. Also, individual states like Punjab, Haryana, and Andhra Pradesh are collaborating with a private promoter to either build or expand biotech parks in their respective states. Currently, both the Indian private sector and the government are investing heavily in the agricultural and medicinal applications of biotechnology. India now has a fairly advanced infrastructure in both fields, and has already made important scientific contributions in areas such as biological control of plant pests, diseases and weeds, development of new vaccines and veterinary products from medicinal and aromatic plants, and enhanced the nutritional value of staples such as basmati rice, mustard, mustard oil, wheat, mango, cardamom, chickpea, potato, vegetables, banana, oil palm, and coconut. However, many developing countries, especially the least-developed countries, face formidable challenges. Not only do many lack the necessary resources and infrastructure, but, given the cost and sophistication of biotechnology, implementation and diffusion will inevitably be slow and piecemeal.

While the current proliferation of patchwork approaches to regulation of GMOs allows countries to tailor rules and regulations to suit their interests, it also creates much overlap and confusion – and, as the following paragraphs shows, makes enforcements difficult. To fully realize biotechnology's potential, the various stakeholders will need to compromise and come to negotiated agreements on a number of critical issues. For starters, the international community needs to formulate a broad globally accepted standard for evaluating the safety of biotechnology food products. Specifically, a science-based evaluation system that would objectively determine the benefits and risks of each individual GMO is important. Such a system will necessitate an approach that carefully addresses concerns regarding the biosafety of each product or process prior to its release, including the benefits and risks. Careful monitoring of the post-release effects of these products and processes is also essential to ensure their continued safety to human beings, animals and the environment.

While the Codex Alimentarius Commission (or Codex), created in 1962 and jointly administered by UN agencies – the Food Agriculture Organization (FAO) and the World Health Organization (WHO) – serves as an international standard-setting body for food safety, Codex principles are not binding on national governments. The Codex Alimentarius Commission has been developing draft principles for human health risk analysis of biotechnology food products, besides considering the labeling of foods derived from biotechnologies to allow the consumer to make informed choices. Nevertheless, while Codex may be able to more effectively promote fair food trade practices and the coordination of all food standards work undertaken by international governmental and NGOs, it remains a first step in the resolution of some more contentious issues.

As the frontiers between discovery and invention have become blurred (the case of Golden Rice has seen various industries claim some 40 different patented steps at the time of release), a broad global agreement on intellectual property rights issues related to biotechnology is essential. While governments in the advanced industrial countries have extended near-exclusive property rights to new technologies, including genes and germplasm to multinational corporations and private interests in an effort to encourage private-sector investments, in many developing countries this has created fears that the granting of such rights will eventually transfer resources from the public sphere to Northern private interests via the legal enforcement of intellectual property rights. Not surprisingly, many developing-country governments, especially advocacy groups and NGOs, have vociferously argued that enforcing intellectual property rights on biotechnology-related products is "biopiracy," because it is tantamount to stealing the proprietary rights of indigenous peoples and poor farmers who have not only nurtured the crops and seeds on which today's biotechnology depends, but who also have used these "traditional products" for centuries. The debate on this topic is both emotional and complex. Consider the case of *haldi*, or turmeric. *Haldi*, an essential ingredient in curry powder, has been used in India for centuries as an antiseptic on wounds. In 1993, when two American scientists obtained a patent for *haldi*'s wound-healing properties, the Indian government mounted a successful challenge and had the patent revoked after proving (using ancient Sanskrit texts) that this was no discovery. However, such "success" has been rare. For example, despite protest by the Indian government and NGOs, that basmati rice was the product of informal breeding by Indian farmers, a US company, Ricetec, was granted patent rights for developing "basmati 867." Ricetec successfully argued that it had developed a new higher-yielding strain. Similarly, a number of Western labs were granted patent to *sarson* seeds (mustard), used for centuries in *ayruvedic* medicine, after successfully extracting the mustard oil used for certain medicines. And last but not least, a patent for the extract from leaves of the *neem* plant, used as toothpaste and as an antiseptic for centuries in India, was granted to several American and European labs, despite the Indian government's challenge.

Given this background, NGOs such as the Third World Network, Oxfam and Greenpeace, among others, have claimed that granting foreign corporations' near-monopoly rights over public resources will result in the further expropriation of the Third World's resources by the rich Western countries. In response, private business interests, in their efforts to protect their investments and proprietary knowledge, have demanded exclusive patent rights rather than the less strict plant-breeders' rights.[22] Predictably, as Victor and Runge (2002) note, "the result has been a proliferation of patent claims and counterclaims by companies who fear losing out on potentially lucrative developments." Resolving the sometimes competing interests of investors and developing countries who claim to represent the "wider public interest" (in particular, the hapless poor unable to purchase transgenic seeds from greedy multinationals), will not be easy. Under the World Trade Organization's Agreement on Trade Related Aspects of Intellectual Property Rights (TRIPS), most processes and many products of biotechnology research are patentable. Since most biotechnology research is conducted in OECD countries, often by private companies, developing countries may have to pay to use a new procedure or product. Although TRIPS exempts advanced life forms from patentability, it nevertheless, requires countries to establish some form of protection for plant varieties. This approach has hardly pleased anyone. Even the trade-liberalization advocates who support the standard of science-based risk assessment incorporated in the WTO agreement on Sanitary and Phytosanitary (SPS) measures are deeply divided over biotechnology.[23] It seems that, at a minimum, the WTO's emphasis on science-based regulatory standards will require strengthening regarding the underlying scientific capacity of developing countries.

Future progress will require the United States to take a more proactive role in international discussions regarding genetic resources, biodiversity, and biotechnology. Specifically, although the US is one of 168 signatories of the UN Convention on Biological Diversity (CBD) signed at Rio in 1992, its failure to ratify it has not only send a negative message, but also has had negative implications.[24] For example, against US opposition, in January 2000 parties to the CBD completed a supplementary agreement, known as the Cartagena Protocol on Biosafety (or the Biosafety Protocol), giving governments the right to regulate GM foods.[25] The Protocol, ratified in 2003 by 82 countries (including the EU and Japan, but not the United States), seeks to protect countries from risks associated with imports of genetically modified organisms. Because the US had not ratified the CBD, it participated in the Biosafety Protocol negotiations only as an observer – and therefore could not vote or officially participate. This is unfortunate, because the Biosafety Protocol would be a legally binding environmental treaty designed to safeguard biological diversity from the potential risks posed by transboundary movements of certain biotechnology food products that are capable of transferring or replicating their genetic material. Specifically, the core requirement of the Protocol is an "Advanced Informed Agreement" procedure before shipment of biotechnology products (such as seeds), including more limited requirements for shipments of biotechnology-derived agricultural commodities destined for food, feed or processing. In fact, the Protocol would make it a mandatory requirement that exporters seek consent from the competent national authority in importing countries before shipping certain biotechnology products intended for release into the environment.[26] In addition, the Protocol requires exporting countries to provide information about the manner scientists modify the GM foods, label all genetically modified products and adhere to the importing country's national biosafety laws and risk-assessment procedures, and establishes an information-sharing regime to enable countries to understand potential environmental risks and make informed trade decisions.

Equally significant, while it was not drafted to be subordinate to any other international agreement, the Biosafety Protocol preserves countries' rights under other international agreements, including the WTO. The Protocol recognizes that trade and environment agreements should be mutually supportive. Nevertheless, the Biosafety Protocol would offer benefits beyond those afforded by the WTO. Specifically, the Biosafety Protocol would require that regulatory decisions under the Protocol be based on risk assessments carried out scientifically, including taking into account recognized risk-assessment techniques. The Protocol, by reaffirming the use of the "precautionary principle" (which is also a key element of the CBD), authorizes countries to deny entry to undesired biotechnology imports – even in cases of insufficient scientific data, analysis, or information to support the denial.[27] Not surprisingly, during the negotiations, the US and several other nations argued that enforcing the precautionary principle too strongly would allow countries to ban imports of GM food simply because of protectionism.

Indeed, the United States fought against its inclusion, but given its weak observer status, the concerns of the United States were easily rejected by the delegates from the EU and developing countries. However, given the patchwork approach to regulating GMOs, in 2003 the United States, Canada and Argentina began the WTO process of challenging the legality of the European Union's moratorium on GMOs. In other words, the United States, Canada and Argentina turned to the WTO, the other body of international law concerning GMOs. Since the WTO aims to prevent discrimination on nationality, the WTO requires a country refusing imports to base its decision on scientific evidence of food and environmental safety. Thus, as long as these patchwork approaches exist, countries will not agree to a single set of standards.

Conclusion

Finally, it is important to put the discussion on GMOs in some perspective: In 1996 there were only a few million acres planted with GM seeds. By 2002 there were more than 130 million acres under cultivation. But this only constitutes

1.3 percent of the total global cropland. In addition, some 95 percent of the total GM acreage is confined to only four countries: the United States with 68 percent, Argentina with 22 percent, Canada with 6 percent and China with 3 percent (Pringle 2003). However, if the current trend is any guide, the acreage under GM crops is bound to sharply increase.

However, the passionate debates surrounding GMOs are not going to go away anytime soon. For that to happen a wide range of complex issues will need to be resolved. Yet, it is important to recognize that biotechnology offers both promise and perils. In the absence of viable alternative strategies, and in light of the expected increases in global population, biotechnology seems to hold the best promise to overcome the future food needs of the world. However, as discussed, to reap the benefits of biotechnology, the various stakeholders will need to work towards some broad negotiated agreements. Here the various UN agencies can greatly assist in bringing the recalcitrant stakeholders together. Already, the FAO's support of a science-based evaluation system that would objectively determine the benefits and risks of each individual GM food, including its call for a cautious case-by-case approach to address legitimate concerns for the biosafety of each product or process prior to its release, and careful monitoring of the post-release effects of GM products, enjoys broad support among countries in both North and South. If developing countries are to reap the fruits of biotechnology they must adopt a prudent and cautious approach for the successful adoption of the new technology. This means that the old technologies and traditional farming methods should not be discarded, but used to complement the new biotechnologies. In addition, governments must develop a clear policy framework for the dissemination and regulation of the new technology, including setting adequate biosafety guidelines for field testing, and providing clear rules regarding how and which particular technology should be used, and where. Since most developing countries will not be able to undertake effective agricultural biotech research for their own urgent needs without the scientific and financial support of developed countries, international agencies such as the Consultative Group on International Agricultural Research (CGIAR), and private industries, it is imperative that both governments and the private sector in developing countries expand their involvement in the research and/or collaboration with groups on biotech projects. This will not only be crucial for overcoming the contentious intellectual property rights issues, it will also serve to greatly assist developing countries meet their obligations via increased technical assistance and capacity building. Most importantly, it can help ensure poor cultivators reasonable accessibility to the new technology. Yet, if experience is any guide, the success of biotechnology (or any technological improvement for that matter), must be accompanied by a favorable macroeconomic environment. Successful implementation will ultimately depend on good governance, the efficient functioning of the agricultural sector, including transparent extension systems, credit, and marketing.

5   The Doha Development Agenda
Realizing the promise of global trade

In the wake of 11 September 2001, the trade ministers of the World Trade Organization (WTO) gathered in Doha, Qatar, in November 2001 and launched the eighth round of multilateral trade negotiations dubbed the "Doha Round."[1] The subtext was that since the previous rounds had benefited the rich industrial countries at the expense of developing nations, the Doha Round would remedy this. For this reason, the Ministerial Conference in Doha adopted the so-called "Development Agenda" which placed the needs of the developing countries at the heart of the WTO's work. After several interim deadlines were missed in spite of the expectations (especially at the Hong Kong SAR Ministerial in December 2005), all eyes were on the Geneva meetings set for late July 2006.[2] Geneva was seen as "make or break" as the Doha Round was set to expire on 31 December 2006.

Despite the palpable hope generated by WTO Director-General Pascal Lamy's optimism, not to mention weeks of intense negotiations, the Doha Round collapsed in Geneva. Lamy suspended the talks indefinitely on 23 July 2006 after it became clear that the major trading countries, especially the G-6 (Australia, Brazil, India, Japan, the EU, and the United States) could not reach agreement on the modalities (or specific formulas and deadlines) for cutting farm subsidies and lowering agricultural tariffs.[3] While Doha is not dead (only "suspended" or, in the words of Lamy, under a "time-out"), and while all WTO members have uniformly expressed their commitment to the multilateral trading system and to a successful completion of the Doha Round, it is not clear how or when the negotiations would be revived. If the experience of past Rounds is any guide (the last, the Uruguay Round, began in 1986 and ended in 1993), it could take anywhere from months to years to complete the Doha Round – and the bet is years, thanks to the expiration of President George W. Bush's special fast-track trade negotiating authority, the Trade Promotion Authority (TPA) – thereby leaving the Round to the next US administration.[4]

This is most unfortunate as the Doha Round, covering 148 WTO members who altogether account for over 97 percent of world trade, is the first set of multilateral trade negotiations in which the needs and interests of developing countries have been officially declared a priority and whose conclusion is deemed essential. However, the trade talks now being suspended means there will be no progress in several policy domains important to developing countries: agriculture, non-farm trade, access to patented drugs, "special and differential treatment" and dispute settlement, among others.[5] It also means that areas of particular interest to the OECD countries such as the "Singapore issues" dealing with investment, competition, trade facilitation, and government procurement, are now also stalled.[6]

What explains the "collapse" of the Doha Round? What are the implications for global trade, especially for developing countries? And what needs to be done to revive the stalled negotiations? The following sections examine these questions, highlighting the economic implications of the failure, as well as the trade-offs member governments need to make to ensure progress. After all, the Doha Round's commitment to multilateral, reciprocal and non-discriminatory trade liberalization offers the best single chance for the international community to achieve the development promise of trade and make progress towards the MDGs. Clearly, the stakes are high. The following sections will argue that to realize the potential of Doha, the OECD countries must take the lead by further opening their markets to developing countries in agriculture, textiles and apparel. Since agriculture could account for some two-thirds of the potential gains from trade liberalization, meaningful reduction in agricultural protection may be the single greatest contribution rich countries can make to the Doha Round. Similarly, the middle-income countries must also do their part and reduce barriers in their protected agricultural markets, besides bringing down their relatively high tariffs in manufactures. In fact, since trade restrictions are much higher in developing countries, further liberalization, especially by the middle-income developing countries, is essential. Finally, the international community, through the WTO and other multilateral institutions, can help the weaker developing countries, particularly the LDCs (who face particular vulnerabilities and structural difficulties), to adjust to trade liberalization and maximize their capacity to take advantage of the opportunities offered by expanding trade and open global markets. But first, some context and background is necessary.

From Doha to Cancun

The Fourth WTO Ministerial Conference in Doha, Qatar, in November 2001 was a great success compared to the paralysis and breakdown at the Third WTO Ministerial Conference held in Seattle in late 1999. Following the debacle in Seattle and three years of extensive behind-the-scenes preparations, including an intense week-long meeting, trade ministers from the 142 member countries of the WTO completed their marathon session by agreeing to launch a new round of multilateral trade negotiations (Schott 2000). The Doha Declaration set an ambitious timetable: negotiations were scheduled to conclude no later than 1 January 2005 as part of a "single undertaking" – meaning that "nothing is agreed until everything is agreed." To achieve these goals the WTO members set a deadline of 31 March 2003 for producing formulas, numerical targets, and other modalities for countries' commitments. Member countries agreed to a September 2003 deadline (coinciding with the Fifth WTO Ministerial Conference, to be held in Cancun, Mexico) to submit comprehensive draft commitments based on these modalities. During the 12-month period of work to produce modalities (March 2002 to March 2003), extensive consultations engaged all WTO members. The developing countries participated actively through their own South–South caucuses, North–South caucuses (such as the Cairns Group of agricultural exporters[7]), and frequent bilateral consultations with the United States, Japan and the European Union. Throughout the year, member countries submitted proposals, some of which contained formulas and numerical targets for reducing tariffs, export subsidies, and domestic support.

The developing countries, in particular the so-called "G-21," led by Brazil, India, South Africa, China and Mexico, along with the G-33, the G-90 and the "Group of 71" representing the least-developed countries or the ACPs (African, Caribbean and Pacific nations), created a new negotiating dynamic at Doha by demanding and playing an important role in shaping the agenda.[8] In fact, in Doha a series of deadlines were agreed for a number of issues, sequenced in such a way that major areas of concern to developing countries would be dealt with first. The G-21 felt this was necessary to address the problems that arose in the implementation of the 1994 Uruguay Round trade accords – especially the difficulties many developing countries faced in putting current WTO agreements into place (Bouet *et al.* 2005; Elliott 2006).

Most significantly, the Doha Declaration recognized that for developing countries to become full partners in the global trading system, trade measures alone were not enough to fulfill the development promise of Doha (Aksoy and Beghin 2004; Newfarmer 2005; Winters and Hertel 2005). Rather, trade must be part of a larger development strategy for each country – a strategy that also paid equal attention to education, health and good governance, including open markets and fair trade rules reinforced at both the global and the national level by sound macroeconomic and financial policies. In a bold move, the Declaration invited the IMF, the World Bank and related multilateral organizations to join with the WTO as part of a wider approach to a more coherent global and domestic policymaking. In fact, OECD trade ministers made extensive commitments to provide technical and capacity-building assistance to enable developing countries to better defend their interests, respond to trade opportunities, and more effectively implement the administratively costly WTO rules. They made special commitment to addressing "the particular vulnerability of the least-developed countries and the special structural difficulties they face in the global economy," and agreed to a series of items in the Declaration which dealt specifically with these concerns.[9]

The Declaration also confirmed that the existing WTO provisions must afford countries flexibility in addressing public health problems – in particular, access to generic medicines for poor countries with no production capacity. Member countries agreed to address negotiating modalities dealing with public health by December 2002, agriculture by March 2003 and non-agricultural (especially industrial goods, including textiles and clothing) negotiating modalities by July

2003. This sequence was deliberately designed to ensure that developing countries' concern would come before any decision was made on how to negotiate the "Singapore issues" (investment, competition policy, transparency in government procurement, and trade facilitation) – important to the OECD countries, especially the EU and Japan. As the Doha program went further than the previous negotiating rounds in the commitment made to developing countries, the Ministerial was soon dubbed the "Doha Development Agenda" to signify the importance of the role that developing countries and development objectives would play in the multilateral trading system. Finally, the Ministerial Declaration explicitly spelled out the terms of reference and negotiating objectives for the new round of trade talks, as well as directives to guide the work of WTO committees and working groups. The ambitious agenda included (World Bank 2003d):

Agriculture: substantially improve market access, reduce all forms of export subsidies, with a view to phasing them out, and substantially reduce trade-distorting domestic support.[10] Note the need for "special and differential treatment" for developing countries and the need to take into account the demands of these countries in terms of food security and rural development.

Services: further liberalize all categories of services and modes of supply.

Industrial goods: further reduce tariffs, including tariff peaks, high tariffs, and tariff escalation, as well as non-tariff barriers, particularly on products of export interest to developing countries.[11]

Antidumping measures and subsidies: clarify and improve disciplines, while preserving the basic concepts, principles, and effectiveness of these agreements and their instruments and objectives.

Regional trade agreements: clarify and improve disciplines and procedures under existing WTO rules applying to regional trading agreements.

Trade-Related Aspects of Intellectual Property Rights Agreement (TRIPS): establish a multilateral system of notification and registration of geographical indications for wines and spirits, as well as the protection of geographical indications of other products addressed under review of implementation of TRIPS agreement.

Dispute settlement mechanism: improve the implementation of rulings and participation of the developing countries.

The environment: negotiations limited to the relationship between existing WTO rules and specific trade obligations set out in multilateral environmental agreements, and to the reduction or elimination of tariff and non-tariff barriers to environmental goods and services.

Singapore issues: (investment, competition policy, transparency in government procurement, and trade facilitation) subject to a decision on the negotiating modalities at the Fifth Ministerial Conference in Cancun.

Finally, the Doha Ministerial also approved the protocols of accession for both China and Taiwan – who became WTO members in mid-December 2001, and agreed that the Doha negotiations should be carried in "a single undertaking" – that is, no trade agreement without resolution of all issues.

The breakthrough at Doha eased many of the post-Seattle fears. At a time of economic and political uncertainty, ministers from 142 governments underscored that global trade problems could be addressed through a multilateral framework. No doubt, the launch of the Doha Round bolstered confidence in the WTO and its trading system. This was particularly felt in the developing countries, which now believed they would see greater market access for their products (Commission for Africa 2005). Although the 31 March 2003 deadline passed with no agreement on formulating modalities for agricultural negotiations, the offer by the US in June 2003 to reduce agricultural subsidies (which for many developing countries was the *sine qua non* for a successful Ministerial) and trade protection, in particular getting the pharmaceutical industry to further relax patent protections on medicines under TRIPS (thereby making cheap medicines available to poor countries, such as generic drugs to meet medical emergencies like HIV/AIDS,), greatly encouraged developing countries.[12] Therefore, when the trade ministers from the 146 member countries of the WTO met for the Fifth WTO Ministerial in Cancun during 10–14 September 2003, there was much expectation that the WTO would deliver on the Doha commitments.

However, the negotiations in Cancun broke down unexpectedly on 14 September 2003. Although Cancun was not the end of the Doha Round but simply an ongoing round (in fact, an intermediate stage where negotiators were to take stock and make sure that the round was on target for completion at the end of 2004, as scheduled), the collapse of the talks once again raised concerns about the efficacy of the WTO and the multilateral trading system (Baldwin 2006). The stalemate meant that the negotiating countries could not be bound to a set of agreed guidelines for the continuation of the negotiating process, besides more or less guaranteeing that the January 2005 deadline for completing the Doha Development Agenda would not be met.

As the news of the collapse spread, anti-globalization groups, many of whom had been demonstrating in the streets and around the convention center against the trade talks, celebrated with impromptu cheering and dancing. Philippine Trade Minister Manuel Roxas triumphantly summed up the common sentiment when he noted that "we are elated that our voice has now been heard." Lori Wallach (2004, 2000), director of the Washington (DC) based NGO Global Trade Watch, welcomed the collapse of "WTO's corporate-globalization agenda," noting that "the US agenda ignored poor nations in favor of the large corporations bankrolling President Bush's reelection effort." Anuradha Mittal (2003) of Food First, a San Francisco-based NGO, noted (also see Jawara and Kwa 2003; Narlikar and Wilkinson 2004),

> this was not necessarily bad news: As protesters in Cancun's streets learned the news, festivities started on the barricades. They rightly saw the breakdown as proof of a new resolve and tough-mindedness among developing countries. The talks failed – for the second time in four years – for a simple reason: irreconcilable differences between the rich, developed nations and the poorer and developing nations. The rich 20 per cent of WTO

membership continues to ignore every promise made to the other 80 per cent. Once the rich countries' strong-arm tactics kept the poorer countries coming back to the table ready for compromise. Those tactics just won't work any more. And understanding why is our only hope for finding a way forward.

However, many others saw the failure of the Fifth WTO Ministerial Conference with deep regret, since developing countries have a huge stake in the success of the Doha Round (Cline 2004; FAO 2003; Newfarmer 2005; World Bank 2003d; WTO 2004). Recent history is replete with examples of how the polarized North–South standoff undermines the economic interests of both sides – especially the South. Indeed, studies indicate that while every country loses from the setback in Cancun, the big losers are the developing countries, in particular the LDCs, which have the most to gain from a new global agreement to strengthen trade rules, lower tariffs, and eliminate other barriers to the free exchange of goods and services (Anderson and Martin 2005; Cline 2004; World Bank 2004; 2004c). Thus, any "victory" was pyrrhic, as the deadlocked multilateral trade negotiations would not only have an adverse impact on global economic growth, but would also negatively impact developing countries – many of whom are poorly positioned to stimulate their own growth (Hills 2005; WTO 2004). The concern was that, with lost momentum in Cancun, the push for free trade deals between individual countries, or small groups of countries, would only accelerate, with the world's poorest nations becoming even more marginalized (Hills 2005; Bhagwati 2004).

Why the Cancun Ministerial failed

In keeping with former Director-General of the WTO Mike Moore's apt description that the WTO is like a car with one accelerator and 145 hand-brakes, smooth operation is a challenge. The talks failed because several of the OECD, as well as developing countries, engaged in political brinkmanship, acrimonious negotiations, unrestrained recriminations, and "winner-take-all" positions on a number of important issues. This served to undermine compromise, especially on two politically sensitive issues. The first and more contentious was over how to free up trade in agriculture; the second was whether to negotiate the four Singapore issues.[13] The collapse on the final day of the talks came as the G-21 and other developing nations refused to enter into what they perceived (with some justification) as the *quid pro quo* demands of the EU and Japan that any further movement on agriculture be accompanied by movement on foreign investment rules and other Singapore issues.[14] Although in the final hours the EU agreed to an "unbundling" of the Singapore issues and to take up only trade facilitation and transparency in government procurement (while agreeing to continue the "educative process" in the case of investment and competition), it proved to be too little too late.[15]

It seems that when the developed countries agreed to make the Doha Round of trade negotiations the "development round," they created legitimate expectations among developing countries that major concessions on trade liberalization, specifically aimed at helping developing countries, were on the way (Narlikar and Tussie 2004; Newfarmer 2005). Not surprisingly, on the first day of the talks the G-21 demanded an immediate end to the huge subsidies given to farmers in the United States, the EU and Japan, including the demand by four poor West African countries (Mali, Chad, Burkina Faso, and Benin) that the US and EU phase out their cotton subsidies and pay compensation for lost trade during the phase-out. They poignantly pointed out that while cotton provides the main source of cash income for millions of smallholders in the four countries, cotton prices had fallen to their lowest since 1994 because of the subsidies producers receive in rich countries. For example, they highlighted that farmers in the four West African countries can produce cotton at $0.47 per kg (far below the $1.61 it costs to produce a kilogram of cotton in the United States); however, the roughly $3.9 billion in guaranteed subsidies the 25,000 American cotton producers received in 2002 (after the US Congress passed the Farm Security and Rural Investment Act, which increased subsidies for farmers by up to 80 percent for commodities such as cotton and involved a total which was greater than the national income of each of the four countries) was systematically impoverishing African farmers and undermining their already weak economies.[16] The G-21 blamed the intransigence of the United States but especially targeted the EU and Japan over agricultural protection, accusing them of hypocrisy for urging poor countries to open their markets but not being prepared to open their own markets or reducing the huge subsidies given to their farmers. The G-21 argued that because agriculture is of particular importance to the economic prospects of many developing countries, reforming the current practices in global farm trade holds perhaps the most immediate scope for bettering the livelihoods of the world's poor. Yet, they pointed out that the rich countries impose tariffs on agriculture that are eight to ten times higher than those on industrial goods (Commission for Africa 2005). Also the fact that many OECD continue to use various forms of export subsidies to drive down world prices and take markets away from farmers in poorer countries was not lost to the G-21. They argued that agricultural support costs the average household in the EU, Japan, and United States more than US$1,000 a year. Much of this support depresses rural incomes in developing countries while primarily benefiting the wealthiest farmers in rich countries.

Moreover, the G-21 blamed the EU, Japan, and South Korea (which it saw as the three most protectionist countries on agriculture) for trying to introduce out of sequence the Singapore issues dealing with foreign investment and competition policy.[17] The G-21 argued that by bringing these issues, the rich nations were trying to divert attention from the traditional market access issues – the subject on the top of the agenda of the current talks.[18] They adamantly maintained their position that negotiations must proceed according to sequence. That is, any negotiations on the Singapore issues, particularly investments, should not take place without first resolving areas of concern to developing countries. In addition, the ACP countries voiced their strong opposition to launching negotiations on the Singapore issues because of their alleged limited benefits to poor countries and the potentially significant implementation costs. In hindsight, it seems that the insistence by the EU, Japan, and South Korea that developing countries make commitments on the Singapore issues, without the G-21 fully knowing what they would get in return on agriculture (since the US–EU proposal was ambiguous and contained no deadlines for either subsidy or tariff reduction[19]), and non-agricultural market access modalities, doomed the talks. Their rather intransigent position made it possible for the G-21 countries to maintain a common bargaining position despite intense external pressures, especially from the US, for compromise (Bouet *et al.*, 2005; Narlikar and Tussie 2004).

On the other hand, the United States and the EU blamed the G-21 for the failure. Robert Zoellick, the US trade representative, and Pascal Lamy, the EU's trade commissioner, blamed the G-21's lack of commitment to reciprocity, their unwillingness to compromise and zealous determination "to transform the WTO into a forum for the politics of protest" for the breakdown. Zoellick noted "whether developed or developing, there were 'can do' and 'can't do' countries here. The rhetoric of the 'won't do' overwhelmed the concerted efforts of the 'can do.' 'Won't do' led to impasse" (cited in Bhagwati 2004a: 53). Zoellick was particularly incensed because he felt it was through his efforts that the EU had acceded to demands by the United States to reduce and eventually eliminate agricultural export subsidies – a major achievement given the formidable clout of domestic protectionist lobbies.[20] In return, the US encouraged developing countries to support the EU's proposals for new negotiations on environment, investment and competition policy. Zoellick bitterly noted that without these trade-offs, neither the United States nor the EU could accept the Doha Declaration, and threatened to "shift Washington's focus away from multilateral pacts and towards bilateral agreements with 'will-do' nations" (Bhagwati 2004a: 53). Sounding more conciliatory, Lamy defended the EU's "unique track record on agricultural reform," noting that the EU's Common Agricultural Policy (CAP) had undergone tremendous changes. For example, under the Agenda 2000 CAP reforms a large part of the EU's support for farmers was in either the WTO's "blue box" (support that is linked to production limitations and therefore less trade-distorting) or its "green box" (support that is minimally trade-distorting) – in other words, contrary to popular belief the EU had come a long way in liberalizing its agricultural sector. Lamy noted that the EU would only return to the talks when the G-21 was prepared to negotiate in good faith.

Beyond this North–South divide, it is important to recognize that negotiating trade issues can be an exceedingly slow and complex process. Indeed, it can be argued that the Doha Round has fared no worse than previous rounds, as no recent trade round has proceeded without divisions (Baldwin 2006; Bhagwati 2004; Sutherland 2005; Winham 1986). As Table 5.1 shows, the Uruguay Round which was signed in 1994 took eight years to complete, and the Tokyo Round took six years (1973–1979). Some of the agreements of the Uruguay Round, launched over 15 years ago, are still being implemented.

Compounding this, negotiating WTO accords has become a much more complex and unwieldy process than prior GATT rounds as the agenda on what needs to be done has increased (Evenett and Hoekman 2005; Hills 2005; Schott 2000). Table 5.1 highlights the ambitious nature of the Doha Round when compared to the earlier rounds.

With the incorporation of ever more countries, especially developing countries, as well as numerous NGOs and other actors who serve as advisors and interlocutors, the priorities of the WTO have undergone a shift, upsetting the traditional mechanism of WTO negotiations: reciprocity. The change has made coalition-building more difficult and consensus even more elusive (Bouet *et al.* 2005; Schott 2000). More often than not, the 148 member nations have different and competing agendas – not always amenable to accommodation and agreements. Yet, since the WTO still operates by consensus, the task of crafting a set of agreements that meets the demands of the large and increasingly disparate membership has become extremely challenging.

Second, previous multilateral rounds produced agreements in areas of primary interest to the OECD countries that dominated these discussions. It was only with the conclusion of the Uruguay Round in 1994 that international trade rules were brought to areas previously excluded or subject to weak rules, such as agriculture, textiles and clothing, services, trade-related investment measures, trade-related intellectual property rights (TRIPS), and the dispute settlement

Table 5.1 The GATT/WTO trade rounds

Year	Place/name	Subjects covered	Number of countries
1947	Geneva	Tariffs	12
1949	Annecy	Tariffs	13
1951	Torquay	Tariffs	38
1956	Geneva	Tariffs	26
1960–1961	Geneva (Dillon Round)	Tariffs	26
1964–1967	Geneva (Kennedy Round)	Tariffs and antidumping measures	62
1973–1979	Geneva (Tokyo Round)	Tariffs, non-tariff measures, "framework" agreements	102
1986–1994	Geneva (Uruguay Round)	Tariffs, non-tariff measures rules, services, intellectual property, dispute settlements, textiles, agriculture, creation of WTO	123
2002–2004	Doha	All goods and services tariffs, non-tariff measures, antidumping and subsidies, regional trade agreements, intellectual property, environment, dispute settlement, Singapore issues	144

Source: McGuirk (2002: 6).

mechanism – areas of particular interest to developing countries (Hoekman *et al.* 2002; Martin and Winters 1996). However, these also constitute the most difficult issues to resolve, given protectionist interests in both developed and developing countries. Therefore, the Doha Agenda raised the most complex and contentious issues which defy easy resolution. As Schott (2004: 3) notes,

> achieving a negotiated balance of concessions is further complicated by the fact that the United States and the European Union have very little left to give at the negotiating table in terms of market access, except things that are very difficult to give, i.e. the protection in agriculture and textiles that has survived eight previous rounds of multilateral trade negotiations and that is of major export interest to developing countries.

To get the United States, Europe, and Japan to

> commit to significant reforms in long-standing protection in agriculture and in some manufacturing sectors, other WTO members, including middle-income developing countries need to offer concrete reductions in their protection as well. But the developing countries object to lowering their own generally much higher trade barriers without increased and more secure access to industrial markets.

Finally, the fact that the Doha negotiations are a "single undertaking" and given the WTO consensus rule (the all-or-nothing requirement) which means that sufficient progress must be made on all key issues or nothing gets done, and that all new issues are included in the single undertaking, leaves little room for trade-offs, compromises and accommodation.[21]

What is at stake?

First, the implications for the world's poor in trade policy are large. As discussed in Chapter 2, international trade can be a key to reducing poverty by providing jobs and driving economic growth. Countries that have entered export markets through trade and intensified their links with the global economy have tended to grow faster than those that have not. Several studies, including the well-cited one by the World Bank (2004c, 2003d), document the benefits that would flow to developing countries and the world's poor from a liberalization of international trade (see Anderson 2005; FAO 2003; Goldin and Reinert 2006; Hoekman *et al.* 2002). A successful Doha agreement that substantially lowers agricultural and manufacturing tariffs and reduces agricultural subsidies provides real opportunities for substantial gains from reciprocal trade. World Bank projections suggest that the static welfare gains from removing barriers to merchandise trade would amount to between $250 billion and $620 billion a year – with developing countries capturing one-third to one-half of these gains, largely by opening their own markets.[22] This is far more than the annual flow of aid to these countries.

Similarly, William Cline (2004) estimates that if all global trade barriers were eliminated, approximately 500 million people could escape poverty over a period of 15 years. Developing countries would gain approximately $200 billion annually in income – and at least half of this amount would stem from the removal of protection against their export products in industrial countries.[23] Cline's study provides a comprehensive analysis of the potential for trade liberalization to spur growth and reduce poverty in developing countries. It quantifies the impact on global poverty of industrial-country liberalization, as well as liberalization by the developing countries. Half or more of the annual gains from trade would come from the removal of industrial-country protection against developing-country exports. By removing their trade barriers, industrial countries could convey economic benefits to developing countries worth about twice the amount of their annual development assistance. By helping developing countries grow through trade, the OECD countries could lower costs to consumers for imports and realize other economic efficiencies. Cline's study estimates that free trade could reduce the number of people earning less than $2 per day by about 500 million over 15 years. This would cut the world poverty level by 25 percent. Cline notes that developing countries were right to risk the collapse of the Doha Round at Cancun by insisting on much deeper liberalization of agriculture than the industrial countries were then willing to offer. He calls for a two-track strategy: first, deep multilateral liberalization involving phased but complete elimination of industrial-county protection and deep reduction of protection by at least the middle-income developing countries, albeit on a more gradual schedule; and second, immediate free entry for imports from "high risk" low-income countries (heavily indebted poor countries, least-developed countries, and sub-Saharan Africa), coupled with a ten-year tax holiday for direct investment in these countries.[24]

The big challenge: reducing protectionism in agriculture

With roughly 70 percent of the poor people in developing countries living in rural areas, agricultural sector reforms, in particular global trade liberalization, will be crucial in giving them opportunities for better lives. As discussed in the previous chapter, growth in agriculture has a disproportionately positive effect on poverty reduction because, in the aggregate, developing countries have a strong comparative advantage in agriculture. Since the vast majority of the population in developing countries live in rural areas, the agricultural sector is important for income generation in these countries. Also, liberalization of value-added activities is crucial for expanding employment and income opportunities beyond the rural sector. Yet, while manufacturing protection has declined worldwide following reforms of trade policies, especially in developing countries, most OECD countries continue to tenaciously protect their agricultural sector – often at high levels through a combination of subsidies to producers, tariffs and other non-tariff measures such as import restrictions and quotas.[25] On the other hand, over the past two decades many developing countries have liberalized their agricultural sectors, in addition to eliminating various forms of import restrictions, quantitative restrictions, export taxes, including abandoning multiple exchange rate systems that penalized agriculture.[26] Overall, the average agricultural tariffs, the main source of protection in developing countries, have declined significantly from 30 percent in 1990 to 18 percent in 2000 (Aksoy and Beghin 2005: 42). In fact, Finger and Winters (2002) note that the average depth of tariff cuts by developing nations has been greater than that agreed to by high-income countries.

However, the so-called "reactive protection" in response to industrial-country support to agricultural producers began to increase in many middle-income countries, especially in food products. These developments are unfortunate, as over the past two decades many developing countries, including many LDCs, have been investing to increase their agricultural production and productivity. However, for many these gains will not be fully translated into growth and poverty reduction unless the OECD and several middle-income countries reduce agricultural trade protection. In the absence of reduced protection, increased productivity in agriculture will give rise to overproduction and price declines for many commodities, undermining competitive poor countries' efforts to expand exports and rural incomes. It also increases pressure for greater protection globally. Projections indicate that without significant reforms, the agricultural trade surpluses of industrial countries will increase while the developing countries will face increasing agricultural trade deficits – with adverse consequences for the world's rural poor. Not surprisingly, agricultural protection continues to be among the most contentious issues in global trade negotiations. Why is this so?

Prior to the completion of the Uruguay Round, agriculture was largely excluded in trade negotiations (Croome 1998; Preeg 1995). The Uruguay Round Agreement on Agriculture (URAA), enacted in 1995, marked an important first step by members of the WTO towards liberalizing agricultural trade policies. The Uruguay Round made four major contributions to liberalizing agricultural trade: (1) rules-based trade was established for agriculture, with a core framework; (2) market access; (3) domestic supports; and (4) export competition. A transparent rules-based approach to market access was established that converted non-tariff barriers, including variable levies and quotas, into bound tariffs – termed "tariffication" in trade jargon. This process provided a framework that allowed the negotiation of initial and future tariff cuts. The reduced use of export subsidies has meant reduction in both the spending on export subsidies and the volume of subsidized goods. Previously, export subsidies distorted agricultural trade by reducing world prices, hurting farmers both in the importing country and in non-subsidizing exporting countries. Overall, the conversion of all non-tariff measures into bound tariffs with reduction commitments and the introduction of minimum access commitments in the form of import quotas (as a share of domestic consumption) are seen as two of the most important achievements of the URAA (Elliott 2006; Martin and Winters 1996).

Nevertheless, the levels of import protection and trade-distorting domestic support in agriculture in the United States, the EU, and Japan – all of whom artificially increase production and distort trade – while lower than it was during the 1986–1988 base period (which established domestic support ceilings for the Uruguay Round) – still remains high. As Hathaway and Ingco (1996) note, this was largely because tariffication provided many opportunities for backsliding, thereby greatly reducing the effectiveness of the agreed disciplines (also see Hoekman *et al.* 2002). Thus, despite the progress under the URAA, agriculture continued to be among the most distorted sectors in international trade (Martin and Winters 1996). For example, the average agricultural bound tariff world-wide is estimated to be 62 percent, with a large variation of import protection rates among commodities and countries. Roughly 28 percent of domestic producers in OECD countries are protected by import quotas with high out-of-quota tariffs. Tariff peaks remain very high – over 500 percent in some cases – and tariffs in many countries increase by degree of processing, creating an escalating tariff structure that limits imports of processed food products. For example, Watkins (2003: 6) notes that

> if Latin American tomato exporters make the mistake of processing the vegetable into sauce, the tariff they face rises by a factor of six percent. Average EU tariffs on fully processed foods are twice as high as on products in the first stage of processing. Tariff escalation serves the deeply pernicious purpose of keeping poor countries trapped in low value-added segments of the agricultural trading system.

Other examples include, "in New Zealand this 'development tax' imposes a 5% tariff on coffee beans and a 15% tariff on ground coffee – and in Japan a 0.1% tariff on unprocessed textiles and an 8.6% tariff on fully processed textiles" (UNDP 2003: 155). Furthermore, agricultural imports into the OECD also face an array of sanitary and phytosanitary measures and other technical requirements. These measures, though ostensibly designed to protect human, animal and/or plant life, are also used to restrict trade (Hoekman *et al.* 2002; Newfarmer 2005).

The study by Aksoy and Beghin (2005) provides a comprehensive analysis of how large trade distortions in specific commodities – sugar, dairy, rice, wheat, groundnuts, fruits and vegetables, cotton, seafood, and coffee – impede trade flows, depress world prices, and discourage market entry or delay exit by non-competitive producers. Their study shows that reforms will lead to large gains, confirming the results of global models. Moreover, the study finds that border barriers are high in most of the commodity markets. For example, the global trade-weighted average tariff for all types of rice is 43 percent and reaches 217 percent for Japonica rice. Many Asian countries remain bastions of protectionism in their agricultural and food markets. Subsidies have similar effects, depressing world prices and inhibiting entry by inducing surplus production by non-competitive and often large producers. As noted earlier, cotton subsidies in the United States and the EU, for example, have reached $4.4 billion in a $20 billion market. The EU alone subsidized sugar production by $2.3 billion in

2002 – becoming the world's second largest sugar exporter even though its production costs are more than double those in many developing countries. Domestic support and protection policies have substantial negative effects on producers in developing countries, because of the sheer size of the subsidies relative to the size of the market. Such large support programs shield non-competitive producers and penalize efficient producers, often in poor countries. Recent studies provide vivid examples of the impact and implications:

> Sugar in the European Union, Japan, and the United States is commonly protected through a combination of quotas, tariffs, and subsidies allowing domestic sugar producers in those countries to receive more than double the world market price. OECD governments support sugar producers at the rate of US$6.4 billion annually – an amount nearly equal to all developing country exports. Prices are so high that it has become economic to grow sugar beets in cold climates and to convert corn to high fructose corn syrup. Sugar imports in the OECD have shrunk to next to nothing.... Rice support in Japan amounts to 700 percent of production at world prices, stimulating inefficient domestic production, reducing demand, and denying export opportunities to India, Thailand, Vietnam and other countries.
>
> (World Bank 2004c: xvii)

> To be fair, even the US is hard-pressed to match the EU's capacity for double standards in agriculture. Consider the CAP sugar regime. Europe is among the world's highest-cost producers of sugar. It is also the world's biggest exporter of white sugar. The reason: subsidies and tariffs. EU farmers are paid three times the world price for sugar, and EU taxpayers and consumers then foot the bill for dumping the resulting surplus – 7 million tons of it – on world markets. Non-subsidizing exporters such as Malawi and Thailand suffer the twin consequences of lower prices and lost market shares. Meanwhile, high tariffs keep the EUs own market firmly out of bounds.
>
> (Watkins 2003: 6; also see Oxfam 2005)

Furthermore, within OECD countries, total transfers to farmers (from taxpayers and consumers) averaged about $235 billion per year in 2000–2002 (World Bank 2003b).[27] Agricultural subsidy regimes in rich countries often increase protection when commodity prices fall, throwing the burden of production on to global prices and poor countries. "The effect is to stimulate overproduction in high-cost rich countries and shut out potentially more competitive products from poor countries." Thus, "subsidies make the relatively rich even richer and the poor even poorer" as more than 70 percent of subsidies in rich countries were directed to large (corporate) farmers with incomes often substantially higher than average incomes in countries like Europe, Japan and, to a lesser extent, the United States (World Bank 2004c: xvi–xvii; Ingco and Nash 2004). The enormous agricultural subsidies in OECD countries not only deter developing countries from maximizing the gains they can reap from agricultural trade, but consumers in countries that provide these market-distorting supports are denied the benefits from competitively priced food and agricultural products while taxpayers are forced to subsidize the high cost of production. A simulation study by IFPRI (the International Food Policy Research Institute) (Diaz-Bonilla and Gulati 2003: 3) shows that the policies of the industrialized countries have displaced about US$40 billion in net agricultural exports per year from developing countries and reduced agricultural incomes in those countries by nearly US$30 billion – counting both primary and manufactured agricultural products but not related activities such as trade, commerce, and other services.[28]

Therefore, meaningful reform in agriculture is the most significant step OECD countries can take to promote global economic growth and development. Agriculture is central to the development promise of the Doha Round because it is the driving force in almost all developing economies. Not only do 70 percent of the world's poor live in rural areas and earn their livelihood from agriculture, the agricultural sector accounts for over one-third of export earnings for almost 50 developing countries, and for about 40 of them this sector accounts for over half of export earnings (World Bank 2004c). Given these realities, growth in agriculture will have a disproportionately positive effect on poverty reduction. However, if progress is to be made on this contentious issue, the OECD countries must demonstrate their willingness to reduce and eliminate both the absolute value of subsidies it provides its farmers, and the tariffs and other non-tariff barriers, including sharp limits on the use of trade-distorting domestic support.

As Schott (2004: 3) notes, at a minimum the rich countries must be willing to make substantial cuts in domestic subsidies for each major product sector as well as the

> elimination of agricultural export subsidies, including the subsidized component of official export credits, by a fixed date preferably with accelerated phase-outs for products of export interest to developing countries. Such a framework would mean ending most export subsidies soon after the completion of the Doha Round; real reductions in domestic subsidy disbursements by the United States and the European Union on cotton and other major products; deep cuts in high farm tariffs and larger import quotas for Japanese and Korean rice; and meaningful, albeit less comprehensive, reforms by middle-income developing countries of their farm trade restrictions.

The UN Millennium Project (2005: 213–14), aptly calling "agriculture – the biggest and costliest aberration" argues that

> export subsidies should be totally and definitively eliminated ... by 2010. This will send a powerful signal to developing countries, which will follow suit with their own deeper market opening without the danger of export subsidies greatly distorting trade and competition. All countries should

decouple all support payments to farmers by 2010 and cap all domestic support measures at 10 percent of the value of agricultural production (on a byproduct basis) by 2010 and at 5 percent by 2015 ... By 2015 no bound farm tariff should exceed 5 percent for OECD countries. Market access negotiations must address both the unacceptably high tariff peaks that remain in agriculture and tariff escalation, which continues to frustrate developing country efforts to move up the value chain. All non-tariff barriers, including tariff rate quotas, should be removed by 2010.

Yet, as Aksoy and Beghin (2005) note, how reforms are actually implemented will have important consequences for developing countries. They argue that the best approach is coordinated global liberalization of policies, in particular the importance of a multi-commodity approach to reform, as gains and losses tend to differ greatly by market. Such an approach would allow countries to trade off gains in some commodities against the losses in others. For example, world sugar price increases alone would offset about half the lost quota rents, or about $450 million, for countries with preferential access. Their analysis shows that losses in rents would be much less than is commonly expected, as high production costs eat up much of the potential benefit from preferential access to the high-price markets.

What about the barriers to agricultural imports that remain high in many developing countries, creating obstacles to South–South trade, besides implicitly taxing their own consumers? As Newfarmer (2005) and Diaz-Bonilla and Gulati (2003), among others, note, in the Doha Round developing countries have been either "playing offense" by trying to limit the industrialized countries from subsidizing and protecting their agriculture or "playing defense" by asking for additional exemptions via the "special and differential treatment" (SDT) to subsidize and protect agriculture in developing countries. While these strategies vary by country, partly reflecting whether they are net food exporters or importers, the G-33 (which includes both food importers and food exporters) has stuck to its position that developing countries should be allowed to exempt 10 percent of their agricultural tariff lines from reduction and an additional 10 percent for agricultural tariff lines deemed "special products" be subject to cuts of 5 to 10 percent.[29] Clearly, the many large developing countries, in particular the Cairns Group of agricultural exporting countries (which includes 14 developing-country members), who have long been "playing offense" cannot have it both ways. As potential major beneficiaries of agricultural liberalization, they cannot demand that the OECD countries dismantle their distortions while they continue to maintain theirs. As Schott (2004) notes, these countries need to make "meaningful, albeit less comprehensive reforms" if the negotiations on agricultural liberalization are to move forward.

Second, what about the legitimate concerns of many of the LDCs, including the small island economies in Africa, the Caribbean, and the Pacific (ACP)? As noted, these countries joined forces to form the Group of Ninety (G-90) because of their concerns about the impact of "preference erosion" on their economies.

Most ACP countries already enjoy duty-free access for their exports in key markets, such as the EU and the United States, in the context of preference schemes designed to encourage export growth and development in these poor countries. Currently, both the United States and the EU have a number of preferential regimes arising from free trade agreements or in the framework of non-reciprocal regimes, such as the EU's Everything but Arms (EBA) initiative which covers LDCs and the Cotonou Agreement with Africa–Caribbean–Pacific countries (ACP). The United States, for example, has implemented the African Growth Opportunity Act (AGOA) and the Caribbean Basin Economic Recovery Act, among others – all of which remove tariffs on a wide range of goods imported from the world's poorest countries. In addition, every OECD country also grants non-reciprocal preferences on a wide range of products to some 144 developing countries within the framework of the Generalized System of Preferences (GSP).

The multilateral reduction of trade barriers has the potential to erode the price advantage that trade preferences provide and expose countries whose exports rely on this advantage to competition from more cost-efficient producers. Specifically, it is argued that the level of agricultural protection in a given country is not a very useful measure. Rather, measurement must be relative to the structure and composition of exports from each country, and the price sensitivity of various commodities to liberalization. Seen this way, evidence indicates that protection is concentrated in a few sectors, and many poor countries could lose market share and face an increased cost of food imports due to preference erosion. No doubt, shocks from preference erosion could be significant for countries with undiversified exports sectors, especially those with heavy dependence on sugar, bananas, and – to a lesser extent – textiles and clothing. This is because sugar and bananas account for three-quarters of the current preference margins – or the difference between the most favored nation tariff and the preferential tariff for a market. Jensen and Gibbon (2007: 5) point out that

> preference erosion, for instance, is a real threat to Africa. A lowering of Most Favored Nation (MFN) rates will increase the competition that Africa faces, especially in the EU market, and might lead to competitive middle-income exporters such as Brazil replacing African ones.[30]

Bureau *et al.* (2006) point out that multilateral liberalization will erode preferences for the LDCs – but the main obstacles to LDC exports will appear in the non-tariff area (sanitary, phytosanitary standards), which increasingly originate from the private sector and are not dealt with under the Doha framework. Not surprisingly, the G-90 has called for various "compensatory remedies," including technical and financial assistance to allow G-90 exports benefit from an equitable share of the world market.[31]

Does this mean that developing countries, especially the LDCs, have little to gain from additional market access? Not necessarily. At the outset it is important to note that as OECD countries reduce tariffs on imports from all of their trading partners under the WTO's most favored nation terms, the value of these trade preferences will erode. Nevertheless, research also shows that the impact of preference erosion would be significant for only a small number of G-90 countries heavily dependent on a handful of products. For example, Alexandraki and Lankes (2004) point out that, depending on the elasticities of export supply, the magnitude of the potential shock is rather small – between 0.5 percent to 1.2 percent of the total exports of the 76 middle-income countries they studied (also see Newfarmer 2005; Subramanian 2003). They add that the effects are likely to be spread over time in accordance with liberalization schedules established under the Doha Round. Given this, remedial measures could be targeted only to countries and sectors that are the most vulnerable. It is important to keep in mind that preferential policies are discriminatory because they are not extended to all countries. Developed countries grant preferences voluntarily rather than as part of a binding multilateral negotiation. Donor countries often determine which country, eligibility, product coverage, the size of preference margins, and its duration. Approved preferences often come with all kinds of restrictions, product exclusions and administrative rules. Also, preference programs usually cover only a share of exports from developing countries, and among those eligible countries and products, only a fraction of preferences are actually utilized. Products and countries with export potential often do not receive preferences, whereas eligible countries and product categories often lack export capacity. Last, but not least, with respect to preferential access schemes for exports from low-income countries they might actually reduce recipient countries' incentives to reduce their own trade barriers.

Third, what impact will agricultural liberalization have on developing countries, especially the LDCs who are net importers of food? No doubt, the benefits of agricultural liberalization to developing countries are likely to be much smaller than predicted and distributed unevenly. The reduction in subsidies in the United States and the EU may give a boost to exports in only a handful of middle-income countries such as Argentina and Brazil. According to recent studies the expectations that liberalization will lead to a dramatic improvement in trade opportunities for the poorest countries have been overestimated (Bureau *et al.* 2006). Liberalization of agricultural trade is expected to drive up prices for most agricultural commodities, although prices are expected to rise more steeply for the food products that developing countries import than for the commodities they export. This has led some to conclude that poor countries who import agricultural products will suffer from higher prices – further worsening the balance of payments of these countries and exacerbating poverty levels (Panagariya 2003, 2005).

However, this problem needs to be put in proper perspective. According to the World Bank (2004c: 134–6; also Tokarick 2003), of the 58 countries classified as low-income in 2000–2001, 29 were net importers, and of the 89 classified as middle-income, 51 were net importers. Among the middle-income countries, the total net imports of the net importers were almost $56 billion – with 46 percent of the imports by relatively high-income countries such as Hong Kong,

South Korea, Singapore and Taiwan. Another 35 percent went to the oil export-ing countries, including Saudi Arabia, the United Arab Emirates and Algeria. The bulk of the remaining imports were accounted for by Egypt and Oman. Thus, the overall impact of agricultural price increases on the middle-income countries would be limited, particularly as a proportion of their trade. Among low-income countries, oil-producing Angola, Nigeria and Yemen account for almost 32 percent of the total deficit. Twelve conflict-ridden countries account for another 21 percent. Only 14 low-income countries are real net food importers with total net imports of roughly $2.8 billion in 2000–2001. In this group, three countries – Bangladesh, Pakistan, and North Korea – account for 80 percent of the net imports. The rest of the low-income countries have a deficit of just $565 million which makes up a small percentage of their trade.

Overall, most developing countries are expected to benefit from the reduc-tions in tariffs and subsidies in developed countries. Improved access to markets in the OECD countries and reduced trade distortions should boost rural incomes and employment and stimulate production and supply from local agriculture, particularly of food for domestic markets. Developing countries would gain from price increases not only because their exports are predominantly agricul-tural, but also because the agricultural trade policies in OECD countries have had a stifling effect on agricultural and agro-industrial production in all develop-ing countries, regardless of their net trade position. Aksoy and Beghin (2005) note that consumers in highly protected markets will benefit greatly from trade liberalization as domestic (tariff-inclusive) prices fall and product choice expands. Consumers in poor, net-food-importing countries could face higher prices if these markets were not protected before liberalization, because of higher import unit costs. However, they note that in practice, such concerns have often been exaggerated. For example, dairy consumption in the Middle East and North Africa would be little affected by trade liberalization because, while world prices would rise, high import tariffs would be removed, so that the net impact on dairy consumer prices would be negligible. Similarly, rice prices will decline for consumers in most rice importing developing countries in Asia and Africa. As Diaz-Bonilla and Gulati (2003: 3–4) note,

> given that these sectors [agricultural] are the main economic activities in many developing countries, particularly poor ones, and that growth in these sectors is usually multiplied throughout the whole economy, poor develop-ing countries, even net importers, may have lost a substantial source of dynamic benefits. In fact, depressed world prices of many food products caused by agricultural protectionism and subsidies in industrialized coun-tries may have contributed to some developing countries becoming net food importers, pushing them into a more extreme specialization in tropical products.

Thus, there is the possibility that the net-importing countries could become net exporters if world prices rise sufficiently following liberalization. Nevertheless, development assistance to compensate for agricultural price effects and other welfare-enhancing measures, including safety-net mechanisms to cushion the negative effects, could help LDCs adjust to the possible balance of payments problems.

Non-agricultural market access

Non-agricultural tariffs are also high. While some 50 years of tariff reduction under eight multilateral rounds have reduced average developed-country industrial tariff rates to around 4 percent, these residual tariffs offer little protection. Rather, they impose $16 billion in annual costs on traded goods. The low average tariff rate also disguises high tariff peaks and escalations imposed on individual products, in particular low-cost manufactured goods produced in the poorest, least-developed countries. Developed-country tariff rates on developing-country imports are four times higher than the tariff rates on imports from other OECD countries. Thus, many developing countries continue to face major obstacles to selling manufacturing exports to rich countries because of high tariffs, quotas, specific duties and barriers that discourage value-adding. For example, while the Uruguay Round Agreement on Textiles and Clothing was supposed to phase out quotas progressively by 1 January 2005, in reality the phase-outs have been heavily back-loaded with more than 50 percent of quotas, often covering the most commercially valuable products, yet to be removed.

In addition to disproportionately burdening developing-country imports, rich-country tariff policies raise the cost of many basic necessities for their own consumers. Developing countries – largely insulated from earlier trade rounds by special and differential exceptions – have also retained high tariff walls. Duties imposed on North-to-South trade average 10.9 percent, while duties imposed on South-to-South trade average 12.8 percent. With more than 40 percent of current world trade now flowing between developing countries, the World Bank (2004c) estimates that 70 percent ($57 billion) of the tariff burden faced by manufactured goods from developing countries is imposed by other developing countries. The high tariffs also increase the price of inputs, offsetting much of the market advantage these developing countries gain from low labor costs. It is in the interest of developing countries to liberalize South-to-South trade because they are important markets for each other. Similarly, while still less than full reciprocity, the LDCs should also bind their tariffs at uniform and moderate rates.

Clearly, a strong commitment to eliminate tariffs on all goods is crucial for global economic growth. According to the World Bank (2004), free-flowing world trade has the potential to create $500 billion in global income, two-thirds of which would go to developing countries. Furthermore, to the extent that there is any revenue loss to governments, it will be made up by the returns from increased domestic economic growth and reciprocal market access opportunities. As for industrial development, tariffs are a blunt economic policy tool, usually causing more collateral harm than direct benefit. Successful and sustainable development will be achieved not by protection, but by liberalization paired with domestic structural reforms. The WTO members must make a commitment to the elimination of tariffs on all consumer and industrial goods. The elimination of tariffs will open market access opportunities for all members and stimulate economic growth and development. Specifically, the members must make a real effort to abolish tariffs – that includes the elimination of all duties on a full range of industrial and consumer goods, with the aim to ensure that market access opportunities are created for all members and that all members participate in the liberalization process. Furthermore, any elimination of tariffs also requires concurrent efforts to remove non-tariff barriers since it interferes with market access gained from tariff reductions. For many industries, non-tariff barriers are as obstructive, if not more so, than tariff barriers. Identifying and addressing these barriers as part of overall non-agricultural market access negotiations will be a vital component of the final Doha outcome.

The Doha Round stalemate also means that the economic incentive for services liberalization is now stalled. This is unfortunate, as in the past decade growth of trade in services has increased at a greater rate than manufacturing, and services trade now accounts for nearly a quarter of total cross-border trade. The OECD countries are the largest exporters of services, but developing countries have much to gain as well from increased market access. Services exports are an important source of foreign exchange earnings for these countries. Many have already demonstrated a comparative advantage in sectors such as tourism and natural resource-based services, and others compete in more human and capital resource intensive services such as software. Furthermore, while developed countries will probably dominate certain services sectors in the near term, the technology spillover effect from foreign firms can facilitate development of local service providers in these sectors. Thus, removing barriers to trade in services would significantly increase global welfare given the dominant role of the service sectors in most economies and the still large trade barriers typical of these sectors. The World Bank (2004) estimates that lowering services barriers by one-third will raise developing countries' incomes by $95 billion. Moreover, services liberalization increases by 4.5 times the gains to developing countries from goods liberalization alone – the effective protection created by inefficient sheltered domestic services eliminates the increased market access opportunities created by tariff reductions on finished goods in foreign markets; and inefficient technology, transportation, financial, distribution, and express delivery services erase the advantage created by lower-cost inputs. Clearly, expansion of the services agenda should be at the top of the developing-country negotiating list.

Constructive ways must be found to deal with the Singapore issues where developing countries are reluctant to make new commitments. To allay fears, cooperative approaches such as the IMF–World Bank Financial Sector Assessment Program, designed to strengthen the international financial system, can help. Beyond these, it is important to recognize that developing countries have much to gain from greater transparency of government regulations and policies on all four issues under review. Studies show that greater transparency would yield important dividends in terms of combating corruption, reducing uncertainty about rules for accessing and competing in national markets, and encouraging investment. Open and transparent domestic regulatory policies and processes with public accessibility and participation, coupled with effective due process procedures, are essential to sound regulatory practice – ensuring a level playing field for all market players and securing consumer protection. Regulatory transparency is particularly important to cross-border service providers because of the high transactional complexity and costs. Since good regulatory practices strengthen trade liberalization and increase the economic benefits that derive from competitive service sectors, it is in the interest of developing countries to undertake commitments on regulatory disciplines in services.

The continued difficulties in completing the Doha Round may result in disillusionment with the WTO and accelerate the trend towards bilateral or regional free trade agreements (FTAs), leaving many poor countries isolated from major markets and vulnerable to the demands of the more powerful trading nations (Bhagwati 2004a; Hills 2005). In fact, following Cancun, the US advocated bilateral agreements as a way to open markets and sought extensive concessions that it was unable to secure during the Doha talks. While both approaches can potentially promote trade creation and even establish the framework for later multilateral liberalization, such balkanized systems of integration are clearly a poor second-best alternative to global multilateral liberalization. Bilateral agreements will invariably accentuate the weight of the already powerful – like the United States, the EU, and Japan – which the WTO with its emphasis on consensus-building helps mitigate. Also, if poorly designed, bilateral and FTAs can lead to trade diversion, administrative complexities, and a series of trade rules that compete with those under the WTO framework.[32] Global trade and economic integration requires predictable rules and representative institutions that enable countries to facilitate trade, resolve disputes and more effectively distribute the gains of economic growth. The WTO is indispensable as it provides a negotiating forum in which countries make trade policy commitments that improve access to each other's markets and establish rules governing trade. The WTO, by requiring every member to play by common rules and in providing a multilateral dispute settlement mechanism that prevents policy reversals and backsliding, brings credibility and confidence to a multilateral agreement and ultimately greater stability and predictability to the global economy. While not always appreciated, a rules-based system protects the weak against the unilateralist tendencies of the more powerful trading nations.

Finally, while building trade-facilitation capacity requires concerted national action, the OECD countries and multilateral development agencies can help poor countries move towards best practice. Streamlining and simplifying regulations to remove technical and custom barriers, providing assistance in developing appropriate legal and regulatory frameworks, training more personnel and upgrading the availability of telecommunications technology, including global positioning technology and other electronic measures, will over the long term reduce costs and accelerate both cross-border and global trade. It will also enhance the surveillance and detection of illicit activities, including terrorism and fraud.

Much is at stake: Hong Kong to collapse at Geneva

After the breakdown at Cancun, negotiators set themselves the challenge of restarting talks by 15 December 2003. But, on the eve of that deadline, the coalitions were as far apart as ever on the main issues. It seemed that the Doha Development Agenda would be put off indefinitely. However, in early January 2004 in an effort to put the talks back on track US trade representative Robert Zoellick sent a letter to his ministerial colleagues clarifying US interests and objectives in the Doha Round and committing to substantial reforms in US policies in the context of a substantive package of WTO accords. Similarly, EU commissioner Lamy sent signals that the EU could be persuaded to drop the request to have three of the four Singapore issues on the agenda (keeping only the least controversial, trade facilitation) and agree to an elimination of export subsidies, provided all forms of export competition were subject to the same commitment. The talks formally resumed in March 2004, with the members agreeing on a 31 July 2004 deadline on a framework for agriculture. Following intense negotiations, the WTO General Council on 1 August 2004 finally reached a broad consensus on several "framework agreements," called the "July Framework Agreement" (FA) or the "July Package," as a guide to further negotiations. The FA included a framework for negotiations on agriculture and industrial goods, recommendations on services, and modalities for negotiating improved customs procedures. On agriculture, the agreement did not make precise commitments. Rather, it proposed to eliminate "by a credible end date" all forms of export subsidization and for a progressive reduction of tariffs and domestic support. However, the formula to be used for tariff and domestic support reduction and the cuts to be made were not specified – thereby leaving these contentious issues for future negotiations.

Under the FA the WTO members were expected to reach an agreement on most of the modalities before August 2005 and then reach a consensus on an advanced draft before the Sixth WTO Ministerial Conference in Hong Kong SAR on 13–18 December 2005, where a final compromise on the resolved issues was to take place. While the FA accepted in principle many of the key demands of the developing countries, little progress was actually made in the months following. In fact, the parties were unable even to agree on a "first approximation" of the modalities by the end of July 2005. Therefore, the question remained whether they could deliver results consistent with the initial ambitions of the Doha Development Agenda in Hong Kong. In light of this, when the trade ministers from the 149 member countries of the WTO convened in Hong Kong they knew that they had to quickly breathe new life into the stalled Doha trade negotiations. Concluding the long-stalled round by the targeted deadline of year-end 2006, and before the expiration (on 30 June 2007) of President George

W. Bush's special fast-track trade negotiating authority, the TPA, gave the ministerial added urgency as the window of opportunity was fast closing.

The week-long Hong Kong Ministerial began amidst a dizzying array of public (and closed-door) activities as some 6,000 delegates, 2,000 NGO representatives and nearly 4,000 journalists attempted (sometimes prematurely) to put their spin on the prevailing state of the negotiations and their preferred (and possible) outcomes. Despite the often competing and contradictory viewpoints, the festive atmosphere was hard to miss as the ministerial began. Director-General Lamy (the former EU trade commissioner), a man well versed in WTO policies and politics, underscored during several press briefings that all WTO member-states were determined to "put Doha back on track" and avoid the kind of stonewalling and disarray that had occurred at Seattle in 1999 and Cancun in 2003. Lamy noted that his optimism stemmed from the fact that since the July Framework Agreement there had been a strong desire among countries rich and poor, North and South, large and small, to resolve their differences amicably and achieve meaningful progress.

Although the Hong Kong Ministerial Declaration (approved and adopted on 18 December 2005 by all WTO members) boldly reaffirmed the members' commitment to "renew our resolve to complete the Doha Work Program fully and to conclude the negotiations launched at Doha successfully in 2006," the ministerial again failed to achieve the kind of breakthrough that was considered possible just weeks earlier.[33] As Hufbauer and Schott (2006: 2) note, what Hong Kong did achieve was "more in spirit than in substance and placed more emphasis on negotiating process than on policy reform." Indeed, the WTO trade ministers accepted an agreement that only incrementally advanced the WTO negotiations, but left the most politically difficult decisions for 2006. Put bluntly, while some basic compromises and trade-offs were reached at Hong Kong, the more difficult issues were simply postponed for a later date. This was most evident on the contentious agricultural issues.

As discussed in previous sections, reaching an acceptable trade-off between greater market access for developing countries' agricultural products in return for their commitments to lower barriers to manufactured goods and services from the rich nations has been the Achilles' heel of the Doha Round.[34] Finding a common ground on these issues again proved elusive at Hong Kong. While there was no progress on the thorny issue of domestic farm subsidies and border restrictions, the ministerial did agree to eliminate the so-called "minor irritants" like agricultural export subsidies by 2013 – a date acceptable to the EU, which accounts for about 90 percent of such spending.[35] This was the absolute minimum that members had agreed to at the July 2004 Doha Round accord. However, export subsidies are small (about $5 billion) compared with the trade-distorting domestic farm supports – which range anywhere from $100 to $300 billion.[36] In addition, the WTO members agreed to grant least-developed countries free access to OECD markets for at least 97 percent of agricultural and manufacturing tariff lines by 2008. Specifically, the declaration requires the provision of duty-free and quota-free market access for most products from 32 least-developed countries "by 2008 or no later than the start of the implementa-tion period" of any negotiated agreement. It requires such access for at least 97 percent of products as defined by the tariff schedule. The United States had pressed for exceptions to duty-free, quota-free for specific products that already trade competitively on the global market because – as Hufbauer and Schott note (2006: 1), countries like "the United States already allows duty-free and quota-free imports for some 83 percent of LDC trade. Exempting 3 percent of tariff lines actually affects a much larger share of trade because it would cover the least competitive domestic production."

However, the difficult negotiations on the core agricultural issues – domestic support and tariffs – remained incomplete. On tariffs, the Hong Kong declara-tion simply adopted existing working language by setting four bands – from the highest to lowest – but set no level of ambition (or "targets") for cuts – although the US had pressed for cuts at the highest level. Moreover, the declaration out-lined no specific language on limiting the number of sensitive products excluded from tariff cuts. Again, the United States had pressed for a limit of 1 percent of products, as defined by the tariff schedule, but the EU rejected this and sought 8 percent or about 160 products. While on trade-distorting domestic support, the declaration adopted some new language setting three bands for cuts (with the sharpest cuts to be made in the highest band); it outlined no specific level of ambition.

With little real progress, Lamy and others were quick to highlight the few potential achievements. For example, much was made of how the US delegation worked in good faith with negotiators representing Burkina Faso, Benin, Mali, Chad and Senegal – who had threatened to block any Doha agreement without satisfactory resolution of the cotton issue. In the end, the United States agreed to eliminate export subsidies on cotton in 2006 – in large part after the Appelate Body of the WTO Dispute Settlement Mechanism ruled the "cotton case" in favor of Brazil in 2005. The declaration stated as an objective that any negoti-ated cuts in domestic support spending for cotton farmers in countries that have such programs would have to go deeper and be implemented faster than any other domestic agricultural subsidy cuts. Lamy called for the quick resolution of other contentious issues because, as he appropriately argued, this measure would provide for duty-free, quota-free access to cotton from the poorest least-developed countries – but only once implementation starts on any final agree-ment reached in the Doha negotiations.

Real progress on agriculture blocked progress in the other critical area, non-agricultural market access (NAMA) and services. Regarding industrial tariffs, the EU now demanded that the Ministerial Declaration require that tariff cuts in industrial goods achieve a comparably high level of ambition as agricultural tariff cuts. In effect, the EU threw down the gauntlet by insisting that for Doha to succeed there had to be balanced ambition in all areas of the negotiation and a proportionate contribution from all players from across the full range of eco-nomic activity – agriculture, goods and services. For developing countries, such an ultimatum was unacceptable. They referred to the July 2005 framework where member countries had agreed, in principle, to cutting tariffs in accordance with the Swiss formula.[37] While no progress was made in Hong Kong on industrial tariffs, the WTO members did agree to the Swiss formula for the industrial tariff cuts, requiring the sharpest cuts for the highest tariffs. They also set a 30 April 2006 deadline for establishing modalities, for NAMA, and a 31 July 2006 deadline for countries to submit concrete offers. The Hong Kong Ministerial Declaration also set deadlines for the services negotiations, requiring countries to make offers to open their markets for financial services, telecommunications and other services by 31 July 2006, in addition to requiring countries to submit their final complete list of proposed commitments on services by 31 October 2006.

However, as the Hong Kong Ministerial came to an end without real progress, Lamy and WTO ministers began to shift focus to the 30 April 2006 deadline that negotiators had set for agreeing on the modalities for the agricultural and non-agricultural goods. Lamy instructed all parties to engage in vigorous, continuous negotiations to achieve tangible results before the next deadline – noting that the talks were in a "red zone" and could fail unless a deal is struck soon. However, without an agreement on the outstanding issues at Hong Kong, negotiators at Geneva could not flesh out specific commitments for the final WTO package. Rather, they had to revisit the unresolved issues at Geneva. The stumbling blocks were the same: if the United States and the EU offered very little in the way of liberalization of their heavily protected and subsidized agricultural sector, developing countries like India and Brazil failed to make reciprocal offers in manufacturing and services.

In the end, Lamy could not narrow the divide among the six major participants over opening agricultural markets and cutting agricultural subsidies – the same issues that have blocked progress since negotiations were launched. Moreover, to his credit, he refused to settle for a minimalist deal in order to save Doha. He aptly reasoned that a watered-down "Doha light" would produce only modest liberalization and reforms and constitute a wasted opportunity given that so much effort had already gone in the Round. Thus, on 24 July 2006 he announced an indefinite suspension of the negotiations. In specific terms this meant that the talks can now only resume when real progress is made on the outstanding issues. Till then, the suspension will apply to all negotiating groups. It also means that the progress made to date on the various elements of the negotiating agenda are to be put on hold pending the resumption of the negotiations.

Implications and what needs to be done

Without doubt, the Doha Round is the most complex and ambitious set of commercial negotiations ever launched. A successful outcome to the negotiations will preserve and strengthen the world trading system. On the other hand, failure will gravely weaken the WTO – the only multilateral organization that has the power to enforce global trade rules, settle trade disputes among nations, and encourage the further expansion of world trade through rule-based negotiations.

The loss of confidence in the WTO could see the proliferation of bilateral and regional trade agreements – each with different (and often contradictory) rules, and each with the potential to create more red tape and increase costs to businesses and workers, without necessarily extending meaningful benefits. After all, "trade" agreements are about more than just trade. Regional and bilateral trade agreements between the rich and developing countries are build on an exchange: developing nations, including the LDCs, receive preferential access to rich-country markets, but the price can mean extensive concessions to rich-country demands – such as capital market opening or protection for intellectual property rights. The biggest losers would be developing countries, in particular the world's poorest countries. This is because although rapid global growth benefits all, it particularly benefits new entrants in world markets. Many low-income countries have yet to experience the full benefits of their own trade liberalization. These benefits are greater (and adjustment costs less) when undertaken against the backdrop of a healthy world economy. A successful Doha Round will consolidate the progress made over the past 60 years and avoid the damage that would be inflicted on the world economy by a slide back towards protectionism.

Optimists are quick to remind that there have been eight successful rounds of multilateral trade negotiations under the auspices of the GATT. The last round, launched in Montevideo in 1986 and concluded in 1994 in Marrakech, Morocco, led to the creation of the GATT's successor, the WTO. As is well known, none of these rounds went smoothly. Rather, each was characterized by high drama – periods of jubilant breakthroughs followed by heart-wrenching near collapse and recriminations. But, in the end, all the rounds were successfully completed. Following this logic, optimists argue that while the Doha Round has experienced its share of setbacks, it is faring no worse than previous rounds. While, they are cognizant of the challenges ahead, they insist that there is too much at stake for the parties to walk away, and once the member-states find the right mix of political will and self-interest, the Doha Round will also end triumphantly. On the other hand, skeptics note that the early rounds were comparatively easy as they covered only reductions in tariffs and quantitative import restrictions. However, the Doha Round is much broader – adding a number of contentious issues that are almost impossible to resolve to everyone's satisfaction. Moreover, the number of countries participating in the earlier rounds were small (averaging 25), in contrast to the 149 countries engaged in the Doha Round negotiations. The large numbers of developing countries acceding to the WTO in recent years, especially the growing muscle of the so-called "group of 20" influential developing countries led by Brazil, China, and India, have made consensus difficult, as they are prepared to walk away from negotiations if it does not go their way.

Even if history is on the side of optimists, reviving and then completing the Doha Round will require significant movements by all the G-6 countries. Without doubt, breaking the impasse on agriculture is critical. But how can this be achieved? It is important to reiterate that even if the commitments made at Hong Kong are fully implemented, agricultural protection will remain high and concentrated in OECD countries. The United States, the EU and other OECD countries have made only limited progress in reducing high tariffs and trade-distorting subsidies in agriculture. Clearly they must show more leadership: that is, the EU needs to improve its offer of agricultural market access and the US needs to improve its offer on agricultural domestic support to the point where there is real market access. In fact, the OECD "concessions" may not prove to be as negative as they think. Growth in agricultural exports has been particularly strong in recent years, and as incomes and purchasing power rise in countries like China and India, the demand for more agricultural commodities will only grow.

While the US and EU intransigence is usually blamed for the impasse, it is also important to note that both have stated that they are willing to entertain deeper tariff reductions, provided the richer developing countries make recipro-cal cuts on foreign investment rules and other Singapore issues. However, the G-20, especially India, refuses to improve its offer on non-agricultural market access. Rather, the G-20, especially India, demands an immediate end to all forms of subsidies given to farmers in the United States, the EU and Japan. This *quid pro quo* stance is not only bad politics: it is not in the developing countries' economic interests to have such an uncompromising "all or nothing" stance on agricultural liberalization. First, emerging market countries such as Brazil, Thai-land and India cannot assume that the Doha Round is a non-reciprocal agree-ment. These and many other developing countries themselves maintain high protection in agriculture. A significant reduction in agricultural subsidies and other barriers would enable them to sell products more successfully in each other's markets. Also, as increasingly prominent players in world trade, these large developing countries must also further open their markets. Their tariffs on industrial products are three to four times as high as those of industrial countries.

In fact, large continent-sized developing countries like India and Brazil have long used the Third World coalition while it suited their interests, but have done little to support the particular needs of the LDCs. Therefore, the LDCs should not throw their support blindly behind the G-20 countries as the G-20 does not always represent their interests. Rather, the LDCs should engage in more stra-tegic bargaining to further advance their interests. For example, rather than aligning with India – which has some of the highest industrial tariffs in the world and a protected pharmaceutical market that has never freely given generic drugs to LDCs – these least-developed countries should try to persuade China to open its market for their manufactured goods. China, whose trade barriers are low compared to those of India and Brazil, may be quite amenable to this as it has much to lose from a collapse of the WTO system.

At Hong Kong, the LDCs made some important gains, and it is important that they consolidate these gains. For example, the Hong Kong declaration requires the provision of duty-free and quota-free market access for most products from 32 least-developed countries "by 2008 or no later than the start of the implemen-tation period" of any negotiated agreement. It requires such access for at least 97 percent of products as defined by the tariff schedule. However, it was the United

States, and not the G-20, that pressed for exceptions to duty-free and quota-free for specific products that already trade competitively on the global market. Similarly, in an effort to give the least-developed countries a bigger stake in the global trading system, it was the rich countries that pushed the declaration to make specific commitments to promote trade measures supporting development. For example, the WTO member countries formalized a landmark breakthrough in the rules governing intellectual property rights that balances the needs of protecting patent rights with delivering life-saving medicines to areas hardest hit by disease. This is of great importance to countries struggling to cope with HIV/AIDS, and other health crises.

Finally, even if the Doha Round is revived, there is great deal of work yet to be accomplished before the Round is completed. Negotiators will need to complete the template agreements for trade in agriculture and industrial products, besides accelerating services negotiations in more than 100 sectors including tourism, telecommunications, and financial services. Yet, even if agreement on modalities were reached, negotiators still would have months of hard work to prepare line-by-line tariff schedules, achieve balanced exclusions from tariff cuts for a few politically sensitive products, and elaborate the details about services trade. Moreover, environmental issues addressed only tangentially in Doha are another difficult topic left on the table (Conca 2000; Tarasofsky and Palmer 2006). Although at Hong Kong some progress was made on disciplining fisheries subsidies, discussions and decisions over other environmental issues were postponed. In particular, topics that remain highly controversial include: ensuring a mutually supportive relationship between WTO rules and multilateral environmental agreements (MEAs); identifying environmental goods for the reduction of tariff and non-tariff barriers; and introducing disclosure requirements for inventions using genetic resources and traditional knowledge in the Agreement on Trade-related Intellectual Property Rights (TRIPS Agreement).

The potential for trade liberalization to spur economic growth and reduce poverty worldwide is now well established. By removing their trade barriers, both the developed and developing countries would gain greatly. The Doha Round of trade negotiations can be a powerful tool to realize the MDGs.

6   The truth about foreign aid

In the midst of the tsunami disaster, the UN Undersecretary-General for Humanitarian Affairs, Jan Egeland, suggested that the world's richest nations are "stingy" when it comes to giving international aid, this rankled senior officials in the Bush administration.[1] President Bush expressed his displeasure by sharply noting: "Well, I felt like the person who made that statement was very misguided and ill-informed. We're a very generous, kindhearted nation, and, you know, what you're beginning to see is a typical response from America." However, forgotten behind the furor and acrimony is the paradoxical fact that both protagonists are right: Egeland if we judge the volume of aid given by the rich OECD countries, and the Bush administration if we measure US generosity on a specific yardstick. As Figures 6.1 and 6.2 show, while the United States gives more aid dollars in absolute terms than any other country in the world, when aid is calculated per US citizen, or as a percentage of the economy, the United States is among the least generous in the industrialized world.[2]

No doubt, the rich countries can give more aid. While the aid target set by the United Nations states that high-income countries should contribute 0.7 of 1 percent of GNP in aid, only a handful of high-income countries meet this target.[3] The fact is that official development assistance (ODA) has been on a downward trend.[4] It fell in 2000 to 0.22 of 1 percent of the rich countries' GNP – down from more than 0.4 of 1 percent in the 1960s and slightly more than 0.3 of 1 percent in the 1970s and 1980s. Today, development assistance is at one of its lowest levels at 0.22 percent of GDP, compared to 0.5 percent 30 years ago.[5] Even more troubling, concessional aid, which constitutes the bulk of development assistance to low and middle-income countries, has declined in real terms. If all the G-7 group of countries (the United States, Canada, United Kingdom, Germany, France, Italy, and Japan) met the modest 0.7 percent target it would generate some $142 billion per year. At the meeting of world leaders in Monterrey in March 2002 the rich countries promised to make concrete efforts towards the target of 0.7 percent of GNP as ODA to developing countries – of which 0.15 percent to 0.20 percent of GNP should be earmarked for the least-developed countries. While donors have pledged to increase development assistance by $18.6 billion a year by 2006 (measured from a base of about $58 billion

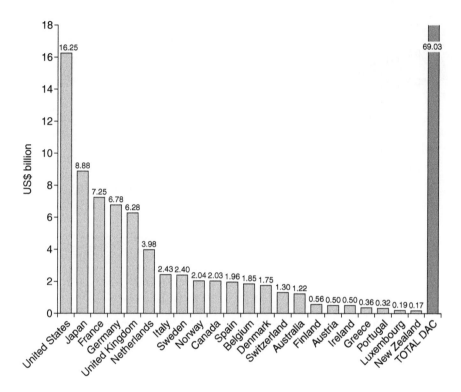

Figure 6.1 Net ODA in 2003 – amounts (source: *OECD-DAC 2004*).

in 2002), not much real progress has been made to date, and the future prognosis is not encouraging.

The decline in ODA is mainly due to the vagaries of domestic politics, to the downgrading of strategic considerations in the post-cold-war period (Lancaster 2006; Grant and Nijman 1998), and to the growing "aid fatigue" amongst both donor governments and their citizens – except for the outpouring of donations by governments, charities and individuals during large-scale humanitarian crises. The main reasons behind aid fatigue are: (1) the widespread belief that "aid does not work" because it is siphoned away by local elites and other vested interests and fails to reach those it was intended for; (2) as Bauer (1972, 1981) and more recently Easterly (2001, 2006), among others, have argued, aid is not effective in either promoting economic development or reducing poverty – its two oft-stated objectives: rather, it has the opposite effect by creating disincentives for investment and reforms; and (3) donor governments are giving away too much in foreign aid at a time they can ill afford to do so, given their own fiscal problems. For example, Cline and Williamson (2005: 420) point out that "on average, Americans believe that the government spends over 20 percent of its budget on foreign aid, whereas the true figure is about 1 percent." To put

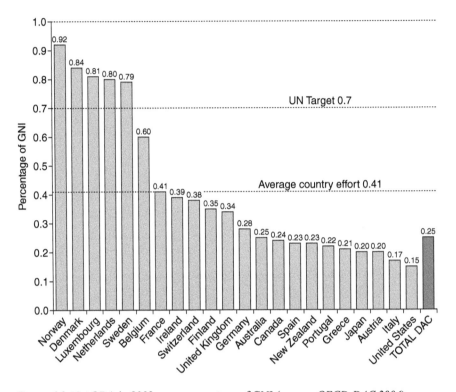

Figure 6.2 Net ODA in 2003 – as a percentage of GNI (source: *OECD-DAC 2004*).

this in some perspective, a Center for Global Development study (2004: 2) states that

> the US devotes less than 1% of the federal budget to development assistance, which amounts to $54 a year or 15 cents a day, for each American. This is a quarter of what the average American spends on carbonated soft drinks each year – $212.

Clearly, rich countries – in particular the wealthiest, the United States – can afford be more generous.

The case for and against aid: then and now

The question of whether foreign aid contributes to economic growth and poverty reduction has long been a subject of scholarly debate.[6] Studies in the 1960s drawing on the Harrod–Domar growth models saw aid as an exogenous net increment to the capital stock of the recipient country. The widely held view was that poor countries remained poor because of market failures and lack of capital.

The underlying assumption was that aid, by contributing to an increase in savings, inevitably spurs growth – that is, aid resources would fill the gap between available savings and required investment. In fact, Paul Rosenstein-Rodan (1961) assumed that a dollar of foreign aid would result in an increase of one dollar in total savings and investment. He argued that the pervasive "low-level equilibrium trap" keeps poor countries caught in a vicious cycle of poverty because income increases do not lead to more savings, but only higher population growth. Aid was seen to fill the badly needed "financing gap" – or the difference between domestic savings and the level of investment required for economic growth. In a similar vein, Walt Rostow (1960) in his provocative *The Stages of Economic Growth* argued that countries could emerge out of economic stagnation and "take-off" into self-sustaining growth with aid-financed increases in investment. Chenery and Strout (1966), in their seminal contribution, formulated the "two-gap model" where they claimed that poor countries trapped in poverty could not save and accumulate capital. This capital shortage was reflected in either their respective investment–savings and/or import–export gaps. That is, the savings gap exacerbated the foreign exchange gap resulting in the inability to export. This only served to ensure balance of payments problems. Chenery and Strout reasoned that an inflow of foreign capital would bridge this gap between actual investment and the investment required to reach a target growth rate. As Easterly (1999) notes, the two-gap model became conventional wisdom and is still used by many donors to calculate their aid allocations.

Now, a generation later, Jeffrey Sachs (2006), in his best-seller *The End of Poverty: Economic Possibilities for Our Time*, is once again advocating an aid-financed "big push" to eliminate mass poverty and generate economic growth in the world's poorest countries. According to Sachs, most of the world's poorest nations are caught in a vicious "poverty trap" – a condition under which poverty begets even more poverty, making a poor country simply too impoverished to achieve sustained economic growth.[7] As Sachs (2006: 56–7) eloquently notes,

> when poverty is extreme, the poor do not have the ability by themselves to get out of the mess.... When people are poor, but not entirely destitute, they may be able to save. When they are utterly destitute, they need their entire income, or more, just to survive. There is no margin of income above survival that can be invested in the future. This is the main reason why the poorest of the poor are most prone to becoming trapped with low or negative economic growth rates. They are too poor to save for the future, and thereby, accumulate the capital that could pull them out of their current misery.

To Sachs, no region of the world suffers more from the debilitating poverty trap than sub-Saharan Africa. As he notes, the facts speaks for itself: sub-Saharan Africa is not only the poorest region in the world, it is also the only region which has seen its per capita income decline since 1980 – in sharp contrast to other regions which have experienced unprecedented growth. Nearly one in two Africans or 300 million are counted as "poor," spending less than a dollar a day on basic necessities. The continent's food production per person has actually been falling, food insecurity is rampant, and Africans' caloric intake is the lowest in the world. Moreover, large segments of its population have been devastated by HIV/AIDS and the resurgence of vector-borne diseases such as malaria.[8] Today, the African continent has the dubious distinction of leading the world in declining life expectancy and ever-increasing rates of child mortality. Home to 10 percent of the world's population, sub-Saharan Africa now accounts for 30 percent of the world's poor.

To Sachs, the heart of Africa's problems lies in its unforgiving "geography [which] has conspired with economics to give Africa a particularly weak hand" (p. 208) – this along with the resultant unfavorable structural conditions that have left the African continent mired in a vicious poverty trap. Specifically, the poor infrastructure coupled with few natural navigable waterways to provide access to coastal ports makes for very high transportation costs and acts as a barrier for trade and market expansion; agriculture is low-productivity (the result of relatively few large rivers and insufficient and erratic rainfall limits the expansion of irrigation and extension of cultivated areas); the harsh climate encourages a disproportionate level of diseases like malaria and measles; adverse geopolitics and slow diffusion of technology from abroad have put Africa in a disadvantageous position. All this means that Africa does not fit the standard model, where an economy with small initial capital stock and a low capital–labor ratio could be expected to grow by increasing its capital–labor ratio.[9] As Sachs notes, poor people simply do not save enough, so physical capital accumulation fails to keep up with depreciation and population growth.

Therefore, if Africa is to escape the deadly embrace of the poverty trap it must increase its physical and human capital stock above the threshold needed for self-sustaining growth. How can this be done? Sachs argues that the oft-recommended remedy, IMF- and World Bank-led assistance, is no solution. This is because these institutions have not only repeatedly failed to grasp the extent and gravity of the poverty-trap problem in Africa, but their misguided policies of structural adjustment and related "regiments of belt tightening" have been largely responsible for exacerbating Africa's economic decline.

For Sachs, given the absence of other viable alternatives, he proposes a one-step massive increase or "big push" in capital stock via a well-targeted infusion of foreign assistance. He argues that this will help poor countries break out of the poverty trap and grow on their own. How "big" should the "big push" be? Sachs points out that the rich countries must double their foreign aid from the current $65 billion to over $130 billion and double the aid package again by 2015. This is necessary to fill the "financing gap" between the poor countries' own resources and needs and what they can afford on their own. Sachs goes to great length to underscore three points. First, the new infusion of aid must be well managed and targeted – coordinated by the United Nations, with the assistance of donor countries and international financial institutions. Second, contrary to popular belief, more aid will not break the bank in the rich countries. Rather, the doubling of the affluent nations' international assistance would only constitute about 0.5 percent of their GNP. Moreover, because these investments do not include other categories of aid such as spending on infrastructure or post-conflict reconstruction, the rich nations should meet their commitments to reach the agreed target of 0.7 percent of GNP by 2015. And third, a big push is justified because aid-financed investment will have a low payoff (actually no payoff in the long run) unless aid is large enough to push the country across the threshold. He notes, "if the foreign assistance is substantial enough, and lasts long enough, the capital stock rises sufficiently to lift households above subsistence ... growth becomes self-sustaining through household savings and public investments supported by taxation of households" (p. 246). Sachs (pp. 144–45) makes it abundantly clear that the aid should be in the form of grants rather than loans, and it should be "targeted to a particular set of investments, and specifically public sector investments, so that the aid cannot be used for consumption."

Sachs's audacious prescription has touched a raw nerve, inevitably rekindling an old debate among economists. In equal measure he has been hailed as a modern-day crusader for justice and human dignity, an indefatigable fighter for the world's poor and marginalized – indeed, the perfect exemplar of the modern intellectual – who uses his dazzling intellect to solve real-world problems. It seems that everyone from the former UN Secretary-General Kofi Annan, British Prime Minister Tony Blair, and pop singers Bono and Bob Geldof, to Microsoft's Bill Gates and several leading economists, including Nobel Laureate Joseph Stiglitz, the UNDP head Kemal Dervis (2005) and the former chief economist of the World Bank Nicholas Stern (Stern *et al.* 2005), and the World Bank (2005a), among others, have all embraced Sachs' bold solution.[10] Indeed, the Commission for Africa (2005), initiated by Tony Blair, in its report released in March 2005 explicitly notes,

> Africa requires a comprehensive "big push" on many fronts at once ... an essential part of this big push will be a major increase in investment ... we have considered ways in which such a quantum increase in investment could be financed other than by an increase in aid. We have found no credible alternative.
>
> (pp. 13 and 298)

Similarly, the European Commission (2005), in its report notes that increase aid would give Africa a "decisive push" in achieving growth.

However, many others, especially fellow economists, have been less charitable, criticizing him for floating extravagant if not wholly unintelligible and naive proposals. Among Sachs's harshest critics is William Easterly, an economics professor at New York University and a former senior research economist at the World Bank.[11] In his bitingly satirical, *The White Man's Burden: How the West's Efforts to Aid the Rest Have Done So Much Ill and So Little Good*, Easterly implicitly sees Sachs as an earnest but misguided "planner" – reminiscent of the early post-war period when the conventional belief was that grand "social engineering" providentially bankrolled by generous and never-ending supply of foreign aid money would enable poor countries to lift themselves out of economic underdevelopment and poverty.

Combining an impressive array of statistical evidence, telling field anecdotes, and country case-studies and drawing on an authoritative body of literature, Easterly makes three solemn observations. First, foreign aid is neither necessary nor sufficient to raise living standards in developing countries. Rich countries have already spent some $2.3 trillion on foreign aid over the last five decades, but the results have been conspicuously disappointing. This is tragically stark in Africa where aid has been highest as a percentage of income, but African growth is the lowest of any continent. To put it more bluntly, Africa has received some $568 billion in aid, yet the typical African country is no richer today than 40 years ago.[12] Second, poor development outcomes are not always the result of poverty traps, and most poor countries are not stuck in some sort of perennial poverty trap from which there is no escape except by massively scaled-up foreign aid. Third, many developing countries have attained economic growth without large infusions of foreign aid. This underscores that economic development happens not through aid, but through the tireless efforts of "homegrown" entrepreneurs and ordinary citizens relying on the indispensable force of free markets.

Who is right, Easterly or Sachs? Paradoxically, they both are. This is because the large questions addressed by both authors remain as inconclusive as ever – it is impossible to conclusively determine the extent to which aid has contributed to the development of particular countries during particular periods, given that so many other factors also played a role in shaping outcomes, and because for every failure of aid, one can also point to a success story. Indeed, as the World Bank's *Assessing Aid: What Works, What Doesn't, and Why* (1998: 1) notes,

> foreign aid has at times been a spectacular success. [several countries] have gone from crisis to rapid development. Foreign aid played a major role in each transformation [but on the other hand] foreign aid has also been, at times, an unmitigated failure. [In several countries] decades of large-scale foreign assistance left not a trace of progress.

Nevertheless, Easterly correctly highlights the litany of failures associated with foreign aid, state planning, and big government in the developing world. While Easterly may at times come across as a heartless cynic whose "actions" betray his cold indifference to the welfare of the world's most vulnerable,[13] his core argument that the lack of economic growth in many developing countries is due to bad governance, not to the lack of foreign aid, needs to be bluntly made because it is a much-needed antidote against Sachs's blatantly naïve belief that massive volumes of aid could be absorbed almost effortlessly and imperceptibly by poor nations without significant improvements in governance. Moreover, Easterly's accusation that Sachs intuitively favors a "top-down" approach to development is not without merit. Sachs's proposal, which fortuitously envisions a vast central-planning apparatus ruled under the administrative fiat of the UN secretary-general and legions of UN staff (to ostensibly help the secretary-general coordinate the efforts of UN agencies, including the International Monetary Fund, the World Bank, and donors) is astonishing naïve. To expect the United Nations to manage massive aid-flows is a recipe for disaster.

Yet, Easterly exaggerates the flaws in foreign aid. His deep-seated pessimism that aid has proven to be an unmitigated disaster, a zero-sum game of no winners, is based on the most selective of evidences. At times, his arguments not only lack nuance, they are also disingenuous as he is fully aware that the empirical literature on aid effectiveness has yielded ambiguous results given the heterogeneity of aid motives, difficulties in distinguishing short- versus long-term impacts and the complex causality chain linking external aid to final outcome.

As is well known, measuring the "effect" of aid on economic growth is problematic, as "effect" implies causality, as different from correlation. So it is not very difficult to find evidence of a negative correlation between aid and growth – but this does not mean that aid is the cause of the lack of growth. For example, if aid is given to a poorly performing economy, the data will show that aid and growth are negatively correlated, although aid did not cause poor growth. In other words, the direction of causation is the reverse. Clemens *et al.* (2004) lucidly illustrate this. In disaggregating ODA and focusing on the types of aid that are actually aimed at affecting growth directly and relatively quickly, such as aid for infrastructure, agriculture, industry and budget support (as separate from humanitarian aid), and those targeted for health and education (the latter aimed at affecting growth over the long term), they find a strong causal relationship between this subset of aid and economic growth – albeit with diminishing returns, including that there is no reason to expect humanitarian aid to result in growth, or aid targeted for health and education to result immediately in growth.

Moreover, one does not have to be an aid-optimist to appreciate the fact that millions of lives have been saved through large-scale health interventions, many of them supported by aid funds. The eradication of smallpox, the enormous progress in fighting debilitating diseases such as tuberculosis, river blindness and diarrhea, and improvements in health and education, have been mostly funded by aid resources. It seems to me that part of the problem is that Easterly never precisely defines what he means by "aid" – which admittedly encompasses the official development aid given by rich countries, as well as much more targeted project aid such as the schools and water wells built in remote villages by NGOs. Broken down this way, the amount of development aid which has reached the poor is in fact quite miniscule when items like emergency food aid (which is not designed as long-term development assistance) and repaid debts are taken into account. In fact, over time the financing for education, infrastructure, and health projects – or the share of aid going to project and program support – has sharply fallen (Sundberg and Gelb 2006).

In what is a searing indictment, Sachs deftly notes that the average amount of real development aid given to each citizen in sub-Saharan Africa was just $12 in 2002. Moreover, Easterly's deterministic claim that aid cannot be redeemed, and that responsibility lies mainly with the recipient, is based on his assertion that the problem in Africa is mainly corruption (code word for poor governance). However, the fact is that not all the 48 countries on the African continent are badly governed (Sachs draws on data from Transparency International to underscore this), and there are many countries in other continents with predatory governments, but they do not suffer from a poverty trap. As Sachs (2006) notes,

> the outside world has pat answers concerning Africa's prolonged crisis. Everything comes back again and again to corruption and misrule. Western officials, including the countless "missions" of the IMF and World Bank to African countries, argue that Africa simply needs to behave itself better, to allow market forces to operate without interference by corrupt rulers.
>
> (pp. 188–9)

But this fails to explain why in sub-Saharan Africa both the well and badly governed are equally mired in a poverty trap. This is an important question because, as discussed in the previous chapter, it underscores that poor governance is not always the result of corruption and malfeasance. Rather, poor governance can also arise when governments are well intentioned but lack the human and financial resources to establish and operate an efficient public administration.

Given this, as Sachs notes, aid can play a crucial role in promoting development of low-income countries that have little access to private capital, provided that donors deliver aid efficiently and require recipients to use it effectively. He correctly points out that many countries with reasonably good governance have received far less aid than they can use effectively, whereas many other poorly governed ones (for mostly geo-political reasons) are "over-aided."[14] Similarly, it is hard to disagree with Sachs's observation regarding the need to improve aid quality. Corroborative evidence indicates that by reducing the number of agencies involved in disbursing aid, harmonizing aid procedures to reduce compliance costs for the recipients, reducing – if not eliminating – tied aid, aligning aid priorities with each country's own development priorities, and having a better understanding of which programs work, and why, can go a long way in improving overall aid effectiveness. However, what is so scrupulously missing in Sachs's narrative – and if included would have made his case stronger – is a viable prescription of how to actually manage the increased aid flows (his UN solution is a non-starter). Clearly, absorbing and spending aid resources effectively, dealing with the unpredictable and volatile nature of aid flows, how to best use funds available through debt relief so as to avoid renewed debt distress, and the appropriate macroeconomic policies – in particular, the coordination of fiscal, monetary and exchange-rate policies – all these should have been spelled out. Finally, while Sachs's prescription sounds technically plausible, there is a major gap in his argument. He does not adequately address the absorptive capacity problem. That is, will Africa be able to use the aid productively? If not, despite all the precautions, aid resources will be wasted. I am not convinced that Africa has the absorptive capacity yet. Perhaps it would be more prudent to give

Africa aid at the pace at which it can be usefully absorbed, rather than a massive, one-time infusion. Furthermore, Sachs fails to elaborate how aid resources will create that virtuous circle of domestic reforms and growth necessary to pave the way for sustained poverty reduction. Yet, it is clear that Africa has run out of options and we must act now to reverse the human tragedy that is unfolding there. My altruism compels me to give Sachs' risky proposals the benefit of the doubt. At least he has a plan, and at the end of the day, what he is asking for will not break the bank.

The case for aid

Clearly, numerous examples can be cited to illustrate how foreign aid often ends up in a bottomless black hole – failing either to promote economic development or to alleviate poverty. While Easterly is among the most vociferous critic of aid, many other analysts are equally critical of aid and the vast "aid industry" (Dichter 2003; Reusse 2002). In the literature on this topic, some of the more interesting include Boone (1996) who relates aid effectiveness to political regimes. He finds that aid does not significantly increase investment or improve human development indicators. Devarajan and co-authors (2001) show that unconditional financial aid in poor policy settings may have perverse incentive effects and undermine otherwise necessary reforms. Djankov and co-authors (2006: 2) state that

> foreign aid has a negative impact on the democratic stance of developing countries and on economic growth by reducing investment and increasing government consumption. Therefore, our empirical findings do not support the democratization effect of foreign aid nor the development effect.

Similarly, Feyziouglu *et al.* (1998) find no significant correlation between aid and levels of investment. They point out that due to fungibility aid seems to stimulate government consumption and spending. Bhagwati (2004) and Panagariya (2006) argue that "aid through trade" is a far better option for developing countries. And perhaps the most controversial, Rajan and Subramanian (2006) conclude that regardless of the situation – whether countries have adopted sound economic policies or improved government institutions, and regardless of the type of assistance involved – aid does not appear to stimulate growth over the short or long term. In fact, they claim that there is "no discernible robust impact of aid on growth, positive or negative." The authors argue that the reason for this is that "aid inflows have systematic adverse effects on a country's competitiveness." Thus, aid can be counterproductive in that it tends to boost the recipient country's exchange rate. This in turn makes its exports less competitive, thereby undermining local manufacturing.

However, the overall ineffectiveness of aid should be seen in context. As Sachs (2005) and Stiglitz (2002) succinctly point out, the obsession with "aid–growth relationship" is not always valid as significant portions of aid such as food aid and emergency disaster transfers are not always directed at promoting economic growth. Not surprisingly, the overall relationship between aid and growth are weak – because the careless mixing of data of both "development" and "humanitarian" aid produces misleading results. Thus, as noted earlier, although aid has a less than stellar record, on average aid has helped to reduce poverty and improve the quality of life of the poor by financing treatment for river blindness, tuberculosis and polio, and eradicating smallpox, as well as dramatically reducing the incidence of diarrheal diseases via the introduction of oral rehydration therapy. Similarly the dissemination of high-yielding varieties of wheat, rice, corn, and many other crops was made possible by international cooperation in which aid played a central role. Therefore, well-targeted aid can have positive outcomes and significantly improve the lives some two billion people who live on less than $1 a day.

While the relationship between aid, good governance and institutions is complex, cross-country evidence shows that foreign aid has a strong positive effect on a country's economic performance (faster growth coupled with poverty reduction and gains in social indicators) if "sound policies"[15] and good governance are in place – but has no measurable effect in countries with poor governance and policies (Burnside and Dollar 2000, 2004; Clemens *et al.* 2004; Collier and Dollar 2002; Svensson 1999, 2000; World Bank 1998, 2002c). For example, Burnside and Dollar's (2000, 2004) skillful analysis of aid flows to 56 developing countries during the period 1970–1993 concludes that with a 1 percent increase of GNP in aid, the growth rate of the good policy performer increases by 0.4 percentage points. Moreover, in good policy environments aid attracts private investment, and aid totaling 1 percent of GDP leads to a 0.9 percent reduction in infant mortality.[16] Similarly, Collier and Dollar's (2002) study of 59 developing countries (including 20 countries from Africa) over the period 1974–1997 found that the impact of aid on growth depends on the quality of economic policies. These authors stress that good governance must mean, among other things, that the recipient country has in place the administrative capacity to manage and use aid flows effectively and the mechanisms to prevent capture of aid resources by vested interests. Radelet (2004) also argues that aid effectiveness depends on the quality of governance in the recipient country.

Therefore, the policy implications are clear: in a good policy environment aid given as financial assistance can serve as a catalyst for faster growth and improvements in human development indicators. Thus, to get the maximum impact on growth and poverty reduction, financial assistance should be directed to countries that have in place sound policies and responsive and accountable governance. It also means that the practice of giving aid indiscriminately to both the egregiously corrupt and the relatively non-corrupt regimes alike, in the hope that "conditionality" (providing aid and then hoping that recipient governments will become politically and economically responsible), simply does not work. Rather, experience shows that governance reforms are almost never taken voluntarily. Thus, throwing money at the accountability gap will not fix the problem. Instead, both bilateral and multilateral donors should regularly and judiciously monitor recipient country performance and base their aid on "selectivity" – that is, target their assistance to supporting countries that implement governance reforms and invest in human capital. It should be made explicit that there will be tangible rewards for countries that perform well in areas of democratic accountability, show respect for the rule of law, and invest in the welfare of their citizens.

Specifically, responsive and accountable governments will receive not only sustained development assistance, more generous debt relief and incentives for foreign investment, but also greater "country ownership" of aid resources in setting national priorities and designing particular programs. In the case of some LDCs, including failed or failing states where policy performance and institutions cannot be strengthened in the short run, donors have two options. First, donors should not cut off aid – in particular, humanitarian relief and assistance. Rather, they should adopt a multi-year "carrot and stick" aid commitment, with financial disbursements conditional on good-faith efforts by recipients to implement their commitments and improvements in governance and economic performance ... *and stick*, cutting off funds when governments fail the test. This may serve to constrain recipient governments from simply making *pro forma* reforms and stalling, and will provide real incentives for recalcitrant governments to qualitatively improve their performance. Second, in environments where a viable and responsible state does not exist, donors could channel resources through non-governmental organizations (including other representatives of civil society) and provide technical assistance, while at the same time assisting in building public institutions and improving the quality of governance. Indeed, in countries such as Uganda, Mozambique and, more recently, Sierra Leone, aid has played a critical role in sustaining vulnerable populations as well as helping build civil and other grass-roots organizations during the long years of civil war (Radelet 2003, 2004).

Since aid is fungible, how can donors mitigate the problems associated with "fungibility?" That is, a donor may give aid to a particular sector (say education, health or infrastructure) but this may not lead to increased spending in that sector if the recipient government reduces its own spending there and spends the funds saved elsewhere. Studies show that aid resources allocated to a particular sector tend to free up for other purposes money that the government would otherwise have spent in that sector. This means that in funding specific projects or sectors, donors may actually be helping to increase spending on sectors they do not want to finance, such as military spending or a particular regime's "patronage politics." Because aid effectively goes to the whole economy, the overall quality of government spending and its ability to use money efficiently is important.[17] However, as Burnside and Dollar (2000) and others have noted, aid is effective only when the overall policy environment is good – not otherwise. No doubt, while building accountable and responsive institutions is critical, in the short term donors can ameliorate the problems associated with fungibility by carefully selecting projects and closely monitoring their implementation. They also have the option of supporting "projects" as opposed to the more fungible budget support. NGOs have long known that resources allocated to specific projects such as schools, health centers or dispensaries are relatively non-fungible as recipient governments cannot easily redirect them. Donors providing budget support should work with recipient governments on setting budget targets, in particular allocating their funds once the recipient government has already outlined its budget priorities. Finally, we know that different types of aid have differential effects on growth. For example, Clemens and coauthors (2004) find that "short-impact" aid flows such as budget and balance of payments support, and investment in economic infrastructure, have a much greater impact on growth than aggregate aid.

According to Abhijit Banerjee (2006) donors know little about the effectiveness of their aid programs because they do not collect solid evidence on what works. He believes one way to know what works and thereby use aid most productively is to perform more controlled experiments. Specifically, he proposes collecting this "hard" evidence using randomized controlled trials and confining aid to projects that the evidence supports. As Banerjee notes, this is how one evaluates new drugs, and we should do the same to assess the efficacy of different aid-financed projects. No doubt, many aid agencies do little to properly evaluate the impact of their projects. Independent audits of aid performance can go a long way in telling which programs work and which do not. As Banerjee notes, donor agencies disbursing large volumes of tax-financed aid ought to use randomized evaluative assessments before committing resources. Yet, it must be recognized that such randomized experiments can be quite costly for smaller private aid agencies. Moreover, such experiments can tell us only so much: that is, what may work in one locality or set of localities may not work in another jurisdiction. Moreover, areas such as governance reforms, including institutional capacity-building or decentralization, are not easily amenable to random evaluations.

Increasingly, donors now recognize the value of independent evaluations. In early 2002, the donors to the World Bank's International Development Association (IDA) – the world's primary source of concessional financing (or "soft loans") for development – made the 13th IDA replenishment contingent on the establishment of a results-based measurement system for all IDA programs.[18] Similarly, President George W. Bush's ambitious initiative announced in March 2002, called the "Millennium Challenge Account" (MCA) designed to provide assistance to poor countries that are "ruling justly, investing in people, and encouraging economic freedom," marks a break with past practices because it explicitly links aid to governments' performance. In the fiscal 2006 budget, the Bush administration allocated $9.5 billion for bilateral humanitarian and development assistance – about $2.1 billion more than the current level – reversing a 40-year downward trend in US foreign aid as a percentage of the gross domestic product and making aid one of the few areas of non-defense spending to get an increase. Nevertheless, even with the increase and funding for the MCA, it is still shy of the $5 billion that Bush initially pledged to spend in 2006. US contributions still total about 15 cents for every $100 in gross domestic product, compared with 80 cents to 92 cents for nations such as the Netherlands, Denmark and Norway.[19] However, all bilateral and multilateral donors, in particular the

OECD's Development Assistant Committee (DAC), need to better coordinate with each other to avoid duplication and wastage. Moreover, limiting aid fragmentation and harmonizing aid with performance will produce more positive outcomes.[20]

Some have argued that the decline in aid can be easily filled by foreign direct investment (FD1) and other forms of private capital flows. According to the World Bank (2004b), in 1997 the net private capital flows to developing countries was at about seven times the net official assistance. In hard numbers, the volume of private financial flows to developing countries increased from about $55 billion to $155 billion between 1990 and 2002. However, the distribution of FDI among developing countries remains extremely unequal. In the second half of the 1990s, more than half of FDI went to just four middle-income developing countries and over one-third to just two countries – China and Brazil. At the end of the 1990s, the top ten middle-income developing countries received 78 percent of FDI. On the other hand, about half of all developing countries received little or no FD1. For example, sub-Saharan Africa (the region with over two-thirds of the world's most poor countries) received only 5 percent of all FDI, with the bulk going to a handful of countries with petroleum- and mineral-based industries.[21] As noted earlier, Africa today is characterized by uniquely high levels of poverty and underdevelopment. The region has become increasingly marginalized, while HIV/AIDS, civil conflict and widespread poverty continue to create barriers to development and growth. Currently sub-Saharan Africa is home to 70 percent of those infected with HIV/AIDS, and as a result average life expectancy has now fallen to 47 years in the region. For nations in sub-Saharan Africa, as for many low-income countries unable to attract private investment, ODA remains the most important source of foreign capital. It is in this context that Sachs (2006) concludes that to build Africa's physical and human capital stock above the threshold for self-sustaining growth and lift the continent out of a debilitating "poverty trap" will require massive external aid that provides targeted investment in infrastructure and human capital. In fact, sub-Saharan Africa is going to need a "scaling-up" of external assistance for many years if the region is to meet its people's most basic needs for health care and education while at the same time building physical infrastructure and effective institutions.

Evidence also shows that private investors can be slow to respond when low-income countries improve their investment climate and social services. It is precisely at this stage that aid can have a great impact on growth and poverty reduction. Sachs and Warner (1995), Stern (2002) and others have compellingly argued that even very modest transfers – just fractions of 1 percent of GNP – from the rich countries to the very poor could enable massive expansions of health services, access to essential medicines, universal primary and secondary education and other benefits. However, transfers of funds to a developing country in amounts that are large relative to the size of its economy, coupled with the reality that most developing countries have underdeveloped financial markets and relatively closed capital accounts, means that they may not be able to effectively absorb the increased aid flows. The fear is that this may lead to adverse macroeconomic effects, including triggering the so-called "Dutch disease" – a term that broadly refers to the harmful consequences of large inflows of foreign currency into a country.[22]

Specifically, an increase in aid generally increases the demand for both traded and nontraded goods. However, if a significant portion of foreign aid were to be spent on nontradable goods, the price of domestic goods and services would go up. The conversion of foreign exchange into local currency for the purchase of domestic products would expand the monetary base. This expansion could fuel an increase in domestic demand (some of which would be met by greater imports), contributing to a weakening of the trade balance. At the same time, demand for nontraded goods would also increase. Since the supply of nontraded goods is less elastic, higher demand will drive up their price relative to that of traded goods and cause the real exchange rate to appreciate.[23] In turn, the real appreciation will lead to reallocation of labor toward the nontradable goods sector, thereby raising real wages in terms of the price of the tradable goods. In time, the profligacy will catch up and the resulting deterioration in competitiveness can lead to a decline in export performance and draw resources away from the traded goods sector, causing it to shrink further. This problem is magnified if the traded goods sector is the main source of productivity growth in the economy.

Clearly, the problems that result from a limited capacity to absorb aid flows cannot be remedied easily. Nevertheless, the problems associated with the Dutch disease can be ameliorated. First, it is important to note that the Dutch disease effects may vary sharply across countries, being a particular threat to countries where aid accounts for a very large share of national income. However, even there, studies suggest that overall aid effectiveness can outweigh the challenges, provided that the policy environment is sound (Bulir and Lane 2002). Second, in countries where aid funds are smaller or temporary, they must be encouraged to budget conservatively – for example, increasing their planned long-term spending by less than the full amount of aid they receive in a given year. This will help keep the exchange rate at a sustainable level. Third, countries should do the obvious by spending aid mainly on traded goods, thereby reducing the adverse impact on the traded goods sector. Fourth, a number of countries have effectively intervened in the foreign exchange market to limit the exchange rate impact of aid inflows (through buying foreign exchange) and via sterilized intervention (by selling government paper). And finally, ending "tied aid" (aid which must be used to procure goods and services from the donor country) can greatly help. Studies have shown that tied aid, often tied down further through unduly complex policies and procedures, increases transactions costs and tends to reduce the value of assistance by about 25 percent (World Bank 1998). A recent study by Sundberg and Gelb (2006: 15) notes that

> tied aid is estimated to be 11–30 percent less valuable than untied aid because of price differentials between what donor country firms charge and what would be available in the market … throughout the 1980s, more than half of all aid was tied in this way.

The authors note that there are "indications that the share of tied aid is declining, but several donors no longer report how much of their aid is tied, making it difficult to confirm."

Aid and debt are intrinsically linked – thus, if aid is to be effective, it needs to be better aligned with debt relief. Although developing countries are a diverse group, the vast majority of the low-income countries depend heavily on official financing. However (as the next chapter shows) excessive debt in many of these countries poses serious problems for them meeting their development objectives. Between 1990 and 2001, external debt as a percentage of gross national income rose from 88.1 percent to 100.3 percent in the "severely indebted" countries. In 2001, the LDCs were spending almost 3 percent of GDP on servicing debt (World Bank 2002a). The growing problem of "debt over-hang" not only undermines urgently needed progress on policy reforms: besides discouraging private investment, it may force lenders to allocate scarce concessional resources to keep high debtor countries afloat – often at the expense of other deserving countries. While the primary responsibility for achieving debt sustainability lies with debtor countries themselves – in particular, they must keep new borrowing in step with their ability to repay, and adopt policies that increase their resilience to exogenous shocks – donors and creditors can do much to help.

First, given the central role of official creditors and donors in providing new resources to these countries, they need to carefully review current financing policies to ensure that they appropriately reflect countries' risk of debt distress – in particular, that the resources provided to these countries are consistent with their long-term debt sustainability and progress towards achieving the Millennium Development Goals. Second, since an approximate mix of concessional loans and grants may improve a country's ability to absorb large, unforeseen exogenous shocks to only a limited extent, creditors and donors need to consider new or modified instruments to deal with such eventualities. Third, since canceling debt repayments from the world's poorest countries would yield only around US$1 billion per year (Besley and Burgess 2003), an increase in the overall concessionality of financing to low-income countries, including a larger volume of grants, is almost certainly required. As Kenneth Rogoff (2003: 56), former IMF Economic Counselor, aptly notes "it is vital that massive aid increases come mainly in the form of grants, not loans. Burdening countries with massive debts won't help and will likely hurt."

However, what about the perennial concern that recipient countries view loans quite differently from grants because they carry the burden of future repayment? This motivates governments to use funds more prudently and to mobilize taxes or, at least, to maintain current levels of domestic revenue collection. On the other hand, grants are usually viewed as "freebies" and used at the discretion of recipients. Over time, grants, including loans given to highly concessional terms (and often forgiven), can create disincentives to adopt good policies, besides fostering aid dependency. Moreover, grant aid is generally more unpredictable and volatile than aid provided through loans. If recipient countries come to depend too much on aid given as grant for their poverty-reduction spending, it could have an extremely negative impact if grant flows suddenly decline or cease altogether. Clearly, the nature of aid composition matters. For most LDCs, grants (as opposed to loans) are most appropriate and the optimal form of aid when aid is intended to raise consumption of the poor. Grants are also appropriate when the magnitude and timing of returns to public investment are long-term and uncertain, and where the government has limited ability to recover them through taxation to service debt. Grants are one sure way to mitigate the debt burdens from future generations in poor countries. Yet, to underscore again, the disbursements of grants should be accompanied by policies to strengthen domestic institutions.

Finally, as aid-dependent countries only know too well: the donors' aid practices and their aid agencies are not always rational and the actual aid disbursements often tend to fall short of their commitments.[24] Moreover, as Sundberg and Gelb (2006: 16–17) note, the administrative costs of aid have gone up dramatically "in part because of the proliferation of agencies and countries involved in delivering aid – whereas 2 agencies and 10 countries provided aid to Africa in 1960, these numbers had increased to 16 agencies and 31 countries." Birdsall (2004) lucidly outlines what she calls the "seven deadly sins" associated with donor aid practices, procedures and policies. These include: a general impatience with institution-building; both an inability and an unwillingness to exit from programs and countries where aid is not successful; failure to carefully evaluate aid programs and projects; the view that participation is sufficient to claim ownership; collusion and coordination failure between various donors; inadequate and unreliable transfers; and under-funding. In a telling example, Sachs (2005: 87) notes, "the United States contributed a meager $4 million to Ethiopia in 2002 to raise its agricultural output – and then gave $500 million in emergency food aid when famine predictably hit the country a year later." Similarly, the aid shortfalls, usually the end result of the donors' shifting budget priorities and because promises are not always kept, make it very difficult for recipient countries to plan their budgets. Of course, over the long term the solution is to reduce one's dependency on aid. However, in the meantime aid-dependent countries must do all they can to insulate themselves from the vagaries of international aid. In this regard they have few options except to base their spending plans on conservative projections of donor funding. In some cases this may mean adjusting spending based on aid funds that actually materialize. Here, donors can play a critical role by reducing the transaction costs of delivering aid by simplifying the complex procedures for aid disbursements (Easterly 2006). Experience shows that, at best, these unduly cumbersome procedures and the competing bureaucracies which manage them impose significant administrative burdens on low-income countries, and at worst, make aid flows unpredictable, besides creating severe problems of economic management. Rather, donors should focus their energies on the delivery of aid, ensuring that it gets to those who need it the most.

7 Optimal debt relief for the poorest

The idea of forgiving the debt of the world's poor nations began gaining momentum several years ago. Beginning in the early 1990s, "Drop the Debt," a British NGO advocated the complete cancellation of all debt owed by poor countries. In 1995, "Drop the Debt" merged with a new organization called "Jubilee 2000." Made up of a broad coalition of religious groups, ordinary citizens, and high-profile celebrities, Jubilee 2000 mounted unprecedented worldwide campaigns for the complete elimination of Third World debt (Pettifor 2006). One of the more memorable campaigns took place in the final weeks of 1999 when tens of thousands of people in over 150 countries would regularly and symbolically form human chains to pray, sign petitions and peacefully protest for an end to global inequality, injustice and poverty. With charismatic pop stars Bob Geldof and the indefatigable Bono of the group U2 as spokespeople, Jubilee 2000 made the cancellation of all debt held by the world's poorest countries the centerpiece of their demands (Pettifor 2006; Roodman 2006).

In their passionate appeals, Jubilee 2000 argued not only that debt was a morally unjust burden on the world's poor who were paying for obligations made by unaccountable and corrupt regimes and imprudent foreign lenders, but that debt cancellation would free resources that could be used to promote economic development and assist in the eradication of mass poverty. They demanded immediate action by urging citizens of the creditor nations to put pressure on their governments and, indirectly, the international financial institutions – namely the World Bank and the IMF – to work towards a complete cancellation of the debt held by all low-income countries by the end of 2000 (Greenhill et al. 2003; Pettifor 2003, 2006). By the end of the campaign and on the eve of the new millennium, over 24 million people from around the world had signed the Jubilee 2000 petition – making it both the first-ever global petition and the petition with the biggest number of signatures ever collected on one single issue (Pettifor 2006). It included not only thumbprints from the poor and the illiterate, but also the signatures of the famous and powerful, including Pope John Paul II, the Dalai Lama, President Bill Clinton, several members of the US Congress and Senate, heads of state from some 147 countries, United Nations Secretary-General Kofi Annan, South Africa's Bishop Desmond Tutu, several Nobel laureates, and Hollywood stars, among others.

In September 2000, "debt relief" (or the lowering of debt burdens and reduction in debt-service payments), including "debt forgiveness" (or the cancellation of official bilateral debt for LDCs), was made one of the cornerstones of the Millennium Development Goals. It was official recognition not only that high levels of external debt posed a serious constraint on the ability of many poor countries to generate growth and achieve the MDGs, but that concerted efforts must be made to deal with the problem. However, there was disagreement on how best to reduce the debt burdens of the LDCs. The rich nations made it clear that the major instrument for debt reduction in low-income countries would continue to be the Heavily Indebted Poor Countries (HIPC) Initiative launched by the World Bank and the IMF in 1996 and "enhanced" in 1999. Designed to relieve the high external debt of some of the world's poorest nations by either writing off their debt or reducing it to sustainable levels, it was believed that the HIPC Initiative would free up scarce public resources for both economic development and poverty reduction.

While the HIPC Initiative did free up resources for development and helped several countries towards debt sustainability, in many low-income countries the debt burden still remained high. To many anti-debt activists this was further proof that the HIPC Initiative was not working, resolving their demand for complete debt forgiveness for all poor countries as well as the heavily indebted middle-income countries (Cheru 2006; George 1998; Pettifor 2003, 2006). Finally, in the face of growing international pressure, the finance ministers from the Group of Eight (G-8), made up of the world's wealthiest countries, during their annual summit at Gleneagles on 6–8 July 2005 announced the creation of the Multilateral Debt Relief Initiative (MDRI), designed to provide an unprecedented 100 percent debt cancellation for some 19 of the world's most heavily indebted low-income countries on eligible debt from three multilateral institutions. That is, under the MDRI, the three multilateral institutions – the IMF, the International Development Association (IDA) of the World Bank (the part of the World Bank that provides zero interest loans and outright grants to the poorest nations[1]) and the African Development Fund (AfDF) – would cancel 100 percent of their debt claims on countries that had reached, or would eventually reach their "Completion Point" under the joint IMF–World Bank Enhanced HIPC Initiative.

While the MDRI is separate from the HIPC Initiative, it is linked to it operationally. The key difference is that while the HIPC Initiative entails coordinated action by multilateral organizations and governments to reduce the external debt burdens of the most heavily indebted poor countries to "sustainable levels," the MDRI goes further by providing full debt relief in order to free up additional resources to help these countries reach the MDGs. Unlike the HIPC Initiative, the MDRI does not propose any parallel debt relief on the part of official bilateral or private creditors, or of multilateral institutions beyond the IMF, IDA, and the AfDF.

Will the latest debt relief initiative finally help the world's poorest countries to grow and meet the MDGs? At the outset it should be noted that while debt relief and debt forgiveness is not an end in itself, it is essential if poor countries are to stimulate economic growth necessary to combat poverty and achieve the MDGs. The HIPC Initiative and the MDRI remain the only internationally agreed framework for providing comprehensive debt relief to poor low-income countries. Moreover, both initiatives are committed to providing deeper and broader debt relief, strengthening the links between debt relief, growth and poverty reduction, and to establishing a transparent and generally well-coordinated action on debt relief by the multilateral financial institutions and both donor and recipient governments. Yet, as the following sections will show, these initiatives may not be enough to push most LDCs out of the poverty trap and towards debt sustainability and economic growth.

Debt relief: theory and practice

The main rationale for debt reduction has rested on the concept of "debt over-hang" – a situation when a country owes more money to its creditors than it is able to pay. The cost of a country's unserviceable foreign debt, coupled with a decline in the economy, creates disincentives for an over-indebted country to invest and adjust. According to Krugman (1988, 1989) and Sachs (1986, 1989), excessive debt burdens cause investors to hold back because they fear that their profits will be taxed to help service the debt, or that the debtor country may resort to devaluation (and inflationary policies) as a way to cope with the unpaid debt. Moreover, debt overhang discourages the debtor country from making necessary but painful macroeconomic adjustments because of their concern that the fruits from reform will go to debt servicing, while they bear most of the socioeconomic and political fallout. This vicious cycle means that a country suffering from a debt overhang will not be able to obtain new funds to stimulate economic activity. Therefore, both Sachs and Krugman agree that the debt must be reduced to sustainable levels before economic development can take place. Indeed, this theory inspired several debt-reduction schemes – albeit mainly for highly indebted middle-income countries for which an active secondary market in their bank-held debt existed, and ranging from small buybacks of debt to the Brady deals.[2]

On the other hand, analysts have long recognized that debt relief, like aid, cannot solve the fundamental problems of economic development (Bulow and Rogoff 1990). The basic argument against debt relief is that even if all debt were forgiven, the inability of the LDCs to stimulate economic growth means that expenditure will again outstrip income growth – putting these countries back into debt (Bhagwati 2004). Moreover, debt relief tends to create perverse incentives for debtor countries as debt-dependence simply allows governments to continue to pursue imprudent economic policies which allegedly got them in debt in the first place (Bhagwati 2004; Easterly 2001, 2006). A more sophisticated case, put forward by Arslanalp and Henry (2006: 208), argues that "the Gleneagles proposal for debt relief is, at best, likely to have little effect at all." This is because the world's poorest countries, unlike the heavily indebted middle-income countries, do not suffer from a debt overhang but lack the

> functional economic institutions that provide the foundations for profitable investment and growth. The Brady countries had functional (if underperforming) economies, viable private sectors – something for foreign capital to be interested in. The low-income HIPC have none of the above … debt relief may be more valuable for Brady-like middle-income countries than for low-income ones because of how it leverages the private sector.

In order to evaluate the efficiency of debt relief, Arslanalp and Henry (2005) employed what they call "an unbiased arbiter" – the stock market. They examined how the stock markets of the 16 middle-income developing countries responded to the news as these nations reached individual Brady Plan debt relief agreements between 1989 and 1995. They found that the value of the Brady countries' stock markets increased by $42 billion during the time they were preparing their debt relief strategies. Stock prices went up because market participants anticipated (correctly) that debt relief would generate tangible economic benefits. Within a year of each country's Brady agreement, foreign capital began flowing back and economic growth resumed. Furthermore, US banks that forgave debt also benefited. Because the debtors were better able to service the reduced financial burden, the stock market value of the banks' shares rose by $13 billion. However, the authors argue that debt relief will not stimulate investment and growth in the HIPCs because, unlike the Brady countries, the HIPCs lack the institutions that provide the foundation for profitable economic activity. In the absence of basic institutions, debt relief is like forgiving debt owed by a firm that makes losses on every unit it sells – a temporary bandaid when radical surgery is required. In other words, when a country's principal problem is inadequate institutions, there is no reason to believe that debt relief will stimulate a rush of foreign capital, generating higher investment and growth. What then is the solution? According to Arslanalp and Henry, a more effective way to help the HIPCs is to provide direct aid to build the institutions that will eventually make them attractive places for both domestic and foreign investment. The authors dismiss the argument that debt relief is equivalent to aid. This is because debt relief is fungible. Thus, there is no guarantee that writing down a country's debt will translate into the country using those resources for institution-building.

No doubt, Arslanalp and Henry (2005; 2005a; 2006) make a compelling case that the LDCs do not suffer from a debt overhang. But does this mean there should be no debt relief for them? The answer is definitely no if we consider two factors. First, if the problem facing most LDCs is not debt overhang, as discussed in the previous chapter, it most certainly is the poverty trap. This means that these countries need all the assistance they can get to escape the trap's deadly grip. As will be discussed, if the HIPC Initiative proved ineffective it was because it was based on the assumption that the world's poorest nations were suffering from a debt overhang. However, the MDRI seems to have correctly diagnosed the problem as the poverty trap. Yet, unfortunately, like the HIPC Initiative before it, the MDRI most likely may prove generally ineffective because the amount of fund it will provide to the LDC is miniscule to the task at hand. Second, lest we forget, it was the sharply rising world interest rates which made foreign commercial banks worry about their loan portfolios in the Brady countries (Lairson and Skidmore 2003). As the short-term payment burden for the debtors became unmanageable and banks rushed to call in their loans, new lending came to a standstill, causing a credit crunch. With no new funds coming in, scarce resources that would normally have funded investment were consumed by debt servicing. Under these conditions, economic growth came to an abrupt stop. However, as the debt burden was gradually relieved, new funds began to arrive. The inflow of funds, along with the expeditious implementation of economic reforms, revived investment and growth. With meaningful debt relief, the same scenario may be possible in the HIPCs. Without debt relief we doom the HIPCs to a certain death – both figuratively and literally. Therefore, the latest debt relief initiatives are worth the effort.

The HIPC Initiative

In contrast to middle-income countries, the debt crisis in poor low-income countries emerged rather slowly as payment difficulties (the first real manifestation of problems) were initially addressed through new net lending and debt reschedulings – first on commercial and subsequently on increasingly concessional terms (Cheru 1989; Lissakers 1991; Onimode 1989). However, gradually it dawned to the various stakeholders that the debt stocks of many of these countries were effectively unsustainable and that indebtedness was acting as a major constraint to growth. In mid-1995, the World Bank acknowledged that the external debt situation for a number of LDCs had become extremely difficult, undermining the prospects for economic development. For these countries, even full use of traditional mechanisms of rescheduling and debt reduction (such as the Naples terms and debt swaps), combined with continued provision of concessional financing, was not proving sufficient to attain sustainable external debt levels.[3]

In September 1996, the Interim and Development Committees of the IMF and the World Bank launched a program jointly proposed by the two institutions to address this problem. Endorsed by 180 governments, the Initiative for the Heavily Indebted Poor Countries (or the HIPC Initiative) was an agreement among official creditors to help the poorest, most heavily indebted countries escape from unsustainable debt, and to stimulate economic growth. Specifically, the HIPC Initiative would provide assistance to eligible countries that pursued economic reforms and where traditional debt relief mechanisms were not enough to help them exit from the rescheduling process. The HIPC Initiative would help by reducing these countries' external debt burden to sustainable levels via reduction in the net present value (NPV) of the future claims on the indebted country.[4] It was believed that such a strategy would enable heavily indebted countries to service their debt through export earnings, foreign aid and capital inflows.

It is not an exaggeration to say that the HIPC marked a radical departure from previous approaches to debt relief – at least for the world's poorest countries. It was the first time in their 50-year history that the debts of the World Bank and the IMF ("preferred creditors" to whom debts have always to be repaid first) were included for write-off. In fact, the HIPC was also the first attempt by creditors to deal with the debts of the poorest countries in a comprehensive way. Previously, debtor nations negotiated separately, and at great cost, with sets of bilateral (government to government) or multilateral (institutions owned by a range of governments) or private creditors. As a result their debts were not viewed as a whole. HIPC changed that, because it required the participation of all multilateral creditors beyond the traditional debt-relief mechanisms provided by official bilateral and private creditors.[5] Moreover, all creditors were to participate in providing assistance beyond current mechanisms as required to reach debt sustainability. Creditors also had to share the costs of HIPC assistance on the basis of broad and equitable burden-sharing and provide relief on a basis proportional to their share of the debt after the full application of traditional forms of debt relief – including the Naples terms from Paris Club creditors, which provide a 67 percent NPV reduction on eligible debt.[6]

While the Initiative did provide encouraging early results (in particular, a much-needed respite from high debt service), it was also felt that it was not delivering its stated goal of providing a "lasting exit" to unsustainable debt burdens for the world's poorest countries. A major review in 1999 resulted in a significant enhancement of the original framework. It was hoped that the "Enhanced HIPC Initiative" would make debt relief "deeper, broader, and faster," besides providing greater protection against external shocks. Furthermore, the Enhanced Initiative explicitly linked debt relief to poverty reduction, with the view that the elimination debt would allow countries to invest more in their future. Thus, the Enhanced HIPC Initiative signaled not just a bigger debt-reduction program but a new way of providing support to poor countries.

HIPC eligibility and process

The World Bank and the IMF made it explicit that in order for a country to be eligible for debt relief under the HIPC Initiative they must: (1) be eligible only for concessional assistance from the IMF and the World Bank, and (2) face an "unsustainable debt burden, beyond available debt relief mechanisms." Specifically, "available debt relief mechanisms" meant debt relief provided by the Paris Club group of creditors. Paris Club creditors usually provide a reduction of up to two-thirds of the net present value of eligible debt – in other words, debt which was contracted before a certain "cut-off date."[7] Aid debt is usually excluded from this, and debt rescheduling is at a lower rate of interest. Other bilateral and commercial creditors are also assumed to provide similar reductions, so (3) eligible countries need to demonstrate the capacity to effectively use the assistance granted by establishing a satisfactory track record under IMF and International Development Association supported programs, including establishing a track record of reform through IMF and World Bank supported programs for three years. That is, before qualifying for the HIPC Initiative (or before they are accepted for debt relief), countries must demonstrate a good track record of economic management policies such as economic stabilization programs, public sector reforms and reorientation of public spending toward poverty reduction, health, education, and pro-poor growth. And (4), since a key input in this process is the Poverty Reduction Strategy Paper (as will be discussed), eligibility required that it be prepared with the broad participation of civil society and serve as the basis for implementing the country's poverty reduction strategy. Funds freed up by this debt relief are to be used for poverty reduction programs rather than repayments. Altogether, 42 countries were initially deemed to be eligible for HIPC assistance:[8] Angola, Benin, Bolivia, Burkina Faso, Burundi, Cameroon, Central African Republic, Chad, Comoros, Democratic Republic of Congo, Republic of Congo, Côte d'Ivoire, Ethiopia, The Gambia, Ghana, Guinea, Guinea-Bissau, Guyana, Honduras, Kenya, Lao PDR, Liberia, Madagascar, Malawi, Mali, Mauritania, Mozambique, Myanmar, Nicaragua, Niger, Rwanda, Sierra Leone, Sao Tome Principe, Senegal, Somalia, Sudan, Tanzania, Togo, Uganda, Vietnam, Yemen, Zambia.

The HIPC Initiative was designed to work in two stages. First, countries reach "Decision Point" when their debts are deemed unsustainable even after the full use of "traditional" debt-relief mechanisms, and they have adopted adjustment and reform programs supported by the IMF and the World Bank and established a satisfactory track record.[9] To facilitate this, the debtor country, the World Bank and the IMF staff prepare a Debt Sustainability Analysis (DSA) to determine whether a country is facing an unsustainable debt situation after the full application of traditional debt-relief mechanisms and how much relief needs to be provided by multilateral, bilateral and commercial creditors. A country's debt is deemed to be unsustainable if the net present value of its total external debt is more than 150 percent of its average exports.[10] It was recognized that for countries which are "exceptionally open" (with an export-to-GDP ratio of more than 30 percent), exclusive reliance on external indicators may not adequately reflect the fiscal burden of external debt. Thus, countries which have a very high debt in relation to fiscal revenues despite a relatively good revenue performance, a "debt-to-revenue criteria" (an export-to-GDP ratio of at least 30 percent and a minimum threshold of fiscal revenue in relation to GDP of 15 percent) would be eligible.[11]

Second, to ensure that debt relief translates into real poverty reduction, debt relief was to be made part of a comprehensive poverty reduction strategy comprised of a range of polices aimed at improved social programs, good governance and equitable economic growth. Under the enhanced framework, debt relief was to be linked to the establishment of national poverty reduction strategies developed by governments to ensure that debt relief made a meaningful difference in improving the lives of the poor. Specifically, countries were required to prepare a "Poverty Reduction Strategy Paper" (PRSP) through a broad-based participatory process that included a broad section of civil society, key donors and regional development banks.[12] The World Bank and the IMF, in coordination with the larger development community, were to assist eligible countries in developing their PRSPs. However, the decision as to whether or not countries reached Decision Point was to be made entirely by the World Bank and the IMF, with no participation of the debtor or creditor governments. Once a country reaches Decision Point, it may immediately begin receiving *interim relief* on its debt service falling due. Thus, at the Decision Point, creditors commit to providing sufficient amounts of debt relief to ensure that debt is reduced to levels deemed sustainable. However, the debt is not actually cancelled until "Completion Point."[13] That is, once countries have passed Decision Point, they are required to establish a further track record of good performance under IMF/World Bank supported programs before they reach Completion Point. The length of this second period depends on (1) the satisfactory implementation of key policy reforms agreed at the Decision Point, (2) the maintenance of macroeconomic stability, and (3) the adoption and implementation for at least one year of the PRSP. Once a country has met these criteria, it can reach its Completion Point – at which time lenders are expected to provide the full relief committed at the Decision Point. Those countries that had reached Decision Point with only an interim Poverty Reduction Strategy Paper (PRSP) were required to prepare a full PSRP and to implement their poverty reduction strategy for at least one year.

At Completion Point, full debt cancellation which was committed at Decision Point is provided. Thus, debt relief becomes full and irrevocable at the end of the Completion Point.[14] In November 2001, the IMF/World Bank agreed that further relief might be provided at Completion Point where external conditions had worsened "significantly" between Decision and Completion Points. This feature, introduced in the Enhanced Initiative, illustrated that the Initiative has some flexibility to review a country's debt conditions at the Completion Point and assess whether additional debt relief is required to cope with the unexpected increases in the debt burden. As the advocates point out, this feature prevents the HIPCs from being penalized for events outside their control. On the other hand, meeting the bar is not always easy. As of March 2003, only Burkina Faso, which has a relatively small external debt, had benefited from so-called "topping-up" of relief.[15] Yet, it is important to reiterate that the HIPC Initiative is the first comprehensive effort to eliminate unsustainable debt in the world's poorest and most heavily indebted countries. It introduced a new approach to debt relief by focusing on overall debt sustainability – appropriately basing debt relief on a country's ability to pay within a total context of poverty reduction and economic growth. Moreover, in enabling all creditors to act together in a coordinated and concerted fashion to reduce debt to a sustainable level, it also provides an opportunity for countries to exit from the debt rescheduling process. But the core question remains: what has the HIPC actually delivered?

Actual debt cancellation under HIPC

To fully appreciate the magnitude of the problem it is useful to have an overall view of the debt problem. All developing (both low- and middle-income) country debt rose from $500 billion in 1980 to $1 trillion in 1985 and around $2 trillion in 2000. In 2002, the external debt of low-income countries stood at about $523 billion. Of this $399 billion was public and publicly guaranteed debt. Low-income countries owed $104 billion to the World Bank (of this, $82 billion was owed to IDA). The 41 HIPC countries saw their total indebtedness increase from $60 billion in 1980 to $105 billion in 1985 and $190 billion in 1990 – in the absence of debt reduction, this would have been near $200 billion in 2000. Seen from another angle, the HIPCs' nominal debt stocks rose from moderate levels in the early 1980s to some 800 percent of exports and 160 percent of gross national income in the mid-1990s (IMF 2003: 6; also George 1998; Lairson and Skidmore 2003: 374–87).

In June 1999, the G-7 leaders pledged that a total of $100 billion of HIPC debt would be cancelled. In December of that year, a further $10 billion was committed through 100 percent cancellation from bilateral creditors. However, half of this ($55 billion) was debt cancellation that had already been committed through cancellation under the Paris Club, or under the original HIPC Initiative. In September 2002, creditors committed a further $1 billion of debt cancellation under HIPC in order to provide "topping-up" for countries affected by worsening commodity prices and lower-than-expected exports when they reached Completion Point. However, assessing the amount of debt which has actually been cancelled is difficult, because under the HIPC Initiative debt cancellation is committed at Decision Point but only delivered at Completion Point. When announcing the amount of relief that has been delivered, the World Bank and IMF usually include all the relief committed to the countries past Decision Point. This is because countries gain relief on their debt service as from Decision Point, meaning that the total stock of debt has little relevance if it does not have to be serviced. However, this can overstate the amount of cancellation that has taken place, particularly given that most countries are facing delays in reaching Completion Point, and countries between Decision and Completion Points can have some of their interim debt relief suspended.

This means that the 27 countries that had qualified under the HIPC Initiative by 2004 still owe about $110 billion – although they will receive about $53 billion in debt relief over the next 20 years. This translates to their debt being cut, on average, by two-thirds in NPV terms.[16] Overall, debt-service obligations (as a percentage of exports) of the countries obtaining debt relief declined from an average of 15.7 percent in 1998–1999 to 9.9 percent in 2002, and annual debt service is projected to be about 30 percent lower during 2001–2005 than in 1998–1999 – freeing about $1 billion in annual debt-service savings (IMF-1DA 2004: 11). As Table 7.1 shows, indicators of debt sustainability such as debt-to-exports ratios and debt-service ratios are forecast to be cut by 50 percent or more after debt relief to levels comparable to, or below, those of other low-income countries.

Table 7.1 Debt indicators for the HIPCs that have reached decision point

	Before enhanced HIPC relief	*HIPC relief at Completion Point*
NPV of debt-to-exports ratio	274	128
NPV of debt-to-GDP ratio	61	30
Debt service-to-exports ratio	16	8

Source: World Bank (2004b: 119)

Notes
Before enhanced HIPC relief: debt stocks after traditional Paris Club relief, but before the HIPC Decision Point. Data refers mostly to end-1998 and 1999 (for debt service, average of 1998–1999).
HIPC relief at completion point: forecast for 2005
NPV of debt-to-exports ratio: exports are defined as the three-year average exports of goods and services up to the date specified
Debt service-to-exports ratio: exports are defined as goods and services in the current year

Evidence from graduating HIPCs indicates that they have benefited from more favorable debt-service profiles (as a result of the longer grace periods for payment) and lower interest rates on restructured debts. Equally important, the HIPC Initiative's emphasis on expenditures in the social services has served to appreciably increase spending in these sectors in national budgets. The savings from the HIPC Initiative are being directed into areas such as health and education and anti-poverty programs (Gautam 2003). The case of Ghana is illustrative. On 13 July 2004, the IMF and the World Bank's IDA concluded that Ghana had taken the necessary steps to reach its Completion Point under the Enhanced HIPC Initiative. Total debt relief under the Enhanced HIPC from all of Ghana's creditors amounted to US$3.5 billion in nominal terms. This assistance was equivalent to a reduction in NPV terms of US$2.2 billion, as agreed at the Decision Point. Ghana qualified under the fiscal criterion and the debt relief was calculated to bring the NPV of debt-to-government revenue ratio down to the HIPC threshold of 250 percent. This meant IDA would provide debt relief under the Enhanced HIPC Initiative amounting to US$1.4 billion in debt-service relief (US$782 million in NPV terms), to be delivered through a 67 percent reduction in debt service on IDA credits from 2002 to 2022. The IMF will provide debt relief of US$112 million in NPV terms on payments falling due to the IMF during 2002 to 2009. The remaining bilateral and multilateral creditors are to provide their share of relief required under the Enhanced HIPC Initiative. In addition, many bilateral creditors also indicated their willingness to provide additional relief beyond the Enhanced HIPC Initiative (estimated to total about US$500 million in NPV terms). Again, this means that between 2004 and 2013, Ghana can save approximately US$230 million annually in debt-service costs, as debt relief, together with bilateral assistance beyond HIPC relief, will lower Ghana's debt-to-export ratio and its debt-to-government revenue ratio. Equally important, resources made available by debt relief under the Enhanced HIPC Initiative have already being allocated to fund pro-poor expenditure programs, as outlined in Ghana's Poverty Reduction Strategy (GPRS) Paper completed in February 2003.

No doubt, all this is in sharp contrast to past practices. Before the HIPC Initiative, eligible countries were, on average, spending slightly more on debt service than on health and education combined. This was no longer the case in the 27 countries receiving HIPC relief in 2005. Under their IMF/World Bank-supported programs, these countries have increased their expenditures on health, education and other social services. For example, in the African countries receiving debt relief under the Initiative, poverty reduction spending has increased from 38.6 percent of government revenue in 1999 to 48.1 percent in 2001. Tanzania, which received $3 billion in debt relief, has used the initial debt-service savings to increase education spending and eliminate school fees for elementary school education. Almost overnight, an estimated 1.6 million children returned to school. Similarly, Mozambique increased health spending by $13.9 million. This means that some half a million children will now receive vaccination against tetanus, whooping cough and diphtheria. Also, $10 million is being spent on electrification of rural schools and hospitals and rehabilitation of infrastructure following the floods. $3.2 million is being used to increase the number of girls attending school, and scores of new primary schools are being built (IMF 2003a). These are important gains, as prior to the HIPC, debt-service obligations, which had risen to consume large shares (in many cases more than half) of poor countries' export earnings, stood as a major obstacle to human development.

Limits of the HIPC Initiative

As noted, a necessary requirement for qualification for HIPC debt relief is a track record of strong policy performance. While under the original HIPC Initiative (1996 to end-1999) only six countries had reached Decision Point and four Completion Point, these countries, nevertheless, had strong policy track records. However, in order to accelerate the implementation of the initiative, the policy performance requirement was progressively weakened in the Enhanced HIPC – particularly, for countries that qualified in 2000. Specifically, the debt-burden thresholds were adjusted downward; creditors, including multilateral institutions were permitted to provide "early assistance" to qualifying countries in the form of interim relief; and "floating Completion Points" were introduced which were contingent on an outcome-based assessment of country performance rather than a fixed track record. Since most of these countries had yet to demonstrate an ability to put effective frameworks in place, it compromised the achievement of the HIPC objectives for these countries.

This problem was further compounded by the fact that several potentially eligible HIPCs face major challenges in reaching their Decision Points. Most of these countries are affected by conflict and several suffer from protracted arrears.[17] Satisfactorily completing the PRSP process has proved to be difficult for these countries as many have large displaced populations and face difficulties in undertaking the broad-based participatory process that the PRSP requires, and the promised assistance from donors has not always materialized. As a World Bank study (Gautam 2003: xiv) sharply noted,

> in fact, there was a sharp decline in global net resource transfers starting about the time the Initiative was created. As a result, although the HIPC as a group are getting an increasing share of the declining global aid resources relative to other poor countries, they are not receiving additional funds in absolute terms compared with what they were receiving before the creation of the initiative (that is, until 1995).

Finally, not all creditors have fully participated in the HIPC Initiative by contributing their share to debt reduction. In particular, participation by commercial creditors has been limited, and nine HIPCs were facing litigation on credits held by commercial creditors in 2003.[18]

While the HIPC has been generally successful in reducing most eligible countries' external debt and their debt service (on average) in par with or below the levels of other poor countries, the initial claim that the HIPC will also provide long-term external debt sustainability through a "permanent exit" from debt rescheduling now seems overly optimistic. Yet, in all fairness it should be mentioned that the HIPC offers only partial debt relief: that is, reduction in a country's debt to a level deemed sustainable by the IMF and World Bank – which is total debt of not more than 150 percent of the value of exports. Therefore, sustainability depends on the country's economic performance. Nevertheless, the assumptions of the World Bank and the IMF regarding what constitutes debt sustainability have been unduly optimistic. In part, this was based on the flawed World Bank and IMF's Debt Sustainability Analysis (DSA). The DSA does not adequately take into account the high vulnerability of the HIPCs to external shocks – such as the volatility of commodity prices, exchange rate devaluations, oil shocks, declining terms of trade, variable donor aid flows and non-economic shocks such as climatic disasters, conflicts, political instability and the devastating impact of HIV/AIDS in sub-Saharan Africa.[19] Seen in this context, one can better appreciate the irony that although the external debt stocks of HIPC Completion Point countries have been reduced, exiting from the HIPC Initiative, by itself, does not guarantee long-term external debt sustainability. Rather, the structural weaknesses (all HIPCs are heavily dependent on primary commodities for their export earnings and government revenue and remain extremely vulnerable to declines in world commodity prices and other adverse exogenous developments), coupled with fragile macroeconomic management can easily push even Completion Point countries back into the debt trap. In fact, it is the boom-and-bust cycles which characterize primary commodity export that have pushed a number of Completion Point countries back into unsustainability.

According to Jubilee Research (the successor organization to the original Jubilee 2000), the DSA projections are usually based on the "best possible case" scenarios rather than a realistic assessment of the political and economic contexts in which the HIPC countries find themselves.[20] For example, the average export growth for HIPC countries in 2000–2001 was 5.1 percent – not 9.4 percent as projected by the IMF. Real GDP growth was 4.3 percent – almost one percentage point less than the levels predicted by the IMF. Analysis of the 24 HIPC countries that had passed Decision Point as of January 2002 showed that IMF projections were out by more than a few percentage points. Similarly, in April 2002, the World Bank admitted that of the six countries that had by then passed their Completion Points, at least two still did not have a sustainable level of debt. Specifically, debt ratios for Uganda and Mali deteriorated after Completion Point as a result of declines in commodity prices, under-delivery of debt relief by some creditors, higher-than-expected new borrowing, and a decline in discount rates (IMF-IDA 2004: 11). Thus, the dissonance between debt payments and growth and the fact that payment and borrowing decisions in HIPC are often predicated on growth projections that do not materialize do not augur well for long-term sustainability. Second, as Jubilee Research has argued, the initiative's definition of debt sustainability is flawed and maybe unattainable because it tends to focus on debt stocks rather than debt service. They argue that debt sustainability must be explicitly linked to the resources needed to achieve the MDGs. That is, "affordable debt service" would be calculated as a residual from the revenue base after taking account of the necessary spending to meet the MDGs and to service domestic debt. In addition, affordable debt service should be determined by an independent review panel with representatives appointed by both the creditor and debtor nations.[21] In fact, to NGOs like CAFOD (the Catholic Agency for International Development) and Jubilee Research, since debt cancellation under the HIPC falls far short of what is needed, it should be replaced by new infusions of aid and a complete write-off of all HIPC debt.

Christensen (2004) adds another wrinkle to the problem. Drawing from the experiences of sub-Saharan Africa, he notes that the unsustainability of domestic debt is just as big a threat as the unsustainability of foreign debt (also Cheru 2006; Onimode 1989). Although domestic debt in most sub-Saharan African countries is much smaller than external debt, interest rates are often higher, and the debt must be rolled over frequently (an average of four times a year), adding to the cost of servicing. This means that some countries spend as much on servicing their domestic debt as they do servicing their external debt. In fact, he notes that almost all HIPC countries spend a significant part of their budgetary revenues servicing domestic debt. While the author correctly notes that domestic debt is not necessarily bad if the funds are invested wisely, he found that in the majority of the 28 low-income countries in his sample, even modest levels of domestic debt tended to crowd out investment in the private sector, thereby deterring economic development. He also notes that since poor countries have a very narrow investor base consisting mainly of commercial banks, governments can quickly become captive to the interests of a few major banks. Unfortunately, as Christensen notes, resolving the problems of domestic debt is not as easy as forgiving external debt, as it may be unreasonable to expect domestic agents to forgive part of the debt as done with foreign debt under the HIPC Initiative.

Furthermore, paying down domestic debt would result in a significant liquidity expansion with the potential to destabilize the economy. Thus, "the first best solution would be for governments to reduce fiscal deficits and eliminate the need for domestic borrowing, or even to pay down domestic debt" (Christensen 2004: 11). Also, donor support, provided through a trust fund that swaps domestic debt for claims on the fund, could be a solution. The author argues that such a fund could reduce the cost of the debt because it would be backed by foreign currency assets. However, short of such donor-supported action, governments could also seek to strengthen their financial sectors, which would help them diversify the debt and lengthen its maturity profile. Christensen notes that since all HIPCs have large public expenditure needs, the fiscal tightening needed to reduce domestic debt will have a hugely negative impact on the vast majority of people. Thus, donor-supported action is critical to deal with this problem.

Clearly, achieving debt sustainability has proved to be extremely difficult. The external debt sustainability of half of the 20 countries which were between Decision Point and Completion Point in 2004 has significantly worsened. In fact, the World Bank at the time concluded that, of these countries in the interim period, eight to ten could have debt-to-export ratios above 150 percent at their Completion Points. That is, even at Completion Point the debt levels of these countries would be deemed unsustainable by the World Bank and IMF's own criteria. The World Bank's own numbers paint a grim picture: instead of pulling themselves out of debt, many poor countries were falling deeper into debt. The external debt of developing countries rose from $1.4 trillion in 1990 to $2.3 trillion in 2002. For the least-developed countries, external debt rose from $137.3 billion in 2001 to $144.9 billion in 2002. In 2002 these countries paid $5.1 billion in interest on that debt, nearly one-third of the $17.5 billion they received as official development assistance (also see Cheru 2006; Mulinge and Mufane 2003). Equally troubling, since these poor countries had to undertake more borrowing in order to service existing debts, the net flow of financial resources from poor countries to rich countries increased. The world's poorest countries in sub-Saharan African collectively owed a crushing $68 billion in debt. This meant that for every dollar these countries collectively received in aid, they paid $1.30 in debt service (World Bank 2004a: 2005).

By 2003, it was becoming evident that achieving debt sustainability would remain a major challenge for the HIPC. Evidence showed that many of the low-income countries needed to continue to borrow to meet their developmental needs; coupled with their limited repayment capacity, this meant that even the HIPCs that reached their Completion Points found it difficult to stay below the debt-sustainability thresholds. It also became evident that even if all of the external debts of the HIPCs were forgiven, most would still depend on significant levels of concessional external assistance – in part because their receipts of such assistance have been much larger than their debt-service payments for many years. These realizations underscored the fact that unmanageable debt was a symptom of deeper structural problems and that the one-time debt relief provided by the HIPC Initiative did not guarantee that the problem will not re-emerge.

To get out of this predicament various remedies were suggested. The World Bank's own review of the HIPC Initiative (see Gautam 2003) noted that while the initiative served to increase health and education spending, such emphasis also posed a major challenge as the initiative's performance criteria were more focused on expenditures than on outcomes – even when increased expenditures may encounter absorptive capacity constraints. The study notes that more focus on growth-enhancing programs is now warranted. Furthermore, for debt reduction to have a tangible impact on poverty, additional resources need to be targeted at the poor. That is, HIPC debt relief can be fully beneficial to a country only if it is provided in addition to increased rates of development assistance. Indeed, comparative review of current debt-service payments and concessional assistance illustrated the importance of continued aid programs. The ratio of gross inflows (from long-term debt and grants) to debt service paid averaged about two-to-one for the HIPCs as a group during the 1990s, and ranged upwards four-to-one in half of these countries. Annual net transfers to the HIPCs on medium and long-term resource flows (including grants) averaged about 10 percent of GNP over 1990–1996. Thus, it was concluded that debt reduction must be additional to development assistance. Not surprisingly, the World Bank's position was that industrial countries can greatly help the HIPCs by meeting the UN target for official development assistance of 0.7 percent of GNP per year rather than their current levels of foreign aid at 0.24 percent of GNP, and that this assistance must be complemented by greater access to industrial-country markets so that poor countries can earn their way in the global economy.

Others, most notably Sachs (2002), while not disagreeing with the above assessment, argued that it was time put an end to the "band-aid" solution – where donors and creditors endlessly played the game of musical chairs spending precious time in frustrating "debt-restructurings" negotiations and haggling over the minutest terms of debt payments no one expected to be repaid. They argued that it not only made sense to provide outright grants (and loans only on highly concessional terms) to help poor countries achieve long-term debt sustainability, but also that the debt-service targets should be tailored to each country's specific needs, rather than set at a uniform 150 percent for all HIPCs, and that the level of debt cancellation provided by the HIPC be much deeper and faster (also see Kraay and Nehru 2004). Still others, including Cheru (2006), demanded that the G-7 stop "playing games with African lives," calling for an immediate and unconditional cancellation in all countries where debt repayment was diverting resources away from needed social spending. Similarly, to Hertz (2004: 196) debt relief was a charade as only 12 percent of the debts of the world's poorest countries had been cancelled. In order to effectively resolve the "debt threat" – which threatens people's lives in poor countries – creditors (rather than just borrowers) must first be held responsible for the accumulation of unsustainable debts, and second, "there are some debts that are so clearly illegitimate ... that countries should never be asked to honor them" (p. 178). The latter is hardly a new demand. Adams (1991), Hanlon (1998) and Jayachandran and Kremer (2002, 2006) have all argued that sovereign debt incurred by "dictators" and "illegitimate regimes" should be declared "odious" and must not be the obligation of civil society or successor governments (also Winters 2002).

The G-8 and total debt relief [22]

The once unthinkable idea that full debt forgiveness may be necessary to give desperately poor countries a chance to escape the trap of poverty and economic stagnation finally began to take hold in the G-8 capitals. At the G-8 meeting in October 2004, finance ministers from the world's richest nations for the first time formally discussed debt cancellation – but came to no agreement. However, on 11 June 2005, the finance ministers from seven of the G-8 (Russia was not invited at the June meeting) agreed on a historic deal to write off more than $40 billion worth of debt owed by some the world's most impoverished nations. It seems the G-8 was finally coming around to the realization that most HIPCs were caught in a vicious poverty trap, making them simply too impoverished to achieve sustained economic growth without massive external assistance, including complete debt forgiveness.

This new deal was the result of a British-led effort designed to assist Africa – "a continent facing grave developmental challenges." Gordon Brown, Britain's Chancellor of the Exchequer, who like the British Prime Minister Tony Blair had worked tirelessly for the deal, and who cajoled his sometimes reluctant colleagues (especially US Treasury Secretary John W. Snow) to broker the deal, noted with satisfaction that the agreement represented a "new deal between the rich and poor of the world."[23] Yet, in the end, it was the warm personal relationship between President George W. Bush and Blair that made the difference. The debt relief proposal initially put forward by Blair during his meeting with Bush in Washington on 7 June 2005 was made possible by a significant concession by the White House – that the debt write-off must not jeopardize future aid funding.[24]

In effect, the G-8 had agreed to an unprecedented 100 percent debt cancellation for countries that have reached, or will eventually reach, the Completion Point under the HIPC Initiative. Although some had hoped that the deal would cover all low-income countries and heavily indebted middle-income countries, the agreement stays within the HIPC framework – meaning that only the 40 countries which had already qualified under the HIPC Initiative were eligible. Almost all of the debt being written off is owed to the World Bank, the IMF and the African Development Bank (AfDB), as most of these countries have already received essentially 100 percent debt forgiveness from other official creditors (such as the G-8 governments). While some of these countries will still owe small amounts of debts to other creditors (mostly non-OECD governments), the bulk of their debts are owed to the multilateral financial institutions. With this deal, for the first time ever, the World Bank, the IMF and the AfDB have agreed to forgive 100 percent of the debts owed to them.

In actual dollar terms, the agreement immediately wiped clean $40 billion worth of debt owed by 18 countries which had already passed the HIPC Completion Point by mid-2005: 14 in Africa and four in Latin America. These include Benin, Bolivia, Burkina Faso, Ethiopia, Ghana, Guyana, Honduras, Madagascar, Mali, Mauritania, Mozambique, Nicaragua, Niger, Rwanda, Senegal, Tanzania, Uganda and Zambia. For these 18 countries, instead of spending a combined total estimated between $1.5 billion and $2 billion a year on interest payments alone, they will now be able to redirect these savings toward health care, education, infrastructure and other pressing developmental needs. Once the remaining countries eventually join the list, the total debt relief package will amount to just over $55 billion.

The June 2005 deal was significant because it not only canceled the debts owed to the World Bank, the IMF and multilateral lenders such as the AfDB, but also wipes the slate clean once and for all – at least for the countries that quali-fied. In the past, one of the major stumbling blocks to blanket debt forgiveness was the potentially negative implications on the balance sheets of multilateral financial institutions, as the world's least-developed countries owe the bulk of their debts to these institutions. If lenders like the World Bank and the IMF write off loans, it means they have less money to finance future projects. This approach was preferred by the Bush administration because it would essentially pay for debt cancellation out of the resources of the lending agencies. That is, not only would the debt be erased, but the financial institutions would finance the shortfall themselves by simply reducing their loans to the countries receiving the write-offs. But Britain and other European nations, concerned that such an approach would greatly undermine the financial strength of the multilateral financial institutions, favored a plan by which G-8 countries would assume the burden of making the debt payments owed by the poor nations. Put bluntly, the British argued that there was no option to the wealthy countries taking over the debts themselves.

The final deal was apparently a compromise in which the lenders agree to write off the debts but receive compensation from donor nations, and therefore do not jeopardize their ability (that is, of the IMF, the World Bank and the AfDB) to meet their current and future obligations. In the communiqué issued by G-8, each G-8 country (with the help of other donors) made a commitment to meet the full costs to the IMF, World Bank and AfDB. Specifically, the G-8 pledged to provide additional funds to compensate the World Bank and the AfDB in full for the assets written off. The costs of debt relief for obligations to the IMF would be met from current IMF resources. However, in situations where other existing and projected debt-relief obligations cannot be met from the use of existing IMF resources, donors agreed to provide extra resources.[25] While this extra commitment covers only 2006–9, the G-8 made the commit-ment to cover the full costs for the duration of the cancelled loans by topping up their regular payments to IDA.

It is estimated that the total cost of the debt write-off will be $1.2 billion a year for during this three-year period, for a total of $3.6 billion. While it is not clear whether all of that sum will be new aid or money redirected from existing aid budgets (since this is a matter for individual countries), Britain agreed to contribute between $700 million and $960 million through 2015 to fund the package, the US between $1.3 billion and $1.75 billion, and Germany between $848 million to $1.2 billion.[26] Therefore, the agreement not only goes much further than the one announced by Bush and Blair on 7 June 2005, but the Bush administration also made a significant concession in agreeing to the idea that rich nations would provide extra money to the multilateral institutions to compensate for those assets being written off, as well as ensure that future aid packages would not be affected.

This was not lost on observers. If previous plans offering partial debt relief provoked criticism from activists – who correctly pointed out that many poor countries were forced to spend more on debt service (paying principal and interest on international loans) than on health care, education or social services, the news of the agreement was generally well received. Irish rocker and debt-relief campaigner Bob Geldof noted that "tomorrow 280 million Africans will wake up for the first time in their lives without owing you or me a penny from the burden of debt that has crippled them and their countries for so long." However, he cautioned that "this is the beginning and the end will not be achieved until we have the complete package ... of debt cancellation, doubling of aid, and trade justice" (quoted in Jochnick and Preston 2006) Similarly, the indefatigable Bono welcomed the agreement while voicing determination to press for more debt forgiveness (ibid.). He noted

> the journey of equality took another step today, and broke free millions of people in some of the poorest countries from the bondage of immoral and unjust debts.... There's long nights ahead of us all to build up the speed and accelerate for a comprehensive debt-aid-trade deal.

Likewise, Jubilee Research noted that while the agreement is an important first step, the deal must be expanded to include all impoverished countries rather than those that fall under the G-8's rather restrictive list (Blustein 2005). Jubilee argued that some of the low- and middle-income nations that do not qualify but need immediate debt relief include Indonesia, Sri Lanka, the Philippines, Kenya, Nigeria, Ecuador and Peru, and that at least 62 countries will need to have 100 percent of their debts canceled to meet the Millennium Development Goals.

The Gleneagles Summit and MDRI

Undaunted by terrorist attacks in London, the G-8 leaders during their annual meeting (Gleneagles, 6–8 July 2005) went a step further by agreeing to what was effectively double assistance to Africa. The G-8 agreed that all of the debts owed by eligible heavily indebted poor countries to IDA, the IMF and the AfDB would be cancelled, as set out in their Finance Ministers' agreement of 11 June 2005. In addition, the G-8 welcomed the Paris Club decision to write off around $17 billion of Nigeria's debt. However, the "challenge" posed by the G-8 host Prime Minister Tony Blair – to double aid to Africa, thereby adding $25 billion annually to the total by 2010, with a further increase of another $25 billion annually to be achieved by 2015 (bringing the global total to $75 billion), preferably through the creation of an International Finance Facility – was only partially met. The G-8 agreed to increase total official development assistance by $50 billion and aid to Africa by $25 billion – especially to countries with strong national development plans and committed to good governance, democracy and transparency. The G-8 made it clear that the World Bank would play a leading role in supporting the partnership between the G-8, other donors and Africa, to ensure that assistance is effectively coordinated.

Despite the fact that the debt-relief program was formally approved at the G-8, Brown acknowledged that there was "still work to be done" to get approval for his International Finance Facility (IFF), a scheme under which it is hoped that rich countries would raise an extra $50 billion a year for development by selling bonds (to be paid off through later aid pledges) on the world's capital markets.[27] However, both the United States and Japan rejected the IFF idea. In fact, the ambitious British proposal was viewed negatively by Washington. Like the United States, Japan preferred its own bilateral aid programs, while France and Germany actively pushed their own initiative – an international aviation tax.[28]

Nevertheless, on 7 November 2005 the Executive Board of the IMF reached consensus on the implementation modalities of the proposal for debt relief, calling it the Multilateral Debt Relief Initiative (MDRI). All countries that reach the Completion Point under the Enhanced HIPC Initiative and those with per capita income below US$380 and outstanding debt to the IMF at end-2004 are deemed eligible for the MDRI. On 5 January 2006 the MDRI became fully effective, enabling the IMF to grant 100 percent debt relief to 19 countries (including remaining HIPC assistance) amounting to US$3.3 billion. These included: Benin, Bolivia, Burkina Faso, Cambodia, Ethiopia, Ghana, Guyana, Honduras, Madagascar, Mali, Mozambique, Nicaragua, Niger, Rwanda, Senegal, Tajikistan, Tanzania, Uganda and Zambia. This represents the first phase of countries that will receive 100 percent debt relief under the MDRI. However, as Table 7.2 shows, countries which have yet to reach the Completion Point under the HIPC Initiative will qualify for MDRI assistance upon reaching the Completion Point. That was the case of Cameroon and Malawi on 28 April 2006 and 1 September 2006, respectively. By end-December 2006, 22 countries had received about $3.7 billion in MDRI relief from the IMF.

Debt relief initiatives: a first step, not a giant leap

Will the debt-relief initiatives finally push poor countries towards debt sustainability and growth? The debt-relief initiatives should be seen as a first step, not the giant leap that is required. The $1 billion to $2 billion per year made available under MDRI is tiny relative to the resources needed. Put bluntly, debt cancellation alone will not produce the large new resources necessary for development (Roodman 2006). At best, it will put an average of $1.5 billion to

Table 7.2 Country coverage of the MDRI

	Eligible under the "MDRI-I Trust" (per-capita income below US$380)	Eligible under the "MDRI-II Trust" (per-capita income above US$380)
Countries eligible for MDRI relief as of end December 2006		
"Completion Point" HIPCs: 21 countries that have reached the Completion Point under the Enhanced HIPC Initiative	Burkina Faso, Ethiopia, Ghana, Madagascar, Malawi, Mali, Mozambique, Niger, Rwanda, Sierra Leone, Tanzania, Uganda	Benin, Bolivia, Cameroon, Guyana, Honduras, Mauritania, Nicaragua, Senegal, Zambia
Non-HIPCs (two) with per-capita income below US$380 and outstanding debt to the IMF	Cambodia, Tajikistan	
Countries that will be eligible once they reach the Completion Point under the Enhanced HIPC Initiative		
"Decision Point" HIPCs: nine countries that have reached the Decision Point under the Enhanced HIPC Initiative	Burundi, Chad, Democratic Republic of the Congo, The Gambia, Guinea-Bissau, São Tomé and Príncipe	Guinea, Haiti, Republic of Congo
Ten additional countries that may wish to be considered for HIPC debt relief. They met the income and indebtedness criteria based on end-2004 data	Central African Republic, Eritrea, Liberia, Nepal, Togo	Comoros, Côte d'Ivoire, Haiti, Kyrgyz Republic, Sudan
	Data on Somalia's per capita income are not available at this juncture. Afghanistan's situation regarding the debt criteria is expected to be reassessed by the end of 2006.	

Source: IMF (2006).

$2 billion a year in the hands of the 19 countries for the next three years. This means that the G-8 will only cover the full costs for the duration of the cancelled loans by topping up their regular payments to IDA. But as the regular replenishments are by no means fixed (the US share of the contributions to IDA fell from 20 percent to around 13 percent from 2005) it is impossible to know whether the funds for debt relief will be additional to the amount IDA would have received anyway after 2008. Thus, the claim that future funds are not going to come at the expense of new aid funds is not entirely true.

Moreover, the roughly $2 billion of annual debt relief provided under MDRI amounts to roughly 0.01 percent of the GDP of the OECD countries. This represents about 2 percent of rich-country aid in 2004 and only a small fraction of the extra $50 billion a year that Blair and Brown *hope* to get from the other G-8 countries. Increasingly, the Brown–Blair plan to get the G-8 to commit $50 billion for aid does not look promising. The Bush administration is already on record as stating that it has tripled aid to Africa since 2000 and is not yet prepared to make another major pledge, pending results from its Millennium Challenge Account (MCA) program which ties aid to pledges of good governance, including the fight against terrorism. Not surprisingly, Arslanalp and Henry (2006: 218–19) aptly note,

> the main beneficiaries of the Gleneagles debt relief proposal would appear to be the rich countries who garner good political press at a trivial cost … the danger is that the Gleneagles declaration may amount to a pyrrhic victory: a symbolic win for advocates of debt relief that clears the conscience of the rich countries, but leaves the real problems of the poor countries unaddressed.

There is also concern that the debt-relief initiatives unduly penalize poor countries which do not qualify under the program. For example, Kenya is a poor, low-income country which has honored its obligations by faithfully servicing its debt. Yet, the initiatives only reward borrowers who fail to honor their obligations at the expense of debtors who do. Contrary to popular thinking, not all countries that have gotten into debt are too poor or growing too slowly to service their debts. Some got into the predicament through reckless borrowing and imprudent use of the funds. Thus, complete debt write-off can potentially send the wrong message to the prudent that reckless and irresponsible borrowing and spending pays. Also, if past experiences are any guide, countries benefiting from debt write-off have the tendency to fall back into the debt trap. This is because the conditions that created the debt crisis in the first place – poor governance, rampant corruption, lack of economic incentives, decrepit and unreliable economic infrastructure, and lack of export markets – are still in place.

Finally, as noted in earlier sections, if the G-8 is serious in helping the LDCs, a successful conclusion of the Doha Round should be a top priority. If there is any broad consensus, it is that trade, not aid or debt relief, will bring real and substantial benefits to poor countries.

8 Postscript

Poor people in developing countries face little hope of emerging from lives of poverty and deprivation unless all stakeholders, in particular governments in both the poor and rich countries take urgent action to address the root causes of economic stagnation and poverty. Today, the global community stands at a critical juncture in its fight against global poverty and injustice. It has less than a decade to translate the Millennium Development Goals into reality. Yet, the first three *Global Monitoring Reports* (World Bank 2006a, 2005, 2004), part of a series of annual reports on the progress made on achieving the MDGs, warn that, based on current trends, most countries will fail to meet most of the MDGs. The Reports show uneven progress toward meeting the first goal of halving the global rate of income poverty between 1990 and 2015. While this goal is likely to be achieved at the global level – largely through progress in the world's two most populous countries, China and India – many countries in Latin America and sub-Saharan Africa will fall well short. In fact, Africa is seriously off-track with just eight countries representing about 15 percent of the regional population likely to achieve the goals. Equally troubling, progress on other MDGs, particularly for health, education and environment, is even bleaker.

The Reports urge immediate action by all stakeholders in order to meet the MDGs. Developed countries need to show leadership by delivering on the promises made at the Monterrey Financing for Development conference in March 2002, where they pledged to match stronger reform efforts in developing countries with increased financial support. Yet, the Reports note that since that Monterrey gathering, and despite recent increases, aid remains at low levels relative to needs and trade barriers continue to undermine developing-country exports. The Reports make it clear that developed countries need to lead by example and deliver a "pro-development" outcome to the Doha Round of trade negotiations. Specifically, they recommend the OECD countries should aim to completely eliminate tariffs on manufactured products; completely eliminate export subsidies and decouple agricultural subsidies from production, reducing agricultural tariffs to no more than 10 percent; ensure free cross-border trade in services delivered over telecommunications links; and liberalize the temporary movement of workers. The Reports note that the liberalization of trade is particularly important in agriculture where average protection in the OECD countries is more than seven times as high as in manufacturing. Similarly, the Reports recommend that aid needs to increase significantly to achieve the MDGs. Although donors pledged to increase development assistance by US$18.5 billion a year by 2006, developing countries could effectively absorb an increase of US$30 billion. Additionally, as the developing countries improve their policies and institutions, the amount of additional aid they could use will rise into the range of US$50 billion a year. The Reports also point out that, although macroeconomic policies in developing countries are improving, they still need to keep to the reform path to promote faster economic growth and delivery of essential services to the poor.

The Reports correctly note that sustainable economic development will require global collective action because it is a global public good. Since all countries gain from economic growth, a global partnership for development is required to achieve the MDGs. Yet, the Reports aptly note that partnership also means sticking to specific obligations, responsibilities and national commitments. For their part, developing nations must keep their pledge to strengthen governance and implement economic reforms by committing to time-bound and specific targets. The rich countries, for their part, must increase aid, deliver on debt relief and expand access to trade and technology for the LDCs. Specifically, the Reports recommend that the OECD countries reinforce their commitments by removing some of their more glaring policy contradictions. That is, rich countries can mitigate contradictions in their policies that often help developing countries on the one hand, but penalize them on the other. For example, while rich countries provide foreign aid they also maintain restrictive trade regimes that limit imports from developing countries.

A theme is that ostensibly missing in the Reports is what to do with the growing problems associated with climate change. This is unfortunate, because the sheer magnitude of the problems linked with climate change has the potential to undermine the whole development agenda. Climate change has emerged as a key global concern, especially after the release of former vice-president Al Gore's award-winning documentary, *An Inconvenient Truth* and the 700-page *Stern Review on the Economics of Climate Change* (2006). The Stern Review provides a comprehensive analysis of the costs and risks associated with climate change – which it calls "the greatest market failure the world has seen." The Review warns that inaction could be catastrophic and notes that the window for capping the level of greenhouse gases in the atmosphere at 450–550 parts per million (ppm) CO_2 is closing fast. Based on current trends, average global temperatures will rise by 2–3 degrees Celsius within the next 50 years. This could translate into rising sea levels, flood risk and eventual water shortages due to prolonged droughts. Vast tracts of agricultural lands could become marginal and the resultant declines in crop yields could leave hundreds of millions of people without the ability to produce or purchase sufficient food.

The Review notes that it is still possible to avoid the worst effects of global warming, provided the international community takes immediate action in mitigating climate change caused by human activity. Three elements of policy are required for an effective response. First is carbon pricing. It argues that through taxation, emissions trading or regulation (so citizens are faced with the full social costs of their actions), the international community should build a common global carbon price across countries and sectors. Second is an effective technology policy towards low-carbon use and high-efficiency products. And third is to remove barriers to energy efficiency and to inform, educate and persuade citizens about what they can do to respond to climate change. The Review estimates that fighting global warming will cost about 1 percent of annual global GDP by 2050, explicitly noting that developed countries should take the lead role in combating climate change – at least initially. However, doing nothing will mean that unabated climate change would eventually cost the equivalent of between 5 and 20 percent of global GDP each year. No doubt, as climate change is now the world's biggest priority, developing countries must incorporate climate change into their development strategies. Yet, how this will be done is not clear. Nevertheless, at a minimum it will mean addressing the all-important question: are the rich and middle-income countries willing to accept restrictions on their carbon emissions, and since the poorest countries are most vulnerable to climate change, are the rich willing to bear the financial costs associated with more sustainable energy use and to honor their pledges to support poor countries? This does not simply mean more development assistance. Rather, if the rich countries are to assist poor nations get on the low-carbon track, it will mean transferring cleaner energy technologies and compensating them for ending the deforestation that leads to carbon emissions as well as a loss of biodiversity.

However, in the end, development is about people, especially how they can live full creative lives with freedom and dignity. While the MDGs are means, not ends, achieving the goals is an important step towards that end. The MDGs serve as benchmarks against which such goals must be measured. It remains to be seen if the MDGs can be turned into reality.

Notes

1 Introduction

1 The so-called *dependistas* were not a homogenous group, but divided into liberal and radical versions. The intellectual root of dependency goes back to 1930s Latin America, especially to Argentine economist Raul Prebisch. For an excellent overview, see Munoz (1981) and Packenham (1992).

2 Neoliberalism refers to an economic model that advocates a minimalist state, market allocation of goods and services and openness to international capital and markets. To neoliberals, economic development can best take place through the discipline of the market – via the liberalization of the domestic market and pursuit of outward-oriented trade and exchange rate policies; reduction in government intervention in domestic markets for goods, capital and labor thereby allowing prices, interest rates and wages to find their natural equilibrium through market discipline (via the interaction of supply and demand); the deregulation of financial markets and the opening up of restricted sectors of the economy to private investment; the dismantling of restrictive legislation such as direct and indirect taxation; the privatization of state-owned enterprises (SOE), the liquidation of unviable or "sick" SOEs; and the complete dismantling of the industrial-licensing system and foreign-exchange controls. Overall, neoliberals called for the transformation of "statist" or control-bound, inward-looking economies into market-conforming outward-looking economies. They claimed that such a strategy will enable the economy to move towards an equilibrium growth path in which patterns of production, investment and capacity creation follow dynamic comparative advantage, thereby minimizing resource costs, increasing competition in domestic markets and eliminating potential channels of corruption.

3 Keynesian ideas were shaped during the great depression by John Maynard Keynes. Keynes questioned neoclassical economics' holy grail – the idea that the market functions like an "invisible hand" and therefore is self-correcting and regulating. Keynes argued that market or capitalist economies are inherently unstable, with fluctuations, recessions, down-turns, periods of chronic unemployment and cyclical instability. Since the self-adjusting and self-correcting mechanism can break down, government intervention and prudent public policy is necessary: that is, governments must formulate and plan policy, and guide macroeconomic development through government spending, borrowing and taxation. Thus, in the Keynesian conception there is greater room for public (i.e. state) authorities in economic management. For a trenchant neoliberal critique, see Lal (1985).

4 For the roughly 1.3 billion desperately poor people (about one-fifth of the world's population) who barely exist under the official poverty line set at $1 per person per day or the estimated 2.7 to three billion people who currently live on less than $2 per person per day, even if the MDGs met only a part of their targets, it would improve their lives immeasurably. It is important to note that the most widely used way to

measure poverty is based on incomes or consumption levels. A person is considered poor if his or her consumption or income level falls below some minimum level necessary to meet basic needs. Of course, what is considered necessary to satisfy basic needs varies across time and countries. While most countries set their own poverty lines, to measure poverty between countries an international poverty line was created. The $1-a-day poverty line was originally chosen as representative of typical poverty lines prevailing in a sample of low-income countries. It has since been updated to $1.08 a day in 1993 prices. To estimate poverty in a country, the $1-a-day line is converted to local currency units using the purchasing power parity (PPP) exchange rates. The PPP rates based on the relative prices of consumption goods in each country are more representative of the actual purchasing power of a dollar than market exchange rates, especially in the least-developed countries. However, aggregate poverty measures based on international poverty lines (such as the $1-a-day measure) should not be confused with estimates based on national poverty lines. Most of the World Bank's poverty analysis is based on national poverty lines. As a general rule, national poverty lines tend to increase in purchasing power with the average level of income of a country. Thus, the $1-a-day line, while representative of poverty lines in very poor countries, underestimates the national poverty line of richer countries, which may be set at the equivalent of $2–3 a day or higher.

2 Promoting development: what works

1 At the Monterrey Conference, President George W. Bush promised that he would request a $5 billion increase in the US foreign assistance appropriations for those countries "making the strongest possible commitment to development."
2 To support this effort, international agencies, including the World Bank, the IMF, and the regional development banks have agreed to share data and analysis of global trends of the MDGs indicators.
3 For a good review of the United Nation's half century of involvement in economic and social development, see Weiss *et al.* (2005).
4 That is, for each goal a set of targets and indicators have been defined to track the progress in meeting the goals, and countries are supposed to report on progress on the goals every five years.
5 Figures are from the World Bank, *Global Economic Prospects 2004* (World Bank 2004c). This poverty line was set by the World Bank in 1985. By 1993 it had risen to $1.08 owing to inflation, but it is still referred to as the "$1/day/line" (World Bank 2003a).
6 The World Bank classifies as low-income countries that have income per capita of $755 or less; as middle-income, $756 to $9,265, and as high-income, $9,266 and above in 2000.
7 The Kuznets hypothesis was based on data derived from cross-sectional data or data from different countries observed at various stages of development at about the same point in time. However, to understand how growth affects inequality, time-series data, which show how inequality changes within countries as they grow over time, are required. When such time-series data became available, they refuted the Kuznets hypothesis (see Ravallion 1995; Deininger and Squire 1996; 1998; Bruno *et al.* 1998; and Ravallion 2005).
8 Economic growth is measured by the rate of change of real income per capita. It is assumed that a country with a growth rate of 1 percent per annum doubles its living standard every 70 years, while a country with a growth rate of 3 percent doubles its living standard every 23 years. Thus, poverty reduction is best achieved through making the cake bigger, not by trying to cut it up in different ways. For a excellent overview see Dollar and Kraay (2002), and Foster and Szekely (2000).

9 While absolute poverty is defined in reference to a poverty line that has a fixed purchasing power determined so as to buy basic needs, relative poverty is determined as a fixed proportion of the mean income.

10 The extent to which growth translates into poverty reduction can vary considerably from one country to another. This can be measured by the "total poverty elasticity of growth" – which is the number of percentage points of change in poverty observed for every 1 percent rise in real per-capita income. A negative figure indicates poverty reduction. Another way of measuring the effectiveness of translating growth into poverty reduction is to examine what the elasticity would have been had income inequality been held constant. This "distribution-neutral growth elasticity" is always negative since positive growth will raise the income of everyone, including the poor.

11 Epaulard (2003) examines how poverty has been affected in a number of boom and bust episodes in developing and transition economies. She shows that the elasticity of poverty reduction to growth depends on the initial levels of both per-capita income and income inequality. The higher the average income level, the higher the elasticity; and the higher the inequality, the lower the elasticity. However, the paper also finds the poverty response to growth to be symmetric across positive and negative macroeconomic shocks.

12 There are two ways to define what constitutes pro-poor growth. The *absolute* concept defines pro-poor growth as any growth in mean income that benefits the poor in absolute terms. Therefore, any increase in GDP that reduces poverty measured by some agreed indicators is pro-poor growth, even if it is accompanied by a worsening of income distribution. On the other hand, the *relative* concept places much more emphasis on the distributional effect of growth – that is, changes in inequality during the growth process. According to Kakwani and Pernia (2000), growth is pro-poor if the distributional shifts accompanying growth favor the poor more than the non-poor.

13 While traditional neoclassical growth theory (Solow 1956, 1957) emphasizes physical capital accumulation (such as the stock of machines, equipment and structures), the endogenous growth theory (Romer 1986; Lucas 1988) argues that investment in human capital (such as the stock of education and the skills of the labor force) and technological progress are the main sources of economic growth. Other models (Mankiw *et al.* 1992) have shown that both physical and human capital are important determinants of growth.

14 Similarly, Ghura *et al.* (2002) argue that in addition to growth, macroeconomic policies, especially those aiming at lowering inflation, deepening the financial sector, and raising educational achievements, are important in reducing poverty.

15 The authors use the Inter-American Development Bank (IDB) database of household surveys from 18 Latin American countries (which include over 90 percent of the population of the region) to construct and decompose poverty indices in each country into between-and-within demographic group components. They find that "having more or less skills is a stronger determinant of poverty than being located in rural areas, being employed in relatively unproductive sectors of activity, belonging to female-headed households, or living in households with relatively young or old heads" (Attanasio and Szekely 2001: 16–17).

16 It is important to reiterate that the experience of the former Soviet Union suggest that relatively good stocks of human capital will not translate into growth and improvements in human welfare in an environment of political and economic repression.

17 Bloom, Canning and Jamison (2004: 11) note that "better health also raises per-capita income through a number of other channels. One way is by altering decisions about expenditures and savings over the life cycle. The idea of planning for retirement occurs only when mortality rates become low enough for retirement to be a realistic prospect. Rising longevity in developing countries has opened a new incentive for the current generation to save – an incentive that can have dramatic effects on national saving rates."

18 A growing body of evidence shows that societies that discriminate on the basis of gender suffer from higher poverty rates, lower quality of life and slow economic growth. Specifically, children are disadvantaged directly by their mothers' illiteracy and lack of schooling. Lack of schooling means poor quality of care, which usually translates into more illness, malnutrition, and higher child mortality. Mothers with more education are more likely to adopt appropriate health-promoting behaviors, such as having young children immunized, which translates into better health and well-being for their children. While raising household income improves child survival rates and nutritional status, the question of who controls this additional income also matters. In the hands of women within the household, it has a larger positive impact because women are more likely than men to spend the additional household income for education, health and food (see Agarwall 1994).

19 For a good overview of competing definitions see Held and McGrew (2000) and Scholte (2000).

20 According to Williamson (1993, 1994) who coined the term, "the Washington Consensus" features ten policy measures: fiscal discipline, investments in health and education, a broader tax base, market-determined interest rates, competitive exchange rates, liberal trade policies, openness to foreign investment, privatization of state enterprises, deregulation and secure property rights.

21 Wolf (2005: 40) quotes Vaclav Havel, the author, playwright, political activist and former Czech president: "Though my heart may be left of centre, I have always known that the only economic system that works is a market economy. This is the only natural economy, the only kind that makes sense, the only one that leads to prosperity, because it is the only one that reflects the nature of life itself."

22 The capital account in a country's balance of payments covers a variety of financial flows – mainly foreign direct investment, portfolio flows (including investment in equities), and bank borrowing. Capital account liberalization refers to easing restrictions on capital flows across a country's borders. Many developing countries open up their capital account to help finance projects with foreign capital.

23 These authors note that even though income per capita is higher for developing countries that have more open economies, it is difficult to find clear evidence that suggests this is exclusively due to the fact they have liberalized their capital account. Rather, some of these countries have experienced costly banking or currency crises when investors suddenly decided to withdraw their funds.

24 The advocates of "new institutional economics" recognize that a good market economy requires not only "getting prices right" but also "getting property rights right" and "getting institutions right." This is because property rights and institutions generally set the rules that affect the behavior of economic agents (North and Thomas 1973; North 1990; Rodrik 2000; and Weingast 1995).

25 Easterly and Levine (1997) find that moving from an ethnically homogenous country to one with greater diversity of ethnic communities corresponded with a decrease in annual economic growth rate of more than 2 percent. They argue that since African countries are among the most ethnically diverse in the world, this explains part of the region's "growth tragedy."

26 An early pioneer in microfinance, the non-profit Grameen Bank developed innovative credit techniques. For example, instead of requiring collateral, it reduced risk through group guarantees and joint liability, appraisal of household cash flows, and small initial loans to test potential clients. These alternatives to collateral are especially important to borrowers who do not have assets to pledge, and for lenders who operate in countries with weak secured-lending laws and enforcement.

27 As Littlefield and Rosenberg (2004: 39) note, "an increasing number of serious studies are suggesting that microfinance can produce improvements in a range of welfare measures, including income stability and growth, school attendance, nutrition, and health. Microfinance has been widely credited with empowering women by

increasing their contribution to household income and assets and, thus, control over decisions affecting their lives."

28 The PSE (producer subsidy equivalent) is a broadly defined aggregate measure of support to agriculture that combines, into one total value aggregate, direct payments to producers financed by budgetary outlays.

29 In other words, at 0.22 percent of donor countries' GDP, aid stands as its smallest proportion since it was first institutionalized with the Marshall Plan in 1947.

3 Good governance and economic development

1 Associated with the growing demand for quantifying the governance performance of countries, a number of datasets measuring quality of institutions, governance and corruption have been created. These include the worldwide aggregate Governance Indicators Dataset, generated by researchers at the World Bank, comprising six different governance components for about 200 countries, by the Corruption Perception Index of Transparency International, and by the measures generated from enterprise surveys carried out by the World Bank and the Global Competitiveness program of the World Economic Forum.

2 Civil society composed of non-governmental organizations, faith-based groups, trade unions, indigenous people's groups, charitable organizations, professional associations, and private foundations has emerged as a major force in international development in the past two decades. The dramatic expansion has been aided by the expansion of democratic governance and globalization. Societal groups by mobilizing thousands of supporters around the world have played an important role in shaping global public policy – exemplified by successful advocacy campaigns involving such issues as the banning of land mines, debt cancellation, and environmental protection. At the national level, giving stakeholders (in particular, the poor and marginalized) a greater voice allows for not only greater local participation but also more innovative ideas and solutions to development problems. For problems associated with civil society, see Encarnacion (2006); Feinberg *et al.* (2006).

3 Also see North (1990) and Nelson (2005).

4 North cautions that uncertainty should not be confused with risk – which is quantifiable and even predictable – whereas uncertainty interferes with one's ability to plan for the future.

5 Furubotn and Pejovich (1973), Heitger (2004),Rosenberg and Birdzell (1986), Torstensson (1994).

6 Years ago Milton Friedman (1962) pointed out that political freedom is a function of economic freedom. Also see Bhagwati (1995), Olson (1993), Rodrik (1999), Rodrik *et al.* (2002).

7 At least, statistically, Przeworski *et al.* (1997, 2000) have noted that democracy is most likely to flourish and survive when a country enjoys more than $5,500 per-capita GNP.

8 Scholars distinguish between the "procedural" and "substantive" definitions of democracy. Procedural or formal democracy focuses on democratic institutions, structures and procedures, while substantive democracy centers on democratic conditions and how to achieve the substantive goals of democracy like liberty, economic equality, and redistributive justice.

9 Of course, this comprehensive list is not easy to meet. In his earlier writings, Dahl (1971) utilized the concept of polyarchy rather than democracy because of his view that no government ever becomes fully democratic. Thus polyarchies are those governments that approach democratic norms and practices. To Dahl a country can be considered "democratic" if there is contested election based on universal franchise, as well as civil and political freedoms of speech, press, assembly, and organization. Arend Lijphart (1984) has identified as many as nine different types of democratic political systems on the basis of two dimensions of majoritarian-consensus democracy. Karl

and Schmitter (1991) have identified three types of democracy: conservative, corporatist, and competitive – on the basis of whether a nation's party system is restrictive, collusive or competitive. Adam Przeworski (1991, 1996) defines it as a system of processing conflicts in which parties that lose elections accept this outcome and wait for the next election, rather than try to destroy the regime to attain their goals.

10　As Dahl (2000: 58) notes, "by the end of the twentieth century, although not all countries with market economies were democratic, all countries with democratic political systems also had market economies."

11　Classical thinkers such as John Locke, John Stuart Mill, and Alexis de Tocqueville not only viewed democracies as the embodiment of reason and advancement, but also assumed that liberal democracies would greatly empower the laboring and disadvantaged sectors of society to press successfully to redress the gross socioeconomic and political disparities.

12　Huntington's (1968) and Huntington and Nelson (1976), noted a "cruel choice" between democracy and development. Specifically, they argued that since socioeconomic modernization increases the political participation of citizens without ensuring that their demands can be met, economic development is best promoted under conditions of "a high degree" of political stability and order. In settings where elites lack in the "art of associating together" and institutions are unable to channel the chaos that accompanies modernization, democracy can be counterproductive since it has the potential to open and destroy the already fragile political institutionalization. In such settings popular participation makes democracies ungovernable, as pluralism tends to create more divisions and encourage consumption at the expense of investment. Hence, contrary to the "assumptions of liberal, technocratic and populist models ... in the early stages of development, the expansion of political participation tends to have a negative impact on economic equality" (Huntington and Nelson 1976: 75). Olson (1982) drawing on the political-economy literature, argued that since special-interest groups unduly influence state policy to advance their particularistic interests, democracy would only exacerbate this problem given that it provides interest groups with a wide scope for organization and lobbying.

13　Schedler (2001) argues that a democratic regime is consolidated when leaders behave democratically, when major political actors acquire democratic attitudes, and when the socioeconomic and institutional foundations for democracy are in place. Also see Linz and Stepan (1996).

14　McFaul (2005: 7) lists seven factors for successful democratic breakthrough in postcommunist settings. These include, "(1) a semi-autocratic rather than fully autocratic regime; (2) an unpopular incumbent; (3) a united and organized opposition; (4) an ability quickly to drive home the point that voting results were falsified; (5) enough independent media to inform citizens about the falsified vote; (6) a political opposition capable of mobilizing tens of thousands or more demonstrators to protest electoral fraud; and (7) divisions among the regime's coercive forces."

15　According to O'Donnell (1994) "delegative democracies" are characterized by low levels of horizontal accountability (checks and balances) and therefore exhibit powerful, plebiscitarian tendencies and dominant executives. Delegative democracies are found in societies where economic crises and institutional weaknesses allow such personalist leaders to govern arbitrarily.

16　As Levitsky and Way (2002: 51) note,

> In recent years, many scholars have pointed to the importance of hybrid regimes. Indeed, recent academic writings have produced a variety of labels for mixed cases, including not only "hybrid regime" but also "semidemocracy," "virtual democracy," "electoral democracy," "pseudodemocracy," "illiberal democracy," "semi-authoritarianism," "soft authoritarianism," "electoral authoritarianism," and Freedom House's "Partly Free."

17 As Donald Horowitz (1985: 291) notes, "by appealing to electorates in ethnic terms, by making ethnic demands on government, and by bolstering the influence of ethnically chauvinist elements within each group, parties that begin by merely mirroring ethnic divisions help to deepen and extend them."

18 The editors of *Foreign Policy* provide a nice working definition:

> How do you know a failed state when you see one? Of course, a government that has lost control of its territory or of the monopoly on the legitimate use of force has earned the label. But there can be more subtle attributes of failure. Some regimes, for example, lack the authority to make collective decisions or the capacity to deliver public services. In other countries, the populace may rely entirely on the black market, fail to pay taxes, or engage in large-scale civil disobedience. Outside intervention can be both a symptom of and a trigger for state collapse. A failed state may be subject to involuntary restrictions of its sovereignty, such as political or economic sanctions, the presence of foreign military forces on its soil, or other military constraints, such as a no-fly zone.
> ("The Failed States Index" 2005. *Foreign Policy*, July/August)

19 During the postwar period, the dominant Keynesian paradigm presumed an active government role in creating desirable levels of growth and employment by managing aggregate demand. On the other hand, classical economic liberalism – the nineteenth-century version of contemporary neoliberalism – maintains that economically backward countries would achieve economic development by specializing in producing goods in which they enjoyed a "comparative advantage." Given their belief in the sanctity of markets, the importance of private initiative and incentives, and minimalist government, neoliberals see any reliance on the state as objectionable. For an excellent overview see Dornbusch (2000).

20 Federalism is traditionally defined as a political system where each level has one or more areas of jurisdiction. For details see, Erk (2006); Lijphart (1999); Solnick (2002).

4 Agricultural development for inclusive growth

1 According to Aksay and Beghin (2005: 18), four countries – Bangladesh, China, India and Indonesia – account for 75 percent of the world's rural poor. In the 52 developing countries for which separate rural and urban income data are available, 63 percent of the population lives in rural areas – slightly more than the 56 percent for developing countries as a whole. Some 73 percent of poor people live in rural areas, and the incidence of poverty is higher in rural areas in all groups of developing countries, regardless of their income level. In the least-developed countries, 82 percent of the poor live in rural areas (Aksoy and Beghin 2005: 18). The literature on the relationship between agricultural development and overall economic development is large. For a good overview, see Chenery and Syrquin (1975), Ferranti *et al.* (2005), Hayami and Ruttan (1985); Johnston and Kilby (1975); Mellor (1976); Mosher (1966); Mundlak (2000).

2 Schultz was awarded the Nobel Prize in Economics in 1979.

3 W. Arthur Lewis's (1958) theory of unlimited supplies of labor argued that the centerpiece of national development was industrial development and that this could be accommodated by shifting farmers to factories. The unlimited labor supply theory posited that agriculture in the South was characterized by an overabundance of labor leading to unemployment and underemployment. Therefore, shifting workers from agriculture to industry could speed up industrialization. Since labor's marginal productivity in agriculture was very low, the opportunity cost of this shift was very low. Lewis's theory provided the theoretical rationale for the pro-industrialization strategy.

4 However, to Schultz, the government should not be involved in determining resource allocation as farmers are fully capable of responding to price signals. For a detailed review, see Pomfret (1992: 52–4).

5 Schultz was the first to systematize the analysis of how investments in education can affect productivity in agriculture as well as in the economy as a whole. Long before it was fashionable, he placed primary emphasis on the productivity effects of education, particularly the education of women, as a source of economic growth.

6 Import Substitution Industralization (ISI) was an inward strategy of industrialization that focused on the production of manufactured goods intended for sale in the domestic/national market. Typically, under ISI the state provided trade protection and other forms of assistance to firms and industries. However, ISI was at the expense of agriculture as resources were extracted from countryside to underwrite industrialization – what Michael Lipton (1977) noted as an "urban-bias" in ISI. Without investments and institutional support, rural households faced serious constraints in accessing essential inputs such as feed, fertilizer, seeds, and capital and in selling their products. As a result agricultural productivity stagnated or declined, resulting in increased food imports.

7 There are two main reasons for the decline in spending on infrastructure. First, the structural adjustment programs in the 1980s and 1990s which required developing-country governments to cut their budgets led to reduced investment in infrastructure. Second, in many regions private investment replaced government spending on infra-structure – but only partially. Because many infrastructure services are public and available to anyone without charge, private investors had no incentive to invest in those sectors or services. With less government support, certain essential services became under-funded. In some cases, the vacuum left by government withdrawal could not be filled by the private sector because of prohibitive risks, high transaction costs, lack of access to information, and the absence of contracts and property rights.

8 Guest (2004) beautifully documents the obstacles that stand in the way of doing busi-ness in Africa. Traveling on the beer run with a truck driver for the Guinness company, he finds that a 360-mile journey that should have taken 18 hours turns into four days – delayed by poor roads and numerous roadblocks demanding (and getting) bribes.

9 Experience unambiguously confirms that community participation in constructing and maintaining rural infrastructure is crucial for its efficient operation and maintenance.

10 Reality is such that, to prevent extinction, conservation of bio-resources will take place through either their "preservation" in gene banks or conservation in their natural habitats through bio-diversity parks.

11 There is no universally agreed definition of smallholder. In India, China and sub-Saharan Africa, farms of less than five hectares can be considered "small." Farms of this size comprise the majority of farms in all these places and are found in large numbers in almost all developing countries. Generally speaking, such farms also have limited capital and other assets.

12 It is important to note that in the pre-green revolution period (1947–1966), the increases in agricultural output in India were almost exclusively due to the expansion of area under cultivation. However, in the post-green revolution period, increases were due mainly to growth in agricultural production and productivity or yield. With aggregate foodgrain production doubling since the mid-1960s, India achieved food self-sufficiency by the early 1980s.

13 The green-revolution technologies were not without their problems. For details, see Evenson and Gollin (2003); Sharma (1999: ch. 5).

14 The United Nations estimates that world population is rising by 78 million every year, or by one billion every 13 years. At this rate, the world's population is projected to rise to over eight billion by 2025. To provide food security for all, the world would have to double food production over current levels.

15 Nobel Laureate Norman Borlaug (2003) describes anti-GM critics as engaged in "hysteria" and "in need of a better education in biological sciences."

16 Bioengineered crops are plants in which the DNA has been altered using modern molecular biology. Other names include transgenic, genetically engineered, living modified organisms (LMOs), and genetically modified organisms (GMOs).

17 In 1994, a small biotech company introduced the first genetically engineered food into US supermarkets – the FlavrSavr tomato, designed to gradually ripen after being harvested.

18 In 1998, the Food and Drug Administration (FDA) approved genetically modified Starlink corn for use in animal feed. However, it withheld approval for human consumption because of concerns that humans might be allergic to a new protein contained in the corn. Yet, Starlink corn somehow found its way into taco shells (October 2000) and into bread (March 2001). In the end, Starlink ceased production and had to recall almost 300 food products from around the world.

19 Critics fear the possibility of "out-crossing," which, they argue, could lead to the development of more aggressive weeds or wild relatives with increased resistance to diseases or environmental stresses and impervious to eradication, thereby upsetting the ecosystem balance.

20 CGIAR was established in 1971 to provide financial support to 16 international agricultural research centers in Asia, Africa, and Latin America. Currently, it has 53 members comprising 21 industrialized countries, 17 developing countries, three foundations, and 12 international and regional organizations.

21 www.fao.org/english/newsroom/2003/13960-en.html (accessed 27 May 2003).

22 A patent gives exclusive rights to the owner of an innovation to prevent a third party from using, reproducing, selling, exporting or importing the product or process that led to the creation of the product. Thus, patents give the inventor a temporary monopoly so that the research and development costs can be met.

23 The WTO Sanitary and Phytosanitary (SPS) and the Technical Barriers to Trade (TBT) agreements are part of a series of agreements establishing the WTO. These agreements are designed to limit the trade-distorting aspects of sanitary and phytosanitary measures taken by countries to protect human and environmental health. Regulations dealing with food safety, food labeling, phytosanitary, animal health, and environmental aspects of biotechnology products thus come under these agreements.

24 The CBD adopted at the 1992 Earth Summit in Rio de Janeiro is an environmental treaty that establishes countries' sovereignty and right to control access to genetic resources and biodiversity. It sets out broad commitments for conservation and sustainable use of the world's biodiversity, including equitable sharing of benefits (monetary and other) arising from the commercial use of genetic resources in areas such as pharmaceuticals and biotechnology. Furthermore, it contains statements promoting the granting of more favorable intellectual property rights terms to promote transfer of biotechnology to developing countries.

25 On 29 January 2000, the Conference of the Parties to the Convention on Biological Diversity adopted a supplementary agreement to the Convention, known as the Cartagena Protocol on Biosafety. The protocol, negotiated under the United Nations Convention on Biological Diversity, is one of the first legally binding international agreements to govern the transboundary transfer of GMOs, primarily for use in agriculture Although a few existing international conventions cover different aspects of the trade in GMOs and voluntary guidelines have been developed by a number of international agencies for safe use of biotechnology, the Cartagena Protocol is the first to mandate the need for consent of an importing country prior to trade in some GMOs, in order to allow for assessment of potential risks posed by such transfers to biodiversity and human health in the importing country. The Protocol seeks to protect biological diversity from the potential risks posed by living modified organisms resulting from modern biotechnology; and as noted, it establishes an "advance informed agreement" procedure for ensuring that countries are provided with the information necessary to make informed decisions before agreeing to the import of

such organisms into their territory. The Protocol contains reference to a precautionary approach and reaffirms the precaution language in Principle 15 of the Rio Declaration on Environment and Development. The Protocol also establishes a Biosafety Clearing-House to facilitate the exchange of information on living modified organisms and to assist countries in the implementation of the Protocol.

26 However, such advanced notification and consent would not apply to shipments of biotechnology food products intended for direct use as food, feed, or processing (although additional restrictions and mandatory requirements could be added later), but would apply to shipments of such products as seeds for planting and fish for field release. Nevertheless, shipments of biotechnology food products intended for food, feed, or processing would be required to be accompanied by documentation stating that such shipments "may contain" biotechnology components and that the products are not intended for intentional introduction into the environment.

27 This differs from the provisions of the WTO SPS Agreement and the Technical Barriers to Trade (TBT) Agreement. Although the SPS Agreement authorizes WTO members to provisionally adopt sanitary or phytosanitary measures on the basis of available pertinent information, the SPS Agreement provides that members adopting such measures seek to obtain the additional information necessary for a more objective assessment of risk and review the sanitary or phytosanitary measure accordingly within a reasonable period of time, besides providing a mechanism for WTO members whose exports are constrained by such provisional measures to seek an explanation for them. The TBT Agreement requires WTO members to avoid technical regulations that create obstacles to trade.

5 The Doha Development Agenda: realizing the promise of global trade

1 The World Trade Organization is an international organization of some 148 countries that deals with the rules of trade between nations. The WTO core task is to help international trade to flow smoothly, predictably, and freely, and provides countries with a constructive and fair outlet for dealing with disputes over trade issues. Therefore, the WTO is not a comprehensive development institution; rather, it is a negotiating forum in which governments make trade policy commitments to improve access to each other's markets and establish rules governing trade. The WTO came into being in 1995, succeeding the General Agreement on Tariffs and Trade (GATT) that was established in 1947.

2 The Ministerial Conference is the WTOs highest-level decision-making body. It meets "at least once every two years" as required by the Marrakech Agreement establishing the WTO, the organization's founding charter. The Ministerial Conference brings together all members of the WTO, all of which are countries or customs unions. The Ministerial Conference can take decisions on all matters under any of the multilateral trade agreements.

3 In WTO negotiations, modalities set broad outlines such as formulas or approaches for tariff reductions to be considered for final commitments.

4 The US Congress granted President George W. Bush the TPA in 2002 for the Doha Round as well as agreements with individual countries. The TPA runs out in the middle of 2007. The Congress passed the TPA with the narrowest of margins in the House of Representatives (215 to 214), and only after the Bush administration placed "safeguard" tariffs on steel and acceded to the Farm Act of 2002. With the new more protectionist Congress, extending the TPA will not be easy (Schott 2006).

5 For a good overview see, Akyuz *et al.* (2006).

6 Named after the site of first WTO meeting where these issues were formally raised.

7 The Cairns Group of agricultural exporting nations was formed in 1986 in Cairns, Australia, just before the beginning of the Uruguay Round. Current membership includes: Argentina, Australia, Bolivia, Brazil, Canada, Chile, Colombia, Costa Rica, Guatemala, Indonesia, Malaysia, New Zealand, Paraguay, the Philippines, South Africa, Thailand and Uruguay.

8 The group initially called the G-20 was created on 20 August 2003 in the final stages of the preparation for the Cancun Ministerial. It included Argentina, Bolivia, Brazil, Chile, China, Colombia, Costa Rica, Cuba, Ecuador, El Salvador, Guatemala, India, Mexico, Pakistan, Paraguay, Peru, the Philippines, South Africa, Thailand, and Venezuela. In Cancun, El Salvador withdrew and Nigeria and Indonesia joined, while Egypt, Kenya and others endorsed the G-20 position. The G-20's main goal is to achieve an ambitious outcome in the market access negotiations, with greater access to OECD agricultural markets. The G-33 led by Indonesia was created on 9 September 2003. Initially known as the "SP and SSM Alliance," its main concern was to ensure that issues of food security remained a core part of the negotiations by embodying the principles of "Special Safeguard Mechanism" and "Special Products" in the agreement. The G-90, an alliance of African, Caribbean, and Pacific Island countries (ACP), shared a common concern about "preference erosion" and the weakening of the "Special and Differential Treatment." Group of 71 countries are those which have preferential trading relations with the EU under the former Lome Treaty, now called the Cotonou Agreement.

9 Because much of the capacity-building agenda lies outside the competence of the WTO, its credibility will depend critically on the response of the international community and whether developing countries make the necessary adjustments. WTO member countries agreed to address the Integrated Framework for Trade-Related Technical Assistance for LDCs and to significantly increase their contributions to WTO technical assistance and capacity programs for the least-developed countries by July 2002. The Integrated Framework for Trade-Related Technical Assistance for Least-Developed Countries is designed to help the LDCs strengthen their domestic policies and institutions and make trade a strategic component of their poverty reduction strategies. Areas of trade-related technical assistance include revenue systems, customs administration, trade facilitation, social safety nets, and the financial sector. The partner organizations in the Integrated Framework are the WTO, the World Bank, the IMF, the UN Conference on Trade and Development, the UN Development Program, and the International Trade Centre.

10 Terms such as *support, subsidy, assistance* or *aid to producers* are often used interchangeably to describe the transfers provided to farmers or the agricultural sector as a whole. The OECD produces several indicators of agricultural support. The most important one is the *Producer Support Estimate* (PSE), which shows the annual monetary transfers to farmers from policy measures that maintain domestic prices for farm goods at levels higher (and occasionally lower) than those at the country's border or market price support, and second, provide payments to farmers based on criteria such as the quantity of a commodity produced, the amount of inputs used, the number of animals kept, the area farmed, or the revenue or income received by farmers. These are known as budgetary payments. However, it is important to keep in mind that support comprises not only budgetary payments that appear in government accounts, but also the so-called *price gap* for farm goods between domestic and world markets as measured at a country's border. When talking about subsidy, the literature generally refers to two general types: *export* and *domestic*. An export subsidy is a benefit conferred on a firm by the government that is contingent on exports. A domestic subsidy is a benefit not directly linked to exports. For details, see OECD (2004b).

11 Tariffs are customs duties on merchandise imports, levied either on an *ad valorem* basis (tariff rate charged as percentage of the price or percentage of value) or on a specific basis (e.g. $7 per 100 kg). Tariffs give price advantage to similar locally produced goods and raise revenues for the government. *Tariff binding* is the commitment not to increase a rate of duty beyond an agreed level. Once a rate of duty is bound, it may not be raised without compensating the affected parties. *Tariff escalation* is higher import duties on semi-processed products than on raw materials, and higher still on finished products. This practice protects domestic processing industries

and discourages the development of processing activity in the countries where raw materials originate. Tariff escalation that results in significant protection for processed products makes it difficult for developing countries to escape the cycle of producing and exporting primary products. *Tariff peaks* are relatively high tariffs, usually on "sensitive" products, amidst generally low tariff levels. For industrialized countries, tariffs of 15 percent and above are generally recognized as "tariff peaks." Finally, *tariffication* describes the procedures relating to the agricultural market-access provision in which all non-tariff measures are converted into tariffs.

12 The WTOs Agreement on Trade Related Aspects of Intellectual Property Rights (TRIPS), which took effect in 1995, obliges countries to extend patent protection to pharmaceutical products and processes after a phase-in period linked to level of development. Under these rules, countries that are able to manufacture the drugs would continue to have legal access to generics if they chose to issue compulsory licenses. These tend to be more advanced developing countries such as India, China, and Brazil. However, countries that lack domestic manufacturing capacity tend to be the LDCs – who may be barred from importing the generic versions of patent-protected drugs once rules take effect. The Doha Round provided a mechanism by which poor countries could import generic drugs protected by patents abroad.

13 The 1996 Singapore Ministerial Declaration mandated the establishment of working groups to analyze issues related to investment, competition policy, and transparency in government procurement. In return for agreeing to a stronger mandate for post-Doha agricultural negotiations, the EU and other main *demandeurs* managed to secure a conditional negotiating track for these Singapore issues. However, opposition from many developing countries made any future negotiations subject to a decision to be taken at the next WTO Ministerial Conference by explicit consensus on their scope and timeframes.

14 A good overview is provided by the President of Tanzania, Benjamin Mkapa (2004).

15 However, it should be noted that South Korea and Japan maintained that they would not compromise for anything less than negotiations on all four Singapore issues, while the African Union stuck to the position that they would not agree to negotiate on any of the Singapore issues.

16 According to the World Bank (2004c: xvii), "US subsidies to cotton growers totaled US$3.7 billion last year [2003], three times US foreign aid to Africa. These subsidies depress world cotton prices by an estimated 10 to 20 percent, reducing the income of thousands of poor farmers in West Africa, Central and South Asia, and poor countries around the world. In West Africa alone, where cotton is a critical cash crop for many small-scale and near-subsistence farmers, annual income losses for cotton growers are about US$250 million a year." However, Watkins (2003: 4–6) is more candid in his assessment. He notes, "Take the case of cotton. When it comes to harvesting subsidies, America's 25,000 cotton barons are first among equals. In 2001 they received $3.6 billion in government support – three times US aid to Africa. Because the US is the world's largest cotton exporter, accounting for 40 percent of the world market, these subsidies lowered world prices: by around one quarter according to the International Cotton Advisory Committee. Farmers in Africa have suffered the consequences. In West Africa alone 10–11 million people depend on cotton cultivation as a source of income. The crop is also a major source of foreign exchange and government revenue. Lower world prices caused by American subsidies mean that desperately poor households have seen their incomes fall, with attendant consequences for poverty. In Benin, the price decline associated with American subsidies translates into a 4 percent increase in the incidence of poverty, or 250,000 people falling below the poverty line. Meanwhile, foreign exchange losses have eroded the benefits of development assistance: Burkina Faso loses more because of US subsidies than it gets in debt relief. What makes the cotton case so egregious is that West Africa is a far more efficient producer than the US. Fewer than 10 percent of America's producers would

be competitive on world markets without support. But in 2001/2002 the subsidy provided to American cotton farmers exceeded the total national income of countries like
Burkina Faso and Mali. In a bizarre throwback to the principles of Bolshevik state
planning, it also exceeded the value of cotton output. In cotton, as in other areas of
agricultural trade, market outcomes owe less to comparative advantage than to comparative access to subsidies." Also see Heinisch (2006); Watkins (2002). Regarding
US sugar subsidies, see Elliott (2005).

17 Procedurally, there was a dispute regarding how the Doha Declaration mandated
negotiations – with the EU insisting Singapore issues were part of the "single undertaking" package, while the G-21 and other developing countries argued that any
negotiation on these issues was subject an agreement by "explicit consensus." In
terms of substantive content, the EU argued that it was imperative to negotiate multilateral rules to govern the treatment of these issues, while many developing countries
disputed the rationale of discussing these subjects under the umbrella of the WTO.

18 This claim is not entirely true. In the Doha Declaration, "trade and labor" was the
only subject explicitly excluded from the negotiations.

19 Also, the proposed subsidy and tariff cuts were put broadly under separate titles:
"trade-distorting" and "non-trade distorting." The EU and the US were only prepared
to show flexibility for "trade-distorting."

20 The OECD countries often argue that trade-distorting agricultural policies are necessary
to support farmers' incomes and to correct the market failures caused by externalities
and public goods problems. However, the United States demonstrated its commitment
to agriculture trade reform, tabling a fairly comprehensive reform proposal addressing
market access, domestic support, and export competition policies; these included liberalization measures such as harmonizing tariffs at substantially reduced levels, expanding tariff rate quotas, and dismantling state trading enterprises, eliminating special
agricultural safeguards, limiting trade-distorting domestic support programs, disciplining export credits, and phasing out export subsidies. However, as noted earlier, the proposals contained no deadlines for either subsidy or tariff reductions.

21 Of course, the single undertaking provision provides an insurance policy for all the
members that their voices will be heard. Schott (2003: 3) provides a good illustration:
For the "European Union [it means] that India and other countries will not block the
start of negotiations on investment and competition policy by refusing to agree on
modalities for those talks. If India or any country attempted to block those talks, it
would elicit reciprocal actions to stall ongoing talks on other issues of priority for the
blocking country. The entire WTO negotiation would quickly founder, and India
would be implicated in the crime just as it would have been if it unilaterally blocked
the launch of the talks at Doha."

22 Most of the estimates of the potential global economic welfare gains from trade are
generated using the computable general equilibrium (CGE) models of the global
economy; the most common is known as GTAP (Global Trade Analysis Project).

23 Also see Anderson (2005); Anderson and Morris (2000); Anderson and Martin
(2006); Fabiosa *et al.* (2006); Goldin and Reinert (2006); Hoekman *et al.* (2002);
Newfarmer (2005); Stiglitz and Charlton (2006); and Winters (2004), among
others.

24 However, more recent accounts have raised questions regarding the validity of the
huge potential gains from an agricultural agreement under Doha. Some have claimed
that the World Bank (amongst other institutions) had used incomplete data which
ignored the fact that most developing countries enjoy large preferential access to
OECD markets. Thus, the so-called large gains for developing countries that would
result from tariff cuts were problematic, as most of the tariffs were already very low –
except in the World Bank's database. Using economic simulations that employ the
new MacMap dataset, these new estimates put welfare gains of full liberalization and
elimination of agricultural subsidies at around $55 billion, with only $12 billion going

to developing countries (see articles in Anderson and Martin 2005, especially the one by Hertel and Keeney).

25 Developed countries only began to reduce distortions in their agricultural trade policies after agriculture was brought into the global trade negotiations for the first time in the 1994 Uruguay Round Agreement (URAA). However, as Aksoy and Beghin (2005: 39) note, agricultural protection in OECD countries still remains high. In developed countries agricultural protection is measured using three instruments. One is market price support, the difference between domestic and international prices caused by border barriers such as tariffs and quantitative restrictions. It measures the total impact of border barriers on the prices of domestic production and is equivalent to border protection weighted by domestic production. Border barriers are the major tool of protection and account for about 70 percent of total protection in OECD countries. A second instrument is direct support – the direct production-related subsidies given to farmers. A third is the general support given to agriculture through research, training, market support and infrastructure. This instrument is not usually included in overall production support estimates.

26 In fact, overvaluation of exchange rates, the main source of the bias against agriculture, decreased or was eliminated during the 1990s in most developing countries.

27 Using a slightly different accounting method, Aksoy and Beghin (2005: 43) note that "the overall support given to agricultural producers in OECD countries through higher domestic prices and direct production-related subsidies was $228 billion during 2000–02. About 63 percent or $143 billion of this came from border barriers and market price support, and 37 percent from direct subsidies to farmers."

28 Diaz-Bonilla and Gulati (2003: 3) note that "these estimates may be low because they do not include dynamic effects from additional investments that better market opportunities may elicit or second-round multiplier effects from those agricultural incomes that never materialized. More than half of these displacement effects have resulted from the policies of the European Union (and other European countries such as Norway and Switzerland), somewhat less than a third from US policies, and about 10 percent mainly from Japanese policies, with the balance resulting from the policies of other industrialized countries."

29 While hardly perfect, developing countries have been able to place mutually agreed limits on the OECD countries via the "Special and Differential Treatment" (SDT) provisions in the WTO which cover three core areas: *preferential access* to developed-country markets, typically without reciprocal commitments from the developing countries; *exemptions* or deferrals from some WTO rules; and *technical assistance* to help implement WTO mandates. The underlying premise of the SDT is that industries in developing countries need assistance for a period of time both in their home market (protection) and in export markets (preferences). Thus, in practice, the SDT is based on commitments by high-income countries to provide preferential access to their markets, the right to limit reciprocity in trade negotiating rounds to levels "consistent with development needs," and greater freedom to use otherwise restricted trade policies. However, as Diaz-Bonilla and Gulati (2003: 2) note, some "countries are trying to coordinate both approaches. India is an interesting case. On the one hand, playing offense seems reasonable for a country that in the past few years has emerged as one of the world's top net exporters of agricultural products. On the other hand, a large percentage of India's poor population lives in rural areas. Concerns about possible negative impacts on the rural poor have therefore underpinned the defensive components in India's WTO proposal."

30 This is because as the MFN tariffs are cut, the value of preferences is reduced.

31 There are various proposals regarding how best to address the problem of preference erosion. Some have suggested the use of trade policy measures that slow down the pace of preference erosion. Others have suggested compensation through complementary financial measures that assist poor countries to cope with its adverse consequences.

32 Under bilateral agreements, the powerful can implement trade and other policy reforms unilaterally, because they can do so and because of the pressures put by domestic protection lobbies.

33 Doha Work Program, Hong Kong. Ministerial Declaration, adopted on 18 December 2005; Geneva, WTO.

34 In WTO talk, *market access* means cutting tariffs, expanding tariff-quotas and various flexibilities for these; *exports subsidies* (officially "export competition") means eliminating these and disciplining export credit, food aid and state trading enterprises to eliminate hidden export subsidies; and *domestic support* means cutting supports that distort trade (by stimulating over-production and artificially raising or lowering prices) and disciplining forms of support that could distort trade.

35 The EU is one of the key players in the WTO. The EU has a common trade policy. While the member-states co-ordinate their positions in Brussels and Geneva, the European Commission alone negotiates on behalf of the Union's 25 member-states at almost all WTO meetings.

36 Moreover, in parallel with export subsidy elimination, the declaration also required negotiated agreement by April 2006 on disciplines for agricultural export credits and credit guarantees; on monopoly state trading enterprises such as grain marketing boards in Canada, Australia and New Zealand; and on food aid. Regarding food aid, the declaration notes that any WTO-negotiated rules would not prevent food from going to hungry people in emergencies, but would prevent displacement of commercial sales by donations of excess commodities. The EU had been pressing to restrict food aid to cash only, a position vigorously resisted by the United States.

37 In the Tokyo Round (1973–1979), a "Swiss" formula was used – under which the highest tariffs were reduced by the widest margin. The July 2005 framework specified the use of two coefficients – one for developing countries which would result in smaller average cuts, and one for developed countries where the cuts would be larger in percentage terms. There would also be flexibilities for developing countries in which they could exempt a percentage of tariff lines from the formula cuts. The compression effect of this formula meant that tariff peaks and tariff escalation would be sharply reduced. This is significant because while developed countries have generally low tariffs, they often apply their highest peaks and use tariff escalation on products of greatest interest to developing countries, such as textiles, apparel and shoes.

6 The truth about foreign aid

1 Jan Egeland, the United Nations emergency relief coordinator and former head of the Norwegian Red Cross, questioned the generosity of rich nations by saying: "We were more generous when we were less rich, many of the rich countries … And it is beyond me, why are we so stingy, really. … Even Christmas time should remind many Western countries at least how rich we have become."

2 In absolute terms the United States provides almost twice as much aid as the next biggest donor, Japan. Overall, these two countries contribute about a third of total aid. However, the real dollar value of US aid in recent years is, on average, roughly the same as it was in the early 1960s.

3 Only five countries (Denmark, Luxembourg, the Netherlands, Norway, and Sweden) have disbursed ODA equaling 0.7 percent or more of their GNI.

4 Official development assistance, or foreign aid, consists of loans, grants, technical assistance and other forms of cooperation extended by governments to developing countries. Financial aid must include a grant element of at least 25 percent. Technical cooperation also includes grants to nationals of aid recipient countries receiving education or training, and payments to consultants, advisers and administrators serving in the recipient countries. Grants do not have to be repaid. Concessional loans have to be

repaid, but at lower interest rates and over longer periods than commercial bank loans.

5   In other words, at 0.22 percent of donor countries' GDP, aid stands at its smallest proportion since it was first institutionalized with the Marshall Plan in 1947.

6   There is a vast body of scholarly literature on the subject. For a range of opinions, see Cassen (1991); Hancock (1989); Hayter and Watson (1985); Lancaster (2000); Mosley, Harrigan and Toye (1991); Tendler (1975); Tisch and Wallace (1994); and Wood (1986).

7   Of course, there are many ways in which countries can be caught in poverty traps. For an insightful review of the literature, see Azariadis and Stachurski. (2005).

8   The earlier gains that were made against malaria (often by draining swamps) have been lost. The problem is further compounded as the *Anopheles* mosquito has developed resistance to insecticides and drug therapies. Typically, people in malarial regions are infected when they are in their infancy. If they survive into adulthood, the parasite remains in their bodies, causing periodic bouts of illness. These are not usually fatal for adults, but they are incapacitating (Sachs 2006).

9   In the classic Solow model in which all countries have the same steady state, all countries converge to a high level of income. However, if saving is low and population growth becomes very high at low income, then a poverty trap will occur at low incomes, driving the equilibrium down to low or zero capital.

10   The UNDP (2005) in its flagship publication, *The Human Development Report 2005*, notes that "aid provides governments with a resource for making the multiple investments in health, education and economic infrastructure needed to break cycles of deprivation" (p. 7). Similarly, the World Bank (2005a) also argues that the low saving and human capital accumulation in low-income countries is the reason why these countries need aid. Also see Payne (2006).

11   By his own admission, Easterly had to leave the World Bank after the publication of his *The Elusive Quest for Growth* (2001). The tour de force provides a devastating critique of the various global efforts (including the venerable World Bank's) to spur Third World growth.

12   "The typical country in Africa," Easterly writes, "received more than 15 percent of its income from foreign donors in the 1990s," but that "surge in aid was not successful in reversing or halting the slide in growth of income per capita toward zero" (2001: 45).

13   Easterly admits that he feels like "a Scrooge" for pointing out that this "well-meaning compassion" has brought about little improvement in the lot of the world's poor (2001: 4).

14   On the basis of measures developed by the University of Maryland to rate the concentration of power in the executive, known as "Polity IV," about half of total aid during 1960–1990 went to countries that had "unlimited executive authority." Only 10 percent went to more democratic countries with "substantial restrictions on the executive."

15   By "sound policies" the authors mean open trade regimes, fiscal discipline and avoidance of high inflation.

16   However, when Easterly *et al.* (2004) repeated the analysis by Burnside and Dollar – albeit on a larger pool of data – they found no evidence that aid works in a good policy environment. In an interesting study by Brautigam and Knack (2004), where the authors investigated the aid and governance relationship in 32 sub-Saharan African countries for the period 1982–1997, they found that a robust statistical relationship exists between high aid levels in Africa and deterioration in governance.

17   Devarajan and Swaroop (1998) point out that when funds are fungible, a donor project may exhibit a very high return but may actually be financing something with a very low return at the margin. To overcome the problem, they recommend that aid be tied to an overall public expenditures program that provides adequate resources to crucial sectors.

18 The International Development Association (IDA) is part of the World Bank. IDA's Articles of Agreement became effective in 1960 and the first IDA loans, known as credits, were approved in 1961 to Chile, Honduras, India and Sudan. IDA is the largest single source of concessional aid to poor countries. Concessional financing is provided at substantially below market rate, with no interest charge and repayments stretched over 35–40 years, including a ten-year grace period before any repayment begins. IDA levies a 0.75 percent service charge on the disbursed balance to cover administrative costs.

19 President Bush's goal to increase US foreign aid to poor nations by $5 billion per year over current assistance levels is by far the largest proposed increase in US foreign aid in several decades. MCA funds would be provided to developing countries as grants, not as traditional US-managed projects, and would be used to help build local governance capacity and project ownership. In March 2005, the first compact between the US and Madagascar was approved with an aid allocation of $110 million over four years. However, as Birdsall and Deese (2004: 2) note, "the administration's well-intentioned focus on performance and results, while innovative, does nothing to address – and may well aggravate – the problem of project proliferation. As currently conceived, both the MCA and Bush's new AIDS initiative will either reinvent or overlap with efforts already underway at the international level, many of which are effective and, indeed, already supported by the United States."

20 Since its inception in 1960, the OECD's Development Assistance Committee (DAC) has functioned as the principal strategy-setting and policy and performance review organ of the major bilateral donors. Every three years, each of DAC's 22 member countries is subject to an examination of its aid policies and performance by the other members of the Committee based on studies by the OECD staff and led by two specifically designated "examiners" drawn from the Committee. These Development Cooperation Reviews, including the conclusions reached by the DAC, have been published since 1994. Also, the DAC's Working Party on Aid Evaluation brings together the heads of the evaluation units of bilateral and multilateral development agencies to work on evaluation capacities in developing countries. DAC members should now work together to further align and harmonize aid and performance.

21 Moreover, although sub-Saharan Africa has received 60 percent of the increases in ODA disbursements during the past five years, most of these funds were allocated to post-conflict situations. The increase in development aid has been small.

22 The "Dutch disease" broadly refers to the harmful consequences of large increases in a country's income. In the 1960s, the Netherlands experienced a vast increase in its wealth after discovering large natural gas deposits in the North Sea. Unexpectedly, this windfall had serious repercussions on important segments of the country's economy as the Dutch guilder became stronger, making Dutch non-oil exports less competitive. This syndrome became known as the "Dutch disease." Although the disease is generally associated with a natural resource discovery, it can occur from any development that results in a large inflow of foreign currency, including a sharp surge in natural resource prices, foreign assistance or FDI. These effects played out in the oil-rich nations in the 1970s when oil prices soared and oil exports rose at the expense of the agricultural and manufacturing sectors. For an early discussion, see Corden (1984); and Van Wijnbergen (1984). Others have argued that oil dependency may generate corrosive effects on governance and accountability and undermine the institutional foundations of growth (Eifert *et al.* 2003).

23 In a country with a fixed exchange rate, the upward pressure of an expanded money supply on domestic demand and prices of nontraded goods would cause the currency to appreciate in real terms as domestic prices rise, while the nominal exchange rate would remain unchanged. On the other hand, in a country with a flexible exchange rate, the increased supply of foreign currency, not fully absorbed by the purchase of imported goods and services, would drive up the value of the domestic currency, resulting in an appreciation in both the nominal and real exchange rates.

24 Alesina and Dollar (2000) provide a good overview of how and why aid is allocated across countries. Reusse (2002), who worked for the FAO for many years, blames the way "aid technocrats" and NGOs – who often share the same mentality – have undermined aid effectiveness. He cynically notes, "With project outputs so far detached from the donor-country taxpayer's control and so opportunistically or passively watched by the Third World population and their overtaxed and frequently bypassed governments, almost anything goes."

7 Optimal debt relief for the poorest

1 Through the International Development Association (IDA), the World Bank provides grants to the poorest countries. While IDA began as the part of the bank that provided financial assistance to the world's poorest countries at zero interest, it is now providing outright grant assistance to low-income countries. However, the predominant method of delivering relief on IDA debt is through the forgiveness of a portion of IDA debt service as it comes due. IDA will forgive a minimum of 50 percent of the annual debt service due on existing IDA debt and, to the extent possible, will deliver its full share of debt relief to the country within 20 years after the Decision Point.

2 In 1989 US Treasury Secretary Nicholas Brady introduced a plan that took his name, under which the principal and some of the interest would be guaranteed with US Treasury bonds in exchange for a write-down of the amounts outstanding. Under the Brady Plan, debt relief agreements were contingent on debtor countries enacting major economic reforms. The Brady Plan debt reduction, coupled with strengthening economies among the so-called "Brady 15" countries, helped a number of distressed middle-income debtors to return to financial stability. Most poor countries did not benefit from the Brady Plan, however, as most of their debt was to the Paris Club creditor countries and multilateral lenders (George 1998; Lissakers 1991; Roodman 2006).

3 Concessional Treatment or concessionality can occur either through a cancellation of part of the claims or through a rescheduling of the claims over a long period of time with an interest rate that is lower than the appropriate market rate. When a debt treatment results in a reduction of the net present value of the claims rescheduled, it includes concessionality. Debt swaps include operations such as debt for nature, debt for aid, debt for equity swaps or other local currency debt swaps. These swaps often involve the sale of the debt by the creditor government to an investor, who in turn sells the debt to the debtor government in return for shares in a local company or for local currency to be used in projects in the country.

4 The Net Present Value (NPV) of debt is a measure that takes into account the degree of concessionality. It is defined as the sum of all future debt-service obligations (interest and principal) on existing debt, discounted at the appropriate market rate. Whenever the interest rate on a loan is lower than the market rate, the resulting NPV of debt is smaller than its face value.

5 That is, the HIPC, for the first time, brought all creditors – bilateral, multilateral, and commercial lenders – within the same coordinated framework. It is important to note that the debt owed by a country can be broken down into a number of different types, e.g. by debtor (which may be a sovereign government, a public company or a private debtor) or by creditor (which may be a multilateral creditor, a government, a private creditor). Over time, the share of private debt (debt owed by private debtors) and the share of private claims (debt owed to private creditors) has increased, reflecting the increased role of the private sector in both the OECD and developing countries.

6 During the debt crisis, creditor governments formed a committee to agree on the needed debt relief. In consultation with the IMF they agreed that all creditors offered terms at least as favorable as those agreed by the committee. Hosted by the French Treasury, this committee became known as the "Paris Club." Paris Club creditors agree to provide additional debt reduction under the HIPC Initiative as part of the

overall effort to enable the country to exit from unsustainable debt. Consistent with current practice, countries receiving assistance from the Paris Club are required to seek treatment on debt owed to other bilateral and commercial creditors on terms at least comparable to those agreed with the Paris Club.

7 When a debtor country first meets with Paris Club creditors, the "cut-off date" is defined and is not changed in subsequent Paris Club treatments, and credits granted after this cut-off date are not subject to future rescheduling. Thus, the cut-off date helps restore access to credit for debtor countries facing payment difficulties.

8 However, Kenya, Yemen, Angola and Vietnam are considered to already have a sustainable level of debt, and are unlikely to receive further debt cancellation.

9 At the Decision Point, the Executive Boards of the IMF and the World Bank formally decide on a country's eligibility, and the international community commits to provide sufficient assistance by the Completion Point for the country to achieve debt sustainability calculated at the Decision Point.

10 Any definition of sustainable debt embodies a value judgment of what is, and what is not, sustainable. The HIPC Initiative now defines a ratio of net present value of debt (NPV) to exports in excess of 150 percent as unsustainable.

11 Also, for these countries the NPV debt-to-export target will be set at a level which achieves a 250 percent of the NPV debt-to-revenue ratio at the Decision Point.

12 Poverty Reduction Strategy Papers (PRSPs) are prepared by governments in low-income countries through a participatory process involving domestic stakeholders as well as external development partners, including the IMF and the World Bank. A PRSP describes the macroeconomic, structural and social policies and programs that a country will pursue over several years to promote broad-based growth and reduce poverty, as well as external financing needs and the associated sources of financing. Given the time which it may take countries to prepare a fully participatory PRSP, countries may submit only an interim PRSP (I-PRSP)

13 To reach the Completion Point, countries must have satisfactorily finished the reforms they agreed to when they entered the formal HIPC Initiative process. The international community commits to provide sufficient assistance by the Completion Point for the country to achieve debt sustainability. Thus, at the completion the country receives the bulk of its assistance under the HIPC Initiative, without any further policy conditions. However, under the enhanced HIPC Initiative, the timing of the Completion Point is linked to the implementation of pre-agreed key structural reforms (i.e. floating Completion Point).

14 Most, but not all, creditors provide interim debt-service relief between Decision Point and Completion Point. However, even after countries have passed Decision Point, the provision of interim relief is not guaranteed.

15 Topping-up: in a subsequent debt reduction, granting more debt reduction on debt the Paris Club has previously reduced to provide even further debt relief (e.g. when increasing the cancellation level from 33.33 percent of Toronto terms to 67 percent of Naples terms).

16 With regard to implications for overall debt reduction, the World Bank estimates that after HIPC and traditional debt relief, including ODA cancellation, the net present value of public debt in the three dozen countries is likely to be cut by two-thirds. For details see IMF-IDA (2004: 11) and www.worldbank.org/hipc/faq/faq.html.

17 Arrears are debt due and not paid as of a given date. Arrears may be late payments as well as debt due a long time before. The late interest rate that accrues on arrears usually includes the original interest rate of the credits, plus a penalty.

18 A recent IMF-IDA (2003: 4) report notes that

some creditors, mostly commercial, have launched litigation proceedings against HIPC debtors to recover their outstanding claims. The actions reflect the fact that the HIPC Initiative does not alter the legal rights and obligations between HIPC and their external creditors. Accordingly, until the HIPC debtors and their creditors reach bilateral legal agreements in line with the HIPC Initiative, creditors are legally entitled to use available legal mechanisms to enforce their credit claims against HIPCs. In some instances, prior to their Decision Points HIPCs have paid commercial creditors in full (and foregone debt relief) either because of the litigation or the threat of it, a desire to avoid disrupting a commercial relationship, or the fear of losing productive assets in cases where commercial debt was secured by collateral.... So far, the number of such lawsuits and the amounts involved have been relatively small, but such proceedings can be burdensome to the debtors concerned, and can in some cases complicate financial and reserve management in these countries.

19 To be fair, the World Bank does admit that its definition of debt sustainability is quite narrow as it does not deal with issues of domestic debt which are important for fiscal sustainability. Nor does it measure the adequacy of public resources to address priority development programs after debt service has been made.

20 According to Jubilee Research the very definition of "sustainability" is flawed. It has argued that the World Bank offers no justification for the arbitrary level of sustainability set by the HIPC Initiative, as 150 percent of exports (Greenhill *et al.* 2003).

21 While Jubilee Research's proposal sounds intuitively appealing, there are problems with it. For example, the need for debt relief and grants would require a country-by-country judgment of what constitutes a satisfactory policy goal. This would not only be very difficult in practice, it would potentially lead to vast differences in the definition of debt sustainability across countries, raising obvious issues of fairness. Also, since the proposals are designed to put onus on the donor community to provide low-income countries with substantial net transfers while simultaneously limiting their debt-service burden, making such a framework operational would require that donor countries be prepared to allocate a potentially unlimited amount of debt relief and grants to eligible countries. Of course, this is not on the cards.

22 Members of the G-8 include the United States, Britain, France, Germany, Italy, Japan, Canada and Russia.

23 Apparently Brown's American counterpart, Treasury Secretary John W. Snow, initially took a dim view of the British proposal. However, he was eventually won over, calling the deal "an achievement of historic proportions" and adding that debt has been "locking these poorest countries into poverty and preventing them from using their own resources," – a situation he called "morally wrong."

24 Actually, the final deal goes further than the "agreement" between Bush and Blair – which only included debts owed to the World Bank and the AfDB, but not the IMF. Apparently, the logjam was broken when it was found that the IMF had several billion dollars available from gold sales in the late 1990s that it could use to cover the losses it would make from writing off debts. Initially, the idea to sell the IMF's gold reserves (which have increased in value in recent years) to help finance its debt forgiveness, was backed by Britain but opposed by the United States and Canada, both gold-producing countries worried about the adverse impact such a sale might have on the global bullion market. While the G-8 finance ministers left the door open to gold sales by the IMF, they agreed the IMF could meet the cost of the latest planned debt write-offs without selling gold.

25 According to the G-8 communiqué, for IDA and AfDF debt 100 percent stock cancellation will be delivered by relieving post-Completion Point HIPCs that are on track with their programs of repayment obligations and adjusting their gross assistance flows by the amount forgiven. Donors would provide additional contributions to IDA and AfDF, based on agreed burden shares, to offset dollar for dollar the foregone principal and interest repayments of the debt cancelled.

26 The G-8 announced that it will also invite voluntary contributions, including from the oil-producing states, to a new trust fund to support poor countries facing commodity price and other exogenous shocks.
27 The IFF "frontloads" aid by issuing and selling bonds on global capital markets. Donors to the IFF would borrow against their own future pledges of development aid and guarantee repayment of IFF bonds over a period of time. The plan allows countries to circumvent their current fiscal constraints and allocate more aid in the short term. However, the danger is that such a scheme could result in a decline in future aid dispersals, since the bonds would eventually have to be repaid 10 or 15 years down the road by funds taken from future aid budgets.
28 Under the French plan, air passengers would have to pay extra for their tickets to help the world's poor. The finance ministers gave their backing to a proposal from France (later joined by Germany) to impose a levy on air tickets. Both claim that the "air ticket contribution" could raise up to $10 billion a year on the basis of a tax of just $1 a ticket. The proposal is likely to meet fierce resistance from the airlines.

Bibliography

Acemoglu, Daron and James Robinson. 2005. *Economic Origins of Dictatorship and Democracy*. New York: Cambridge University Press.

Acemoglu, Daron, Simon Johnson, and James Robinson. 2001. "The Colonial Origins of Comparative Development: An Empirical Investigation" *American Economic Review*, vol. 91, no. 5, December, pp. 1369–401.

——. 2002. "Reversal of Fortune: Geography and Institutions in the Making of the Modern World" *The Quarterly Journal of Economics*, vol. 17, no. 4, pp. 1231–94.

——. 2003. "An African Success Story: Botswana" in Dani Rodrik, ed., *In Search of Prosperity: Analytical Narratives on Economic Growth*. Princeton, NJ: Princeton University Press.

Acemoglu, Daron, Simon Johnson, James Robinson, and Yunyong Thaicharoen. 2003. "Institutional Causes, Macroeconomic Symptoms: Volatility, Crises and Growth" *Journal of Monetary Economics*, vol. 50, no. 1, pp. 49–123.

Adams, Peter. 1991. *Odious Debts*. London: Earthscan Publications.

Adams, Richard. 2003. *Economic Growth, Inequality and Poverty: Findings from a New Data Set*. World Bank Policy Research Working Paper no. 2972, February. Washington, DC: World Bank.

Adelman, Irma and Cynthia Morris. 1967. *Politics and Economic Development*. Baltimore: Johns Hopkins University Press.

——. 1973. *Economic Growth and Social Equity in Developing Countries*. Stanford: Stanford University Press.

Agarwal, Bina. 1994. *A Field of One's Own: Gender and Land Rights in South Asia*. London: Cambridge University Press.

Agenor, Pierre-Richard. 2004. "Does Globalization Hurt the Poor?" *International Economics and Economic Policy*, vol. 1, pp. 21–51.

Aksoy, M. Ataman and John C. Beghin, eds. 2005. *Global Agricultural Trade and Developing Countries*. Washington, DC: The World Bank.

Akyuz, Yilmaz, William Milberg, and Robert Wade. 2006. "Developing Countries and the Collapse of the Doha Round: A Forum" *Challenge: The Journal of Economic Affairs*, vol. 49, no. 6, November–December, pp. 6–19.

Alesina, Alberto and David Dollar. 2000. "Who Gives Foreign Aid to Whom and Why?" *Journal of Economic Growth*, vol. 5, no. 1, pp. 33–63

Alesina, Alberto and Edward Glaeser. 2006. *Fighting Poverty in the US and Europe: A World of Difference*. New York: Oxford University Press.

Alesina, Alberto and Beatrice Weder. 2002. "Do Corrupt Governments Receive Less Foreign Aid?" *American Economic Review*, vol. 92, no. 4, September, pp. 1126–37.

Alexandraki, Katerina and Hans Peter Lankes. 2004. *The Impact of Preference Erosion on Middle-Income Developing Countries*. IMF Working Paper 04/169. Washington, DC: IMF.

Almond, Gabriel and Sidney Verba. 1963. *The Civic Culture*. Princeton, NJ: Princeton University Press.

Amsden, Alice. 1989. *Asia's Next Giant: South Korea and Late Industrialization*. New York: Oxford University Press.

Anderson, Kym. 2005. "On the Virtues of Multilateral Trade Negotiations" *The Economic Record*, vol. 81, no. 255, December, pp. 414–38.

Anderson, Kym and Will Martin, eds. 2005. *Agricultural Trade Reform and the Doha Development Agenda*. New York: Palgrave Macmillan

——. 2005b. "Agricultural Trade Reform and the Doha Development Agenda" *World Economy*, vol. 28, no. 9, pp. 1301–27.

Anderson, Kym and Paul Morris. 2000. "The Elusive Goal of Agricultural Trade Reform" *Cato Journal*, vol. 19, no. 3, Winter, pp. 385–96.

Apter, David. 1965. *The Politics of Modernization*. Chicago: University of Chicago Press.

Arslanalp, Serkan and Peter Blair Henry. 2005. "Is Debt Relief Efficient?" *The Journal of Finance*, vol. LX, no. 2, April, pp. 1017–51.

——. 2005a. "Helping the Poor Help Themselves: Debt Relief or Aid?" in Chris Jochnick and Fraser Preston, eds, *Sovereign Debt at the Crossroads: Challenges and Proposals for Resolving the Third World Debt Crisis*. New York: Oxford University Press, pp. 174–96.

——. 2006. "Debt Relief" *Journal of Economic Perspectives*, vol. 20, no. 1, Winter, pp. 207–20.

Artadi, Elsa and Xavier Sala-i-Martin. 2003. *The Economic Tragedy of the 20th Century: Growth in Africa*. NBER Working Paper no. 9865. Cambridge, MA: National Bureau of Economic Research.

Attanasio, Orazio and Miguel Szekely. 2001. *Portrait of the Poor: An Assets-Based Approach*. Washington, DC: Inter-American Development Bank.

Avelino, G., D. Brown, and W. Hunter. 2005. "The Effects of Capital Mobility, Trade Openness and Democracy on Social Spending in Latin America, 1980–1999" *American Political Science Review*, vol. 49, no. 3, pp. 625–41.

Avery, William. 1990. "The Origins of Debt Accumulation among LDCs in the World Political Economy" *The Journal of Developing Areas*, vol. 24, no. 2, pp. 503–22.

Azariadis, Costas and John Stachurski. 2005. "Poverty Traps" in Philippe Aghion and Steven Durlauf, eds, *Handbook of Economic Growth*. Amsterdam: North Holland.

Bagwell, Kyle and Robert Staiger. 2002. *The Economics of the World Trading System*. Cambridge, MA: MIT Press.

Baldwin, Robert. 2006. "Failure of the WTO Ministerial Conference at Cancun: Reasons and Remedies" *The World Economy*, vol. 29, no. 6, pp. 677–96.

Banerjee, Abhijit. 2006. "Making Aid Work – Effectively" *Boston Review*, vol. 34, no. 4, July, pp. 7–9.

Banerjee, Abhijit, Roland Benabou, and Dilip Mookherjee, eds. 2006. *Understanding Poverty*. New York: Oxford University Press.

Bardhan, Pranab. 1997. *The Role of Governance in Economic Development*. OECD: Development Centre.

——. 2004. *Scarcity, Conflicts and Cooperation: Essays in the Political and Institutional Economics of Development*. Cambridge, MA: MIT Press.

Barro, Robert. 1991. "Economic Growth in a Cross-Section of Countries" *Quarterly Journal of Economics*, vol. 56, no. 2, pp. 407–43.

——. 1996. *Getting It Right: Markets and Choices in a Free Society*. Cambridge, MA: MIT Press

——. 1998. *The Determinants of Economic Growth: A Cross-Country Empirical Study*. Cambridge, MA: MIT Press

——. 1999. "Determinants of Democracy" *Journal of Political Economy*, vol. 107, no. 6, December, pp. 158–83.

——. 2000. "Inequality and Growth in a Panel of Countries" *Journal of Economic Growth*, vol. 5, issue, 1, March, pp. 5–32.

——. 2001. "Human Capital and Growth" *American Economic Review*, vol. 91, no. 2, pp. 12–17.

Barton, John H., Judith Goldstein, Timothy Josling, and Richard Steinberg. 2005. *The Evolution of the Trade Regime*. Princeton, NJ: Princeton University Press.

Basu, Kaushik. 2000. *Prelude to Political Economy: A Study of the Social and Political Foundations of Economics*. New York: Oxford University Press.

Bates, Robert and Anne O. Krueger. 1993. *Political and Economic Interactions in Economic Policy Reform: Evidence from Eight Countries*. Cambridge, MA.: Blackwell.

Bauer, Peter T. 1972. *Dissent on Development: Studies and Debates in Development Economics*. London: Weidenfeld and Nicolson.

——. 1981. *Equality: The Third World Economic Delusion*. London: Methuen.

Bekaert, Geert, Campbell Harvey, and Christian Lundbald. 2001. *Does Financial Liberalization Spur Growth?* NBER Working Paper no. 8245. Cambridge, MA: National Bureau of Economic Research.

Ben-David, Dan and Michael B. Loewy. 1998. "Free Trade, Growth and Convergence" *Journal of Economic Growth*, vol. 3, pp. 43–170.

Berdell, John. 2002. *International Trade and Economic Growth in Open Economies*. Cheltenham, UK: Edward Elgar.

Berg, Andrew and Anne Krueger. 2003. *Trade, Growth and Poverty: A Selective Survey*. IMF Working Paper no. 03/30. Washington, DC: IMF.

Bergsten, Fred. ed. 2005. *The United States and the World Economy*. Washington, DC: Institute for International Economics.

Bernauer, Thomas. 2003. *Genes, Trade and Regulation: The Seeds of Conflict in Food Biotechnology*. Princeton, NJ: Princeton University Press.

Bernhard, William, J. Lawrence Broz, and William Clark. 2003. *The Political Economy of Monetary Institutions*. Cambridge, MA: MIT Press.

Besley, Timothy and Robin Burgess. 2003. "Halving Global Poverty" *Journal of Economic Perspectives*, vol. 17, no. 3, Summer, pp. 3–22.

Besley, Timothy and Louise Cord, eds. 2006. *Delivering on the Promise of Pro-Poor Growth: Insights and Lessons from Country Experiences*. Washington, DC: World Bank.

Bhagwati, Jagdish. 1995. "The New Thinking on Development" *Journal of Democracy*, vol. 6, no. 4, pp. 50–64.

——. 1998. "The Capital Myth: The Difference between Trade in Widgets and Dollars" *Foreign Affairs*, vol. 77, no. 3, May–June, pp. 7–12.

——. 2000. *The Wind of the Hundred Days: How Washington Mismanaged Globalization*. Cambridge, MA: MIT Press.

——. 2002. *Free Trade Today*. Princeton, NJ: Princeton University Press.

——. 2004. *In Defense of Globalization*. New York: Oxford University Press.

———. 2004a. "Don't Cry for Cancun" *Foreign Affairs*, vol. 83, no. 1, January–February, pp. 52–63.

Bhalla, Surjit. 2002. *Imagine There's No Country: Poverty, Inequality, and Growth in the Era of Globalization*, Washington, DC: Institute for International Economics.

Birdsall, Nancy. 2004. *Seven Deadly Sins: Reflections on Donor Failings*. CGD Working Paper no. 50, December. Washington, DC: Center for Global Development.

Birdsall, Nancy and Brian Deese. 2004. "Hard Currency" *Washington Monthly*, March, pp. 1–7.

Birdsall, Nancy and John Williamson with Brian Deese. 2002. *Delivering on Debt Relief: From IMF Gold to a New Aid Architecture*. Washington, DC: Institute for International Economics.

Birdsall, Nancy, Dani Rodrik, and Arvind Subramanian. 2005. "How to Help Poor Countries" *Foreign Affairs*, vol. 84, no. 4, July/August, pp. 136–52.

Birdsall, Nancy, Milan Vaishnav, and Robert Ayers. 2006. *Short of the Goal: U.S. Policy and Poorly Performing States*. Washington, DC: Center for Global Development.

Blanchard, Oliver and Andrei Shleifer. 2001. "Federalism with and without Political Centralization: China and Russia" *IMF Staff Papers*, no. 48, pp. 171–9.

Bloom, David E, David Canning, and Dean T. Jamison. 2004. "Health, Wealth and Welfare" *Finance and Development*, vol. 41, no. 1, March, pp. 10–15.

Blustein, Paul. 2005. "Group of Eight Forgives More Than $40 Billion" *Washington Post*, 11 June, available at www.washingtonpost.com/wpdyn/content/article/2005/06/11/AR2005061100561.html.

Boone, Peter. 1996. "Politics and Effectiveness of Foreign Aid" *European Economic Review*, vol. 42, no. 2, February, pp. 289–329.

Bordo, Michael D., Barry Eichengreen, and Douglas A. Irwin. 1999. *Is Globalization Today Really Different than Globalization a Hundred Years Ago?* NBER Working Paper no. 7195. Cambridge, MA: National Bureau of Economic Research, June.

Borlaug, Norman. 2003. "Science vs Hysteria" *The Wall Street Journal*, 22 January.

Boserup, Esther. 1965. *The Conditions of Agricultural Growth: The Economics of Agrarian Change under Population Pressure*. London: Allen and Unwin.

———. 1970. *Woman's Role in Economic Development*. London: Earthscan.

Bouet, A., J.C. Bureau, Y. Decreux, and S. Jean. 2005. "Multilateral Agricultural Trade Liberalization: The Constrasting Fortunes of Developing Countries in the Doha Round" *The World Economy*, vol. 28, no. 9, pp. 1329–54.

Boughton, James M. 2001. *Silent Revolution: The International Monetary Fund, 1979–1989*. Washington, DC: International Monetary Fund Publication Services.

Bouillon, Cesar, Carlos M. Jarque, and Marco Ferroni. 2005. *The Millennium Development Goals in Latin America and the Caribbean: Progress, Priorities and IDB Support for their Implementation*. Washington, DC: Inter-American Development Bank.

Bourguignon, François and Christian Morrisson. 2002. "Inequality among World Citizens: 1820–1992" *American Economic Review*, vol. 92, no. 4, pp. 727–44.

Brainard, Lael, Carol Graham, Nigel Purvis, Steven Radelet, and Gayle E. Smith. 2003. *The Other War: Global Poverty and the Millennium Challenge Account*. Washington, DC: Brookings Institution Press.

Brancati, Dawn. 2006. "Decentralization: Fueling the Fire or Dampening the Flames of Ethnic Conflict and Secessionism?" *International Security*, vol. 60, no. 3, pp. 651–85.

Bratton, Michael and Nicolas van de Walle. 1997. *Democratic Experiments in Africa: Regime Transitions in Comparative Perspective*. New York: Cambridge University Press.

Brautigam, Deborah. 1997. "Institutions, Economic Reform and Democratic Consolidation in Mauritius" *Comparative Politics*, vol. 30, no. 1, pp. 45–62.

——. 2000. *Aid Dependence and Governance*. Stockholm: Almqvist and Wiksell International.

Brautigam, Deborah and Steven Knack. 2004. "Foreign Aid, Institutions and Governance in Sub-Saharan Africa" *Economic Development and Cultural Change*, vol. 52, no. 1, January, pp. 255–85.

Brecher, Jeremy and Tim Costello. 1995. *Global Village or Global Pillage*. Boston: South End Press.

Broad, Robin. ed. 2002. *Global Backlash: Citizen Initiatives for a Just Economy*. New York: Rowman and Littlefield.

Brooks, Stephen. 2005. *Producing Security: Multinational Corporations, Globalization and the Changing Calculus of Conflict*. Princeton, NJ: Princeton University Press.

Bruno, Michael, Martin Ravallion, and Lyn Squire. 1998. "Equity and Growth in Developing Countries: Old and New Perspectives on the Policy Issues." in V. Tani and K.Y. Chu, eds. *Income Distribution and High Growth*. Cambridge, MA: MIT Press.

Bueno de Mesquita and Hilton Root, eds. 2002. *Governing for Prosperity*. New Haven: Yale University Press.

Bueno de Mesquita, B.A. Smith, R.M. Siverson, and J.D. Morrow. 2003. *The Logic of Political Survival*. Cambridge: MIT Press.

Bulir, Ales and Timothy D. Lane. 2002. *Aid and Fiscal Management*. IMF Working Paper no. 02/112, available at www.imf.org/external/pubs/ft/wp/2002/wp02112.

Bulow, Jeremy and Kenneth Rogoff. 1990. "Cleaning Up Third World Debt Without Getting Taken to the Cleaners" *Journal of Economic Perspectives*, vol. 48, no. 1, Winter, pp. 31–42.

Bureau, Jean-Christophe, Sebastien Jean, and Alan Matthews. 2006. "The Consequences of Agricultural Trade Liberalization for Developing Countries: Distinguishing between Genuine Benefits and False Hopes" *World Trade Review*, vol. 6, no. 2, pp. 225–49.

Burfisher, Mary, ed. 2003. *Agricultural Policy Reform in the WTO*. New York: Nova Science Publishers.

Burnside, Craig and David Dollar. 2000. "Aid, Policies and Growth" *American Economic Review*, vol. 90, no. 4, September, pp. 847–68.

——. 2004. *Aid Policies and Growth: Revisiting the Evidence*. World Bank Policy Research Working Paper no. 3251. Washington, DC: World Bank.

Burtless, Gary, Robert Z. Lawrence, Robert E. Litan, and Robert J. Shapiro. 1998. *Globaphobia: Confronting Fears about Open Trade*. Washington, DC: Brookings Institution.

Byman, Daniel. 2002. *Keeping the Peace: Lasting Solutions to Ethnic Conflict*. Baltimore, MD: Johns Hopkins University Press.

Cardoso, Fernando Henrique and Enzo Faletto. 1979. *Dependency and Development in Latin America*. Berkeley: University of California Press.

Carothers, Thomas. 1999. *Aiding Democracy Abroad: The Learning Curve*. Washington, DC: Carnegie Endowment for International Peace.

——. 2004. *Critical Mission: Essays on Democratic Promotion*. Washington, DC: Carnegie Endowment for International Peace.

——. 2007. "The Sequencing Fallacy" *Journal of Democracy*, vol. 18, no. 1, January, pp. 12–27.

Carr, Edward H. 1961. *What is History?* London: Macmillan.

Cassen, Robert. 1991. *Does Aid Work? Report to an International Task Force*. Oxford, UK: Clarendon Press.

Center for Global Development. 2004. *Rich World, Poor World: A Guide to Global Development*. Washington, DC: Center for Global Development.

Center for International Comparisons. 2004. *Penn World Tables*. Philadelphia: University of Pennsylvania.

Cesarano, Filippo. 2005. *Monetary Theory and Bretton Woods: The Construction of an International Monetary Order*. New York: Cambridge University Press.

Chakravarti, Ashok. 2005. *Aid, Institutions and Development*. Cheltenham, UK: Edward Elgar.

Chambers, Robert. 1983. *Rural Development: Putting the Last First*. New York: Longman.

Chan, Sylvia. 2002. *Liberalism, Democracy and Development*. New York: Cambridge University Press.

Chang, Ha Joon. 2002. *Kicking Away the Ladder: Development Strategy in Historical Perspective*. London: Anthem Press.

Chen, Shaohua and Yan Wang. 2001. *China's Growth and Poverty Reduction: Trends between 1990 and 1999*. Policy Research Working Paper 2651. Washington, DC: World Bank.

Chenery, Hollis and Alan M. Strout. 1966. "Foreign Assistance and Economic Development" *American Economic Review*, vol. 56, September, pp. 679–733.

Chenery, Hollis and Moshe Syrquin. 1975. *Patterns of Development, 1950–1970*. London: Oxford University Press.

Chenery, Hollis, Montek Ahluwalia, Clive Bell, G. Duloy, and Richard Jolly. 1974. *Redistribution with Growth*. London: Oxford University Press.

Cheru, Fantu. 1989. *The Silent Revolution in Africa: Debt, Development and Democracy*. London: Zed Press.

———. 2006. "Playing Games with African Lives: The G7 Debt Relief Strategy and the Politics of Indifference" in Chris Jochnick and Fraser Preston, eds, *Sovereign Debt at the Crossroads: Challenges and Proposals for Resolving the Third World Debt Crisis*. New York: Oxford University Press, pp. 35–54.

Chesterman, Simon. Michael Ignatieff, and Ramesh Thakur, eds. 2005. *Making States Work: State Failure and the Crisis of Governance*. New York: United Nations University Press.

Chhibber, Pradeep, Sandeep Shastri, and Richard Sisson. 2004. "Federal Arrangements and the Provision of Public Goods in India" *Asian Survey*, vol. 44, no. 3, May/June, pp. 339–52.

Chong, Alberto. 2004. "Inequality, Democracy, and Persistence: Is There a Political Kuznets Curve?" *Economics and Politics*, vol. 16, July, pp. 69–81.

Christensen, Jakob. 2004. *Domestic Debt Markets in Sub-Saharan Africa*. IMF Working Paper no. 04/46. Washington, DC: IMF.

Christiaensen, Luc and Lionel Demery. 2007. *Down to Earth: Agriculture and Poverty Reduction in Africa*. Washington, DC: World Bank.

Clark, John. 1991. *Democratizing Development: The Role of Voluntary Organizations*. London: Earthscan.

Cleaver, Kevin. 2004. "Rural Investment, Key to India's Growth" available at web.worldbank.org/WBSITE/EXTERNAL/NEWS/O (accessed 20 February 2004).

Clemens, Michael, Steven Radelet, and Rikhil Bhavnani. 2004. *Counting Chickens When They Hatch: The Short Term Effects of Aid on Growth*. CGD Working Paper no. 44. Washington, DC: Center for Global Development.

Cline, William R. 1995. *International Debt Reexamined*. Washington, DC: Institute for International Economics.

——. 2003. "Trading Up: Trade Policy and Global Poverty" *CGD Brief*, vol. 2, no. 4, September. Washington, DC: Center for Global Development.

——. 2004. *Trade Policy and Global Poverty*. Washington, DC: Institute for International Economics.

Cline, William and John Williamson. 2005. "Fostering Development" in C. Fred Bergsten, ed., *The United States and the World Economy: Foreign Economic Policy for the Next Decade*. Washington, DC: Institute for International Economics, pp. 409–27.

Cohen, Benjamin. 1998. *The Geography of Money*. Ithaca: Cornell University Press.

Cohen, Daniel. 2006. *Globalization and Its Enemies*. Cambridge, MA: MIT Press.

Collier, Paul and David Dollar. 2002. "Aid Allocation and Poverty Reduction" *European Economic Review*, vol. 46, no. 1, pp. 1475–500.

Commission for Africa. 2005. *Our Common Interests: Report of the Commission for Africa*. London: UK Department for International Development (also known as the Blair Report).

Conca, Ken. 2000. "The WTO and the Undermining of Global Environmental Governance" *Review of International Political Economy*, vol. 7, no. 3, Autumn, pp. 484–94.

Corden, Max. 1984. "Booming Sector and Dutch Disease Economics: Survey and Consolidation" *Oxford Economic Papers*, vol. 36, November, pp. 359–80.

Cornia, Giovanni, Richard Jolly, and Frances Stewart. 1987. *Adjustment with a Human Face*. Oxford: Clarendon Press.

Correia, Maria and Ian Bannon. 2006. *The Other Half of Gender: Men's Issues in Development*. Washington, DC: World Bank.

Crook, Richard and James Manor. 1994. *Enhancing Participation and Institutional Performance: Democratic Decentralization in South Asia and West Africa*. London: Overseas Development Administration.

Croome, John. 1998. *Reshaping the World Trading System: A History of the Uruguay Round*. The Hague: Kluwer Law International.

Dahl, Robert. 1971. *Polyarchy: Participation and Opposition*. New Haven, CT: Yale University Press.

——. 1989. *Democracy and Its Critics*. New Haven, CT: Yale University Press.

——. 2000. *On Democracy*, New Haven, CT: Yale Nota Bene Books.

——. 2005. "What Political Institutions Does Large-Scale Democracy Require?" *Political Science Quarterly*, vol. 120, no. 2, pp. 187–97.

Dasgupta, Pratha. 1993. *An Inquiry into Well-Being and Destitution*. New York: Oxford University Press.

Datt, Gaurav and Martin Ravallion, 1998. "Farm Productivity and Rural Poverty in India" *Journal of Development Studies*, vol. 34, no. 4, pp. 62–85.

Datta, Swapan and Howarth Bouis. 2000. "Application of Biotechnology to Improving the Nutritional quality of Rice" *Food and Nutrition Bulletin*, vol. 21, no. 4, pp. 451–6.

De Geus, Marius. 1999. *Ecological Utopias: Envisioning the Sustainable Society*. Utrecht, Netherlands: International Books.

——. 2003. *The End of Over-Consumption*. Utrecht, Netherlands: International Books.

De Soto, Hernando. 1989. *The Other Path: The Invisible Revolution in the Third World*. New York: Harper and Row.

——. 2000. *The Mystery of Capital: Why Capitalism Triumphs in the West and Fails Everywhere Else*. New York: Basic Books.

Deardorff, Alan and Robert M. Stern. 2002. "What You Should Know About Globalization and the World Trade Organization" *Review of International Economics*, vol. 10, no. 3, pp. 404–23.

Deaton, Angus, 2003. "Adjusted Indian Poverty Estimates for 1999–2000" *Economic and Political Weekly*, 25 January, pp. 322–26.

Deininger, Klaus and Lyn Squire. 1996. "A New Data Set Measuring Income Inequality" *World Bank Economic Review*, vol. 10, no. 3, pp. 565–91.

———. 1998. "New Ways of Looking at Old Issues: Inequality and Growth" *Journal of Development Economics*, vol. 57, no. 2, pp. 259–87.

Demirguc-Kunt, Asli and Enrica Detragiache. 1998. "The Determinants of Banking Crises in Developing and Developed Countries" *International Monetary Fund Staff Papers*, no. 45, pp. 81–109.

Dervis, Kemal. 2005. *A Better Globalization: Legitimacy, Governance and Reform.* Washington, DC: Center for Global Development.

Deutsch, Karl. 1961. "Social Mobilization and Political Development" *American Political Science Review*, September, pp. 493–514.

Devarajan, Shanta and Vinaya Swaroop. 1998. "The Implications of Foreign Aid Fungibility for Development Assistance" Washington, DC: World Bank, Development Research Group, October.

Devarajan, Shanta, David Dollar, and Torgny Holmgren, eds. 2001. *Aid and Reform in Africa: Lessons from Ten Case Studies.* Washington, DC: World Bank.

Dhar, B. 2003. *Globalization and the International Governance of Modern Biotechnology: Regulating Biotechnology in India.* Brighton: Institute of Development Studies.

Diamond, Jared. 1997. *Guns, Germs and Steel: The Fate of Human Societies.* New York: W.W. Norton.

———. 2004. *Collapse: How Societies Choose to Fail or Succeed.* New York: Viking.

Diamond, Larry. 1999. *Developing Democracy: Toward Consolidation,* Baltimore, MD: Johns Hopkins University Press.

———. 2002. "Elections without Democracy: Thinking about Hybrid Regimes," *Journal of Democracy*, vol. 13, no. 2, April, pp. 21–36.

———. 2003. "Universal Democracy?" *Policy Review*, no. 119, June–July, pp. 3–25.

Diamond, Larry, Juan Linz, and Seymour M. Lipset, eds. 1988/1989. *Democracy in Developing Countries.* Boulder: Lynne Rienner.

———. 1990. *Politics in Developing Countries: Comparing Experiences with Democracy.* Boulder: Lynne Rienner.

Diaz-Bonilla, Eugenio and Ashok Gulati. 2003. "Developing Countries and the WTO Negotiations" 2002–2003 IFPRI Annual Report Essays, available at www.ifpri.org/pubs/books/ar2002/ar2002_essays.htm.

Dichter, Thomas. 2003. *Despite Good Intentions: Why Development Assistance to the Third World has Failed.* Amherst: University of Massachusetts Press.

Dickson, Bruce. 2003. *Red Capitalists in China: The Party, Private Entrepreneurs, and Prospects for Political Change.* New York: Cambridge University Press.

Djankov, Simeon. Jose G. Montalvo, and Marta Reynal-Querol. 2006. "Does Foreign Aid Help?" *Cato Journal*, vol. 26, no. 1, Winter, pp. 1–28.

Dollar, David. 1992. "Outward Oriented Developing Economies Do Really Grow More Rapidly: Evidence from 95 LDCs, 1976–85" *Economic Development and Cultural Change*, vol. 40, no. 3, pp. 523–44.

———. 2005. "Globalization, Poverty and Inequality since 1980" *The World Bank Research Observer*, vol. 20, no. 2, Fall, pp. 146–75.

Dollar, David and Paul Collier. 2001. *Globalization, Growth and Poverty: Building an Inclusive World Economy.* New York: Oxford University Press.

Dollar, David and Aart Kraay. 2002. "Growth is Good for the Poor" *Journal of Economic Growth*, vol. 7, no. 3, pp. 195–225.

——. 2003. "Institutions, Trade and Growth" *Journal of Monetary Economics*, vol. 50, January, pp. 133–62.

——. 2004. "Trade, Growth and Poverty" *Economic Journal*, vol. 114, no. 493, pp. F22–F49.

Donnelly, Jack. 1984. "Human Rights and Development: Complementary and Competing Concerns", *World Politics*, vol. 36, no. 2, pp. 255–84.

Dornbusch, Rudiger. 2000. *Keys to Prosperity: Free Markets, Sound Money, and a Bit of Luck*. Cambridge, MA: MIT Press.

Drezner. Daniel. 2006. *All Politics is Global*. Princeton, NJ: Princeton University Press.

Easterly, William. 1999. "The Ghost of Financing Gap: Testing the Growth Model of the International Financial Institutions" *Journal of Development Economics*, vol. 60, no. 2, pp. 423–38.

——. 2000. "Can Institutions Resolve Ethnic Conflict?" Washington, DC: World Bank Institute.

——. 2001. *The Elusive Quest for Growth: Economists' Adventures and Misadventures in the Tropics*. Cambridge, MA: MIT Press.

——. 2003. "Can Foreign Aid Buy Growth?" *Journal of Economic Perspectives*, vol. 17, no. 3, pp. 23–48.

——. 2006. *The White Man's Burden: How the West's Efforts to Aid the Rest Have Done So Much Ill and So Little Good*. New York: Penguin.

Easterly, William and Ross Levine. 1997. "Africa's Growth Tragedy: Policies and Ethnic Divisions" *Quarterly Journal of Economics*, 112, no. 4, November, pp. 1203–50.

——. 2003. "Tropics, Germs and Crops: How Endowments Influence Economic Development" *Journal of Monetary Economics*, vol. 50, no. 1, January, pp. 3–39.

Easterly, William, Ross Levine, and David Roodman. 2004. *New Data, New Doubts: A Comment on Burnside and Dollar's Aid, Policies and Growth*. NBER Working Paper no. 9846. Cambridge, MA: National Bureau of Economic Research.

Eichengreen, Barry. 1991. *Globalizing Capital*. Princeton, NJ: Princeton University Press.

——. 2000. "Taming Capital Flows" *World Development*, vol. 28, no. 6, pp. 1105–116.

——. 2002. "Capitalizing on Globalization" *Asian Development Review*, vol. 19, no. 1, pp. 1–46.

——. 2004. *Capital Flows and Crises*. Cambridge, MA: MIT Press.

Eifert, Benn, Alan Gelb, and Nils Borje Tallroth. 2003. "Managing Oil Wealth" *Finance and Development*, vol. 40, no. 1, March, pp. 40–45.

Eizenstat, Stuart, John Edward Porter, and Jeremy M. Weinstein. 2005. "Rebuilding Weak States" *Foreign Affairs*, vol. 84, no. 1, January/February, pp. 134–46.

Elliott, Kimberly Ann. 2005. "Big Sugar and the Political Economy of US Agricultural Policy" *CGD Brief*. Washington, DC: Center for Global Development, April, pp. 1–7.

——. 2006. *Delivering on Doha: Far Trade and the Poor*. Washington, DC: Institute for International Economics.

Encarnacion, Omar. 2006. "Civil Society Reconsidered" *Comparative Politics*, vol. 38, no. 3, April, pp. 357–76.

Epaulard, Anne. 2003. *Macroeconomic Performance and Poverty Reduction*. IMF Working Paper no. 03/72. Washington, DC: IMF.

Erk, Jan G. 2006. "Does Federalism Really Matter?" *Comparative Politics*, vol. 39, no. 1, pp. 103–22.

Escobar, Arturo. 1994. *Encountering Development: The Making and Unmaking of the Third World*. Princeton, NJ: Princeton University Press.

Estache, Antonio and Quentin Wodon. 2007. *Infrastructure and Poverty in Sub-Saharan Africa*. Washington, DC: World Bank.

European Commission. 2005. *EU Strategy for Africa: Towards a Euro-African Pact to Accelerate Africa's Development*. Communication from the Commission to the Council, the European Parliament and the European Economic and Social Committee. Brussels: European Commission, October.

Evenett, Simon and Bernard Hoekman 2005. *Economic Development and Multilateral Trade Cooperation*. London: Palgrave Macmillan.

Evenson, Robert E. and Douglas Gollin. 2003. "Assessing the Impact of the Green Revolution, 1960–2000" *Science*, vol. 30, no. 5620, 2 May, pp. 758–63.

Fabiosa, Jay, John Beghin, Stephane de Cara, Amani Elobeid, Cheng Fang, Mural Isik, Holger Matthey, Alexander Saak, Pat Westhoff, D. Scott Brown, Brian Willott, Daniel Madison, Seth Meyer, and John Kruse. 2006. "The Doha Round of the World Trade Organization and Agricultural Markets Liberalization: Impacts on Developing Economies" *Review of Agricultural Economics*, vol. 27, no. 3, pp. 317–35.

Fan, Shenggen, Linxiu Zhang, and Neetha Rao. 2004. *Public Expenditure, Growth and Poverty Reduction in Rural Uganda*. International Food Policy Research Institute (IFPRI) Discussion Paper no. 4. Washington, DC: IFPRI.

FAO (Food and Agriculture Organization). 2003. *WTO Agreement on Agriculture: The Implementation Experience, Developing Country Case Studies*. Rome: FAO.

——. 2004. *The State of Food Insecurity in the World 2004*. Rome: FAO.

——. 2004a. *The State of Food and Agriculture: 2003–2004*. Rome: FAO.

Feenstra, R.C. 2004. *Advanced International Trade: Theory and Evidence*. Princeton, NJ: Princeton University Press.

Feinberg, Richard, Carlos H. Waisman, and Leon Zamosc, eds. 2006. *Civil Society and Democracy in Latin America*. New York: Palgrave Macmillan.

Feng, Yi. 2003. *Democracy, Governance and Economic Performance*. Cambridge, MA: MIT Press.

Ferranti, David de, Guillermo Perry, Daniel Lederman, Alberto Valdes, and William Foster. 2005. *Beyond the City: The Rural Contribution to Development*. Washington, DC: World Bank.

Feyziouglu, Tarhan, Vinaya Swaroop, and Min Zhu. 1998. "A Panel Data Analysis of the Fungibility of Foreign Aid" *World Bank Economic Review*, vol. 12, no. 1, pp. 29–58.

Fields, Gary. 2001. *Distribution and Development: A New Look and the Developing World*. Cambridge, MA: MIT Press.

Finger, J.M. and P. Schuler. 2001. "Implementation of Uruguay Round Commitments: The Development Challenge" in Bernard Hoekman and Will Martin, eds, *Developing Countries and the WTO: A Pro-Active Agenda*. Oxford: Blackwell.

Finger, J.M. and L.A. Winters. 2002. "Reciprocity in the WTO" in Bernard Hoekman, A. Matoo and P. English, eds, *Development, Trade and the WTO: A Handbook*. Washington, DC: World Bank.

Fischer, Stanley. 2004. *IMF Essays from a Time of Crisis: The International Financial System, Stabilization, and Development*. Cambridge, MA: MIT Press.

Flanagan, Robert. 2006. *Globalization and Labor Conditions: Working Conditions and Worker Rights in a Global Economy*. New York: Oxford University Press.

Fogel, Richard William. 2004. *The Escape from Hunger and Premature Death, 1700–2100: Europe, America and the Third World*. New York: Cambridge University Press.

Foster, James and Miguel Szekely. 2000. "How Good is Growth?" *Asian Development Review*, vol. 18, no. 2, pp. 59–73.

Frankel, Jeffrey and David Romer. 1999. "Does Trade Cause Growth?" *American Economic Review*, vol. 89, no. 3, pp. 379–99.

Frieden, Jeffrey. 2006. *Global Capitalism: Its Fall and Rise in the Twentieth Century*. New York: W.W. Norton.

Friedman, Milton. 1962. *Capitalism and Freedom*. Chicago: University of Chicago Press.

Friedman, Thomas. 1999. *The Lexus and the Olive Tree*. New York: Farrar, Straus and Giroux.

——. 2005. *The World is Flat: A Brief History of the Twenty-First Century*. New York: Farrar, Straus and Giroux.

Fukuyama, Francis. ed. 2004. "The Imperative of State-Building" *Journal of Democracy*, vol. 15, no. 2, April, pp. 17–31.

——. 2005. "Stateness First" *Journal of Democracy*, vol. 16, no. 1, January, pp. 84–8.

——. 2006. *Nation-Building: Beyond Afghanistan and Iraq*. Baltimore, MD: Johns Hopkins University Press.

Furubotn, Eirik and Svetozar Pejovich, eds. 1973. *The Economics of Property Rights*. Cambridge, MA: Ballinger.

Gautam, Madhur. 2003. *Debt Relief for the Poorest: An OED Review of the HIPC Initiative*. Washington, DC: World Bank.

George, Abraham. 2005. *India Untouched: The Forgotten Face of Rural Poverty*. New York: Writers Collective.

George, Susan. 1998. *A Fate Worse than Debt: The World Financial Crisis and the Poor*. New York: Grove Press.

Gerring, John, Philip Bond, William T. Barndt, and Carola Moreno. 2005. "Democracy and Economic Growth: A Historical Perspective" *World Politics*, vol. 57, April, 323–64.

Gerschenkron, Alexander. 1963. *Economic Backwardness in Historical Perspective*. Cambridge, MA: Harvard University Press.

Ghura, Dhaneshwar, Carlos A. Leite, and Charalambos Tsangarides. 2002. *Is Growth Enough? Macroeconomic Policy and Poverty Reduction*. IMF Working Paper no. 02/118. Washington, DC: IMF.

Gilbert, Christopher and David Vines, 2000. eds. *The World Bank: Structure and Policies*. New York: Cambridge University Press.

Gilman, Nils. 2003. *Mandarins of the Future: Modernization Theory in the Cold War*. Baltimore, MD: Johns Hopkins University Press.

Gilpin, Robert. 1987. *The Political Economy of International Relations*. Princeton, NJ: Princeton University Press.

——. 2000. *The Challenge of Global Capitalism: The World Economy and its Discontents*. Princeton, NJ: Princeton University Press.

——. 2001. *Global Political Economy: Understanding the International Economic Order*. Princeton, NJ: Princeton University Press.

Giovanni, Federico. 2005. *Feeding the World: An Economic History of Agriculture, 1800–2000*. Princeton, NJ: Princeton University Press.

Glaeser, Bernhard, ed. 1987. *The Green Revolution Revisited: Critique and Alternatives*. London: Allen and Unwin.

Goldin, Ian and Kenneth Reinert. 2006. *Globalization for Development: Trade, Finance, Aid Migration and Policy*. Washington, DC: World Bank.

Gourevitch, Peter. 1986. *Politics in Hard Times: Competitive Responses to International Economic Crises*. Ithaca, NY: Cornell University Press.

Grant, Richard and Jan Nijman, eds. 1998. *The Global Crisis in Foreign Aid.* New York: Syracuse University Press.

Greenhill, Romilly, Ann Pettifor, Henry Northover, and Ashok Sinha. 2003. *Did the G8 Drop the Debt?* London: Jubilee Debt Campaign.

Grey, David and Claudia Sadoff. 2006. *Water, Wealth and Poverty.* Washington, DC: World Bank.

Griffin, Keith. 2003. "Economic Globalization and Institutions of Global Governance" *Development and Change*, vol. 34, no. 5, pp. 789–807.

Gruber, Lloyd. 2000. *Ruling the World: Power Politics and the Rise of Supranational Institutions.* Princeton, NJ: Princeton University Press.

Guest, Robert. 2004. *The Shackled Continent: Power, Corruption and African Lives.* Washington, DC: Smithsonian Books.

Gurr, Ted Robert. 2000. *People Versus States: Minorities at Risk in the New Century.* Washington, DC: United States Institute of Peace Press.

Hadenius, Axel, ed. 2003. *Decentralization and Democratic Governance: Experiences from India, Bolivia and South Africa.* Uppsala, Sweden: Almqvist and Wiksell International.

Haggard, Stephan and Robert Kaufman. 1995. *The Political Economy of Democratic Transitions.* Princeton: Princeton University Press.

Hall, Robert E. and Charles I. Jones. 1999. "Why Do Some Countries Produce So Much More Output per Worker than Others?" *Quarterly Journal of Economics*, vol. 114, no. 1, February, pp. 84–116.

Halperin, Morton. Joseph T. Siegle and Michael Weinstein. 2005. *The Democracy Advantage: How Democracies Promote Prosperity and Peace.* New York: Routledge.

Hancock, Graham. 1989. *Lords of Poverty: The Power, Prestige and Corruption of the International Aid Business.* New York: Atlantic Monthly Press.

Hanlon, Joseph. 1998. *Dictators and Debt.* London: Jubilee 2000, available at www.jubileeresearch.org/analysis/reports/dictatorsreport.htm.

——. 2006. "Defining Illegitimate Debt: When Creditors should be Liable for Improper Loans" in Chris Jochnick and Fraser Preston, eds, *Sovereign Debt at the Crossroads: Challenges and Proposals for Resolving the Third World Debt Crisis.* New York: Oxford University Press, pp. 109–31.

Hanson, Gordon. 2005. *Globalization, Labor Income and Poverty in Mexico.* NBER Working Paper no. 11027. Cambridge, MA: NBER.

Hathaway, D. and M. Ingco. 1996. "Agricultural Liberalization and the Uruguay Round" in Will Martin and Alan Winters, eds, *The Uruguay Round and the Developing Countries.* New York: Cambridge University Press.

Hausler, Gerd. 2002. "The Globalization of Finance" *Finance and Development*, vol. 39, no. 1, March, pp. 10–12.

Hayami, Yujiro and Vernon Ruttan. 1985. *Agricultural Development: An International Perspective.* Baltimore, MD: Johns Hopkins University Press.

Hayek, Friedrich von. 1944. *The Road to Serfdom.* Chicago: University of Chicago Press.

Hayter, Theresa and Catherine Watson. 1985. *Aid: Rhetoric and Reality.* London: Pluto Press.

Heinisch, Elinor Lynn. 2006. "West Africa versus the United States on Cotton Subsidies: How, Why and What Next?" *Journal of Modern African Studies*, vol. 44, no. 2, pp. 251–74.

Heitger, Bernhard. 2004. "Property Rights and the Wealth of Nations: A Cross-Country Study" *Cato Journal*, vol. 23, no. 3, Winter, pp. 381–402.

Held, David and Anthony McGrew, eds. 2000. *The Global Transformations Reader*. Oxford: Polity Press.

Heller, Patrick. 2001. "Moving the State: The Politics of Democratic Decentralization in Kerala, South Africa, and Porto Alegre" *Politics and Society*, vol. 29, no. 1, March, pp. 131–63.

Hellman, Joel. 1998. "Winners Take All: The Politics of Partial Reform in Post-Communist Transitions" *World Politics*, vol. 50, no. 2, January, pp. 205–20.

Helpman, Elhanan. 2004. *The Mystery of Economic Growth*. Cambridge: Belknap.

Hertz, Noreena. 2004. *The Debt Threat: How Debt is Destroying the Developing World*. New York: HarperBusiness.

Heston, Alan, Robert Summers, and Bettina Aten. 2002. Penn World Table, version 6.1., University of Pennsylvania, Center for International Comparisons (October)

Hills, Carla. 2005. "WTO: Toward the Hong Kong, China Ministerial and Beyond" *Asian Development Review*, vol. 22, no. 1, pp. 1–11.

Hirschman, Albert. 1970. *Exit, Voice and Loyalty: Responses to Decline in Firms, Organizations and States*. Cambridge, MA: Harvard University Press.

Hoekman, Bernard. 2002. "Strengthening the Global Trade Architecture for Development" *World Trade Review*, vol. 1, March, pp. 23–46.

Hoekman, Bernard, Aaditya Mattoo, and Philip English, eds. 2002. *Development, Trade and the WTO: A Handbook*. Washington, DC: World Bank.

Horowitz, Donald. 1985. *Ethnic Groups in Conflict*. Berkeley: University of California Press.

——. 1991. *A Democratic South Africa? Constitutional Engineering in a Divided Society*. Berkeley: University of California Press.

——. 1993. "Democracy in Divided Societies" *Journal of Democracy*, vol. 4, no. 4, October, pp. 18–38.

Hufbauer, Gary Clyde and Jeffrey J. Schott. 2006. "The Doha Round after Hong Kong" *Policy Briefs in International Economics*, no. PBO6–2. Washington, DC: Institute for International Economics, February.

Huntington, Samuel. 1999. *The Third Wave: Democratization in the Late Twentieth Century*. Norman, OK: University of Oklahoma Press.

Huntington, Samuel and Joan Nelson. 1968. *Political Order in Changing Societies*. New Haven: Yale University Press.

——. 1976. *No Easy Choice: Political Participation in Developing Countries*. Cambridge, MA: Harvard University Press.

IFPRI (International Food Policy Research Institute). 2002. *Ending Hunger in Africa: Only the Small Farmer Can Do It*. Policy Brief, Washington, DC: IFPRI,

——. 2002a. *Green Revolution: Curse or Blessing?*. Policy Brief, Washington, DC: IFPRI.

——. 2005. "A Safety Net with Investments in Children" *IFPRI Forum*, March.

IMF (International Monetary Fund). 2003. *Debt Sustainability in Low-Income Countries – Towards a Forward-Looking Strategy*. Policy Development and Review Department. Washington, DC: IMF, March.

——. 2005. "What Does the Future hold for Microfinance" *IMF Survey*, vol. 34, no. 5, 21 March, pp. 66–80.

——. 2006. *The Multilateral Debt Relief Initiative: A Factsheet*. Washington, DC: IMF, November.

IMF-IDA. 2003. *Enhanced HIPC Initiative – Creditor Participation Issues*. Washington, DC: International Monetary Fund and International Development Association, 8 April.

——. 2004. *Heavily Indebted Poor Countries (HIPC) Initiative – Statistical Update.* Washington, DC: International Monetary Fund and International Development Association, 31 March.

Ingco, Melinda and John D. Nash, eds. 2004. *Agriculture and the WTO: Creating a Trading System for Development.* New York: Oxford University Press.

Irwin, Douglas. 2002. *Free Trade under Fire.* Princeton, NJ: Princeton University Press.

Jackman, R.W. 1973. "On the Relation of Economic Development to Democratic Performance" *American Journal of Political Science*, vol. 17, no. 3, pp. 611–21.

Jackson, Robert. 1990. *Quasi-States: Sovereignty, International Relations and the Third World.* New York: Cambridge University Press.

James, Harold. 1996. *International Monetary Cooperation since Bretton Woods.* New York: Oxford University Press.

Jawara, Fatoumata and Aileen Kwa. 2003. *Behind the Scenes at the WTO: The Real World of International Trade Negotiations.* London: Zed Press.

Jayachandran, Seema and Michael Kremer. 2002. *Odious Debt,* Harvard University Working Paper. Cambridge, MA: Harvard University Press.

——. 2006. "Odious Debt" in Chris Jochnick and Fraser Preston, eds, *Sovereign Debt at the Crossroads: Challenges and Proposals for Resolving the Third World Debt Crisis.* New York: Oxford University Press, pp. 215–25.

Jensen, Michael Friss and Peter Gibbon. 2007. "Africa and the WTO Doha Round: An Overview" *Development Policy Review*, vol. 25, no. 1, pp. 5–24.

Jochnick, Chris and Fraser Preston, eds, 2006. *Sovereign Debt at the Crossroads: Challenges and Proposals for Resolving the Third World Debt Crisis.* New York: Oxford University Press.

Johnson, Chalmers. 1982. *MITI and the Japanese Miracle: The Growth of Industrial Policy 1925–1975.* Stanford: Stanford University Press.

——. 1987. "Political Institutions and Economic Performance" in Frederick Deyo, ed., *The Political Economy of New Asian Industrialism.* Ithaca, NY: Cornell University Press.

Johnston, Bruce and Peter Kilby. 1975. *Agriculture and Structural Transformation: Economic Strategies in Late-Developing Countries.* New York: Oxford University Press.

Kahl, Colin H. 2006. *States, Scarcity and Civil Strife in the Developing World.* Princeton, NJ: Princeton University Press.

Kakwani, Nanak and Ernesto Pernia. 2000. "What is Pro-Poor Growth?" *Asian Development Review*, vol. 18, pp. 1–16.

Kanbur, Ravi and Lyn Squire, 2000. "The Evolution of Thinking about Poverty: Exploring the Interactions" in Gerald M. Meier and Joseph E. Stiglitz, eds, *Frontiers of Development Economics: The Future in Perspective.* New York: Oxford University Press, pp. 183–226.

Kapstein, Ethan. 1999. *Sharing the Wealth: Workers and the World Economy.* New York: W.W. Norton.

Karl, Terry and Philippe Schmitter. 1991. "What Democracy Is ... and Is Not" *Journal of Democracy*, vol. 2, no. 3, Summer, pp. 75–86.

Katzenstein, Peter. 1984. *Corporatism and Change: Austria, Switzerland and the Politics of Industry.* Ithaca, NY: Cornell University Press.

Kaufman, Chaim. 1996. "Possible and Impossible Solutions to Ethnic Civil Wars" *International Security*, vol. 20, no. 4, pp. 133–75.

Kaufmann, Daniel and Aart Kraay, 2003. "Governance Redux: The Empirical Challenge" *Global Competitiveness Report*, Geneva: World Economic Forum.

Kay, John. 2004. *The Truth about Markets: Why Some Nations are Rich but Most Remain Poor*. New York: HarperCollins.

Keck, Margaret and Kathryn Sikkink. 1998. *Activists Beyond Borders*. Ithaca, NY: Cornell University Press.

Keohane, Robert. 1984. *After Hegemony: Cooperation and Discord in the World Political Economy*. Princeton, NJ: Princeton University Press.

———. 2002. *Power and Governance in a Partially Globalized World*. New York: Routledge.

Killick, Tony. 1998. *Aid and the Political Economy of Policy Change*. London: Routledge.

Kitschelt, Herbert. 2003. "Accounting for Post-communist Regime Diversity: What Counts as a Good Cause?" in Grzegorz Ekiert and Stephen E. Hanson, eds, *Capitalism and Democracy in Central and Eastern Europe: Assessing the Legacy of Communist Rule*. New York: Cambridge University Press.

Kloppenburg, J.R.J. 2004. *First the Seed: The Political Economy of Plant Biotechnology, 1492–2000*. Madison, WI: University of Wisconsin Press.

Kohli, Atul. 1986. "Democracy and Development" in John Lewis and Valeriana Kallab, eds, *Development Strategies Reconsidered*, New Brunswick: Transaction Books.

Kraay, Aart. 2004. *When is Growth Pro-Poor? Cross Country Evidence*. IMF Working Paper no. 04/47. Washington, DC: International Monetary Fund.

Kraay, Aart and Vikram Nehru, 2004. *When is External Debt Sustainable*. World Bank Policy Research Working Paper no. 3200, February. Washington, DC: World Bank.

Krugman, Paul. 1988. "Financing versus Forgiving a Debt Overhang" *Journal of Development Economics*, vol. 29, no. 1–2, pp. 253–68.

———. 1989. "Market-Based Debt Reduction Schemes" in Jacob Frenkel, Michael Dooley, and Peter Wickham, eds, *Analytical Issues in Debt*. Washington, DC: IMF, pp. 258–78.

———. 1998. "Saving Asia: It's Time to Get Radical" *Fortune*, vol. 138, no. 5, 7 September, pp. 74–80.

———. 1999. *The Return of Depression Economics*. New York: W.W. Norton.

Krugman, Paul and Maurice Obstfeld. 2002. *International Economics: Theory and Policy*. 6th edition. Reading, MA: Addison-Wesley.

Kuper, Andrews. 2004. *Democracy beyond Borders: Justice and Representation in Global Institutions*. New York: Oxford University Press.

Kurtz, Marcus J. 2004. *Free Market Democracy and the Chilean and Mexican Countryside*. New York: Cambridge University Press.

Kuznets, Simon. 1955. "Economic Growth and Income Inequality" *American Economic Review*, vol. 49, no. 1, March, pp. 1–28.

———. 1963. "Quantitative Aspects of the Economic Growth of Nations: Distribution of Income by Size" *Economic Development and Cultural Change*, January, Part 2, pp. 1–80.

———. 1966. *Modern Economic Growth: Rate, Structure and Spread*. New Haven, CT: Yale University Press.

Kymlicka, Will. 1998. "Is Federalism a Viable Alternative to Secessionism?" in Percy B. Lehning, ed, *Theories of Secessionism*. New York: Routledge, pp. 111–50.

Lairson, Thomas and David Skidmore. 2003. *International Political Economy: The Struggle for Power and Wealth*. Belmont, CA: Thomson Wadsworth.

Lake, David and Matthew Baum. 2001. "The Invisible Hand of Democracy: Political Control and the Provision of Public Services" *Comparative Political Studies*, vol. 34, no. 6, pp. 587–621.

Lal, Deepak. 1985. *The Poverty of Development Economics.* Cambridge, MA: Harvard University Press.

Lancaster, Carol. 2000. *Transforming Foreign Aid: United States Assistance in the 21st Century.* Washington, DC: Institute for International Economics.

———. 2006. *Foreign Aid: Diplomacy, Development, Domestic Politics.* Chicago: University of Chicago Press.

Landes, David. 1998. *The Wealth and Poverty of Nations: Why Some are So Rich and Some So Poor.* New York: Norton.

Larsson, Tomas. 2001. *The Race to the Top: The Real Story of Globalization.* Washington, DC: Cato Institute.

Ledgerwood, Joanna and Victoria White. 2006. *Transforming Microfinance Institutions: Providing Full Financial Services to the Poor.* Washington, DC: World Bank.

Legrain, Philippe. 2004. *Open World: The Truth About Globalization.* Chicago: Ivan R. Dee.

Lele, Uma. 1975. *The Design of Rural Development: Lessons from Africa.* Baltimore, MD: Johns Hopkins University Press.

———. 2005. *Addressing the Challenges of Globalization: An Independent Evaluation of the World Bank's Approach to Global Problems.* Washington, DC: World Bank.

Levitsky, Steven and Lucan A. Way. 2002. "Elections without Democracy: The Rise of Competitive Authoritarianism" *Journal of Democracy,* vol. 13. no. 2, pp. 51–65.

Levy, Jonah D., ed., 2006. *The State after Statism: New State Activities in the Age of Liberalization.* Cambridge, MA: Harvard University Press.

Lewis, John P. 1988. *Strengthening the Poor: What Have We Learned?* New Brunswick, NJ: Transaction Books.

Lijphart, Arend. 1981. *Conflict and Coexistence in Belgium: The Dynamics of a Culturally Divided Society.* Berkeley: University of California Press.

———. 1984. *Democracies: Patterns of Majoritarian and Consensus Government in Twenty-One Countries.* New Haven, CT.: Yale University Press.

———. 1996. "Puzzle of Indian Democracy" *American Political Science Review,* vol. 90, no. 2, pp. 258–68.

———. 1999. *Patterns of Democracy: Government Forms and Performance in Thirty-Six Countries.* New Haven, CT: Yale University Press.

Lindblom, Charles. 1977. *Politics and Markets: The World's Political Economic Systems.* New York: Basic Books.

Lindert, Peter and Jeffrey Williamson. 2003. "Does Globalization Make the World More Unequal?" in Michael Bordo, Alan M. Taylor, and Jeffrey G. Williamson eds, *Globalization in Historical Perspective.* Chicago: University of Chicago Press, pp. 227–71.

Linz, Juan and Alfred Stepan. 1992. "Political Identities and Electoral Sequences: Spain, the Soviet Union and Yugoslavia" *Daedalus,* vol. 121, no. 2, Spring, pp. 123–39.

———. 1996. *Problems of Democratic Transition and Consolidation: Southern Europe, South America and Post-communist Europe.* Baltimore, MD: Johns Hopkins University Press.

Lipset, Seymour Martin and Jason Lakin. 2004. *The Democratic Century.* Norman, OK: University of Oklahoma Press.

Lipton, Michael. 1977. *Why Poor People Stay Poor: Urban Bias in World Development.* New York: Cambridge University Press.

Lissakers, Karin. 1991. *Banks, Borrowers and the Establishment: A Revisionist Account of the International Debt Crisis.* New York: Basic Books.

Littlefield, Elizabeth and Richard Rosenberg. 2004. "Microfinance and the Poor" *Finance and Development,* vol. 41, no. 2, June, pp. 38–40.

Londregan, John and Keith T. Poole. 1996. "Does High Income Promote Democracy?" *World Politics*, vol. 49, no. 1, January, pp. 1–30.

Lucas, Robert E., Jr. 1988. "On the Mechanics of Economic Development" *Journal of Monetary Economics*, vol. 22, no. 1, pp. 3–42.

Lumsdaine, David Halloran. 1993. *Moral Vision in International Politics: The Foreign Aid Regime, 1949–1989*. Princeton, NJ: Princeton University Press.

McCalla, Alex and John Nash. 2006. *Reforming Agricultural Trade for Developing Countries* (Vol. 1). Washington, DC: World Bank.

McFaul, Michael. 2005. "Transitions from Post-Communism" *Journal of Democracy*, vol. 16, no. 3, July, pp. 5–19.

McGuire, J.W. 2006. "Democracy, Basic Service Utilization and Under-5 Mortality: A Cross-National Study of Developing States" *World Development*, vol. 34, no. 3, pp. 405–25.

McGuirk, Anne. 2002. "The Doha Development Agenda" *Finance and Development*, vol. 39, no. 3, Summer, pp. 4–8.

MacIntyre, Andrew. 2001. "Institutions and Investors: The Politics of the Economic Crisis in Southeast Asia" *International Organization* vol. 55, no. 1, pp. 81–122.

McKinnon, Ronald. 1973. *Money and Capital in Economic Development.* Washington, DC: The Brookings Institution.

McMillan, John. 2002. *Reinventing the Bazaar: A Natural History of Markets.* New York: W.W. Norton.

Maddison, Angus. 2003. *The World Economy: Historical Statistics.* Paris: OECD.

Malloy, James. 1987. "The Politics of Transition in Latin America", in James Malloy and Mitchell Seligson, eds, *Authoritarians and Democrats: Regime Transition in Latin America.* Pittsburgh, PA.: Pittsburgh University Press.

Mander, Jerry and Edward Goldsmith, eds. 1996. *The Case Against the Global Economy.* San Francisco: Sierra Club Books.

Mankiw, N. Gregory, David Romer, and David N. Weil, 1992. "A Contribution to the Empirics of Economic Growth" *Quarterly Journal of Economics*, no. 107, pp. 407–38.

Manor, James. 1999. *The Political Economy of Democratic Decentralization.* Washington, DC: World Bank.

Marshall, T.H. 1964. *Class, Citizenship and Social Development.* New York: Doubleday.

Martin, Will and Alan Winters, eds. 1996. *The Uruguay Round and the Developing Countries.* New York: Cambridge University Press.

Mauro, Paolo, 2004. "The Persistence of Corruption and Slow Economic Growth" *IMF Staff Papers*, vol. 51, no. 1, pp. 1–18.

Mayda, Anna Maria and Dani Rodrik. 2001. *Why are Some People (and Countries) More Protectionist than Others?* NBER Working Paper 8461, September. Cambridge, MA: NBER.

Meier, Gerald and Joseph Stiglitz, eds. 2002. *Frontiers of Development Economics: The Future in Perspective.* New York: Oxford University Press.

Mellor, John. 1976. *The New Economics of Growth: A Strategy for India and the Developing World.* Ithaca, NY: Cornell University Press.

Mishkin, Federic. 2006. *The Next Globalization: How Disadvantaged Nations Can Harness Their Financial Systems to Get Rich.* Princeton: Princeton University Press.

Mittal, Anuradha. 2003. *Cancun: Why It's Good that the Trade Talks Broke Down.* Oakland, CA: Food First, 17 September.

Mkapa, Benjamin W. 2004. "Cancun's False Promise: A View from the South" *Foreign Affairs*, vol. 83, no. 3, May/June, pp. 133–5.

Montero, Alfred and David Samuels, eds. 2004. *Decentralization and Democracy in Latin America*. South Bend: University of Notre Dame Press.

Montinola, Gabriella, Yingyi Qian, and Barry R. Weingast. 1995. "Federalism, Chinese Style: The Political Basis for Economic Success in China." *World Politics*, vol. 48, no. 1, October, pp. 50–81.

Moore, Barrington. 1966. *Social Origins of Dictatorship and Democracy: Lord and Peasant in the Making of the Modern World*. Boston: Beacon Press

Moran, Theodore. 2006. *Harnessing Foreign Direct Investment for Development: Policies for Developed and Developing Countries*. Washington, DC: Center for Global Development.

Mosher, A.T. 1966. *Getting Agriculture Moving: Essentials for Development and Modernization*. New York: Praeger.

Mosley, Paul, Jane Harrigan, and John Toye. 1991. *Aid and Power: The World Bank and Policy-Based Lending*. New York: Routledge.

Mulinge, Munyae and Pempelani Mufane, eds. 2003. *Debt Relief Initiatives and Poverty Alleviation: Lessons from Africa*. Pretoria: Africa Institute of South Africa.

Mundell, Robert. 1968. *International Economics*. New York: Macmillan.

Mundlak, Yair. 2000. *Agriculture and Economic Growth: Theory and Measurement*. Cambridge, MA: Harvard University Press.

Munoz, Heraldo. 1981. *From Dependency to Development: Strategies to Overcome Underdevelopment and Inequality*. Boulder: Westview Press.

Myrdal, Gunnar. 1968. *Asian Drama: An Enquiry into the Poverty of Nations*, 3 vols. New York: Pantheon.

Nafziger, Wayne E. 2005. *Economic Development*, 4th edition. New York: Cambridge University Press.

Narayan, Deepa. 2005. *Measuring Empowerment: Cross-Disciplinary Perspectives*. Washington, DC: World Bank.

Narlikar, Amrita and Rorden Wilkinson. 2004. "Collapse at the WTO: A Cancun Post-Mortem" *Third World Quarterly*, vol. 25, no. 3, pp. 417–30.

Narlikar, Amrita, Rorden Wilkinson, and Diana Tussie. 2004. "The G-20 at the Cancun Ministerial: Developing Countries and their Evolving Coalitions in the WTO" *The World Economy*, vol. 27, no. 7, pp. 947–66.

Naylor, Rosamund and Walter P. Falcon. 2004. "Biotechnology in the Developing World: A Case for Increased Investment in Orphan Crops" *Food Policy*, vol. 29, pp. 15–44.

Nelson, Richard. 2005. *Technology, Institutions and Economic Growth*. Cambridge, MA: Harvard University Press.

Newfarmer, Richard, ed. 2005. *Trade, Doha and Development: A Window into the Issues*. Washington, DC: World Bank.

North, Douglass C. 1990. *Institutions, Institutional Change and Economic Performance*. Cambridge: Cambridge University Press.

——. 1991. "Institutions" *Journal of Economic Perspectives* vol. 5, no. 1, Winter, pp. 97–112.

——. 2005. *Understanding the Process of Economic Change*. Princeton: Princeton University Press.

North, Douglass C. and Richard Thomas. 1973. *The Rise of the Western World: A New Economic History*. Cambridge: Cambridge University Press.

Norton, Roger D. 2004. *Agricultural Development Policy: Concepts and Experiences*. West Sussex, UK: John Wiley,

Oates, Wallace. 1972. *Fiscal Federalism*. New York: Harcourt, Brace and Jovanovich.

Obstfeld, Maurice. 1998. "The Global Capital Market: Benefactor or Menace" *Journal of Economic Perspectives*, vol. 12, no. 4, pp. 9–30, Fall.

Obstfeld, Maurice and Kenneth Rogoff. 1996. *Foundations of International Macroeconomics*. Cambridge, MA: MIT Press.

Obstfeld, Maurice and Alan M. Taylor. 2005. *Global Capital Markets: Integration, Crisis and Growth*. New York: Cambridge University Press.

O'Donnell, Guillermo. 1994. "Delegative Democracy" *Journal of Democracy*, vol. 5, no. 4, January, pp. 55–69.

O'Donnell, Guillermo and Philippe Schmitter. 1973. *Modernization and Bureaucratic Authoritarianism: Studies in South American Politics*. Berkeley: Institute of International Studies.

———. 1986. *Transitions from Authoritarian Rule: Tentative Conclusions*. Baltimore, MD: The Johns Hopkins University Press.

OECD (Organization of Economic Cooperation and Development) OECD-DAC. 2002. *Agricultural Policies in OECD Countries: Monitoring and Evaluation*. Paris: OECD.

———. 2003. *Agricultural Trade and Poverty: Making Policy Analysis Count*. Paris: OECD.

———. 2004. *Final ODA Data for 2003*, 8–9 December. Paris: OECD.

———. 2004b. *Agricultural Policies in OECD Countries: Monitoring and Evaluation*. Paris: OECD.

Ohmae, Kenichi. 1995. *The End of the Nation State*. New York: Free Press.

Olson, Mancur. 1965. *The Logic of Collective Action*. Cambridge, MA: Harvard University Press.

———. 1982. *The Rise and Decline of Nations: Economic Growth, Stagflation and Social Rigidities*. New Haven: Yale University Press.

———. 1993. "Dictatorship, Democracy and Development" *American Political Science Review*, vol. 87, no. 3, pp. 567–75.

———. 1996. "Big Bills Left on the Sidewalk: Why Some Nations are Rich and Others Poor" *Journal of Economic Perspectives*, vol. 10, no. 2, pp. 3–24.

———. 2000. *Power and Prosperity: Outgrowing Communist and Capitalist Dictatorships*. New York: Basic Books.

O'Neill, Kathleen. 2005. *Decentralizing the State: Elections, Parties and Local Power in the Andes*. New York: Cambridge University Press.

Onimode, Bade. 1989. *The IMF, the World Bank and the African Debt: The Social and Political Impact*. London: Zed Press.

Osterhammel, Jurgen and Niels P. Petersson. 2005. *Globalization: A Short History*. Princeton, NJ: Princeton University Press.

Ostrom, Eleanor. 1990. *Governing the Commons: The Evolution of Institutions for Collective Action*. New York: Cambridge University Press.

Ottaway, Marina. 2003. *Democracy Challenged: The Rise of Semi-Authoritarianism*. Washington, DC: Carnegie Endowment for International Peace.

Oxfam. 2003. *Rigged Rules and Double Standards: Trade, Globalization and the Fight Against Poverty*. Oxford, UK: Oxfam.

———. 2005. *A Round for Free: How Rich Countries are Getting a Free Ride on Agricultural Subsidies*. London: Oxfam.

Oxhorn, Philip, Joseph Tulchin, and Andrew Selee, eds. 2004. *Decentralization, Democratic Governance and Civil Society in Comparative Perspective: Africa, Asia and Latin America*. Washington, DC: Woodrow Wilson Center Press.

Paarlberg, Robert. 2000. *The Politics of Precaution: Genetically Modified Crops in Developing Countries*. Baltimore: Johns Hopkins University Press.

Packenham, Robert. 1973. *Liberal America and the Third World: Political Development Ideas in Foreign Aid and Social Science*. Princeton, N.J.: Princeton University Press

——. 1992. *The Dependency Movement*. Cambridge, MA: Harvard University Press.

Panagariya, Arvind. 2003. "Think Again: International Trade" *Foreign Policy*, November/December, pp. 20–28.

——. 2004. "'Miracles and Debacles': In Defense of Trade Openness" *The World Economy*, vol. 28, no. 8, pp. 1148–71.

——. 2005. "Agricultural Liberalization in the Least Developed Countries: Six Fallacies" *The World Economy*, vol. 28, no. 9, pp. 1277–99.

——.2006. "Aid Through Trade: An Efficient Option" in Nancy Birdsall, Milan Vaishnav, and Robert Ayers, eds, *Short of the Goal: US Policy and Poorly Performing States*. Washington, DC: Center for Global Development.

Payne, Anthony. 2006. "Blair, Brown and the Gleneagles Agenda: Making Poverty History, or Confronting the Global Politics of Unequal Development" *International Affairs*, vol. 82, no. 5, pp. 917–35.

Pearce, Andrew. 1980. *Seeds of Plenty, Seeds of Want: Social and Economic Implications of the Green Revolution*. Oxford: Clarendon Press.

Pearson, Lester. 1969. *Partners in Development: Report of the Commission on International Development*. New York: Praeger.

Pei, Minxin. 2006. *China's Trapped Transition: The Limits of Developmental Autocracy*. Cambridge: Harvard University Press.

Pender, John, Frank Place, and Simeon Ehui. 2006. *Strategies for Sustainable Land Management in the East African Highlands*. Washington, DC: International Food Policy Research Institute.

Pereira, Luiz, Carlos Bresser, Jose Maria Maravall, and Adam Przeworski. 1993. *Economic Reforms in New Democracies: A Social-Democratic Approach*. New York: Cambridge University Press.

Pettifor, Ann. 2003. *Real World Economic Outlook: The Legacy of Globalization – Debt and Deflation*. New York: Palgrave Macmillan.

——. 2006. "The Jubilee 2000 Campaign: A Brief Overview" in Chris Jochnick and Fraser Preston, eds, *Sovereign Debt at the Crossroads: Challenges and Proposals for Resolving the Third World Debt Crisis*. New York: Oxford University Press, pp. 297–318.

Pinstrup-Andersen, Per and Ebbe Schioler, 2000. *Seeds of Contention*. Baltimore, MD: Johns Hopkins University Press.

Phillips, Peter W.B. 2003. *Policy, National Regulation and International Standards for GM Foods*, Policy Brief no. 1. Washington, DC: International Food Policy Research Institute, January.

Pogge, Thomas. 2002. *World Poverty and Human Rights*. Cambridge, UK: Polity Press.

Polyani, Karl. 1944. *The Great Transformation: The Political and Economic Origins of Our Time*. Boston: Beacon Press.

Pomfret, Richard. 1992. *Diverse Paths of Economic Development*. New York: Prentice Hall.

Posner, Daniel. 2005. *Institutions and Ethnic Politics in Africa*. New York: Cambridge University Press.

Prasad, Eswar, Kenneth Rogoff, Shang-Jin Wei, and M. Ayhan Kose, 2003. *Effects of Financial Globalization on Developing Countries – Some Empirical Evidence*. IMF Occasional Paper no. 220. Washington, DC: IMF, September.

Prebisch, Raul. 1950. The *Economic Development of Latin America and its Principal Problems*. New York: UN Economic Commission for Latin America.

——. 1959. "Commercial Policy in the Underdeveloped Countries" *American Economic Review*. Vol. 49, May, pp. 251–73.

Preeg, E.H. 1995. *Traders in a Brave New World: The Uruguay Round and the Future of the International Trading System*. Chicago: University of Chicago Press.

Prendergast, Renee. 2005. "The Concept of Freedom and its Relation to Economic Development: A Critical Appreciation of the Work of Amartya Sen" *Cambridge Journal of Economics*, vol. 29, pp. 1145–70.

Prestowitz, Clyde. 2005. *Three Billion New Capitalists: The Great Shift of Wealth and Power to the East*. New York: Basic Books.

Pringle, Peter. 2003. *Food Inc., Mendel to Monsanto – the Promises and Perils of the Biotech Harvest*. New York: Simon and Schuster.

Pritchett, Lant. 1997. "Divergence, Big Time" *Journal of Economic Perspectives*, vol. 11, no. 3, Summer, pp. 3–17.

Prud'homme, Remy. 1995. "The Dangers of Decentralization" *The World Bank Research Observer*, vol. 10, no. 2, August, pp. 201–20.

Przeworski, Adam. 1991. *Democracy and the Market: Political and Economic Reforms in Eastern Europe and Latin America*. New York: Cambridge University Press.

——. 1995. *Sustainable Democracy*. New York: Cambridge University Press.

Przeworski, Adam and Fernando Limongi. 1997. "Modernization: Theories and Facts" *World Politics*, vol. 42, no. 2, April, pp. 155–83.

Przeworski, Adam, Michael E. Alvarez, Jose Antonio Cheibub, and Fernando Limongi. 2000. *Democracy and Development: Political Institutions and Well Being in the World, 1950–1990*. New York: Cambridge University Press.

Przeworski, Adam, Susan C. Stokes, and Bernard Manin. eds. 1999. *Democracy, Accountability and Representation*. New York: Cambridge University Press.

Putman, Robert. 1993. *Making Democracy Work: Civic Traditions in Modern Italy*. Princeton, NJ: Princeton University Press.

——. 2000. *Bowling Alone: The Collapse and Revival of American Community*. New York: Simon and Schuster.

Pye, Lucian and Sidney Verba. 1965. *Political Culture and Political Development*. Princeton: Princeton University Press.

Quah, Danny. 2002. *One Third of the World's Growth and Inequality*. CEPR Discussion Paper no. 3316. Washington, DC: CEPR.

Radelet, Steven. 2003. *Challenging Foreign Aid: A policymaker's Guide to the Millennium Challenge Account* Washington, DC: Center for Global Development.

——. 2004. *Aid Effectiveness and the Millennium Development Goals*. Working Paper no. 39, April. Washington, DC: Center for Global Development.

Rajan, Raghuram and Arvind Subramanian. 2005. *What Undermines Aid's Impact on Growth?* IMF Working Paper WP05/126. Washington, DC: IMF.

——. 2006. *Aid and Growth: What Does the Cross-Country Evidence Really Show?* IMF Working Paper WP/05/127. Washington, DC: IMF.

Rajan, Raghuram and Luigi Zingales. 2003. "The Great Reversals: The Politics of Financial Development in the Twentieth Century" *Journal of Financial Economics*, vol. 69, Issue 1, July, pp. 5–50.

Ravallion, Martin. 1995. "Growth and Poverty: Evidence for Developing Countries in the 1990s" *Economic Letters*, vol. 48, June, pp. 411–17.

——. 1997. "Can High-Inequality Developing Countries Escape Absolute Poverty" *Economic Letters*, 56, September, pp. 51–7.

——. 2001. "Growth, Inequality and Poverty: Looking Beyond Averages" *World Development*, vol. 29, no. 11, pp. 1803–15.

——. 2005. "A Poverty-Inequality Trade Off?" *Journal of Economic Inequality*, vol. 3, pp. 169–81.

Ravallion, Martin and Shaohua Chen. 1997. "What can the Survey Data Tell us about Recent Changes in Distribution and Poverty?" *World Bank Economic Review*, vol. 11, no. 2, pp. 357–82.

——. 2004. "Learning from Success" *Finance and Development*, vol. 41, no. 4, December, pp. 16–19.

Ravallion, Martin and Gaurav Datt. 1996. "How Important to India's Poor is the Sectoral Composition of Economic Growth?" *The World Bank Economic Review*, vol. 10, no. 1, January, pp. 1–26.

——. 2002. "Why has Economic Growth been More Pro-Poor in some States of India than Others?" *Journal of Development Economics*, August, pp. 381–400.

Rawls, John. 1999. *The Law of Peoples; With, the Idea of Public Reason Revisited.* Cambridge, MA: Harvard University Press.

Remmer, Karen. 1990. "Democracy and Economic Crisis: The Latin American Experience" *World Politics*, vol. 42, no. 3, April, pp. 315–35.

Reusse, Eberhard. 2002. *The Ills of Aid: An Analysis of Third World Development Policies.* Chicago: University of Chicago Press.

Rieffel, Lex. 2003. *Restructuring Sovereign Debt: The Case for Ad-Hoc Machinery.* Washington, DC: Brookings Institution Press.

Risse, Mathias. 2005. "How Does the Global Order Harm the Poor?" *Philosophy and Public Affairs*, vol. 33, no. 4, pp. 349–76.

Roberts, Kenneth and Moises Arce. 1998. "Neoliberalism and Lower-class Voting Behavior in Peru" *Comparative Political Studies*, vol. 31, no. 2, pp. 217–46.

Rodden, Jonathan. 2002. "The Dilemma of Fiscal Federalism: Grants and Fiscal Performance around the World" *American Journal of Political Science*, vol. 46, no. 3, pp. 670–87.

Rodrik, Dani, ed. 1997. *Has Globalization Gone Too Far?* Washington, DC: Institute for International Economics.

——. 1999. *The New Global Economy and Developing Countries: Making Openness Work.* Washington, DC: Overseas Development Council.

——. 2000. *Institutions for High-Quality Growth: What They Are and How to Acquire Them.* NBER Working Paper no. 7540, available at www.nber.org/papers/w7540.

——. 2003. *In Search of Prosperity: Analytic Narratives on Economic Growth.* Princeton, NJ: Princeton University Press.

Rodrik, Dani, Arvind Subramanian and Francesco Trebbi, 2002. *Institutions Rule: The Primacy of Institutions over Geography and Integration in Economic Development.* NBER Working Paper no. 9305, available at www.nber.org/papers/w9305.

——. 2004. "Institutions Rule: The Primary of Institutions over Geography and Integration in Economic Development" *Journal of Economic Growth*, vol. 9, pp. 131–65.

Rogoff, Kenneth. 2003. "Unlocking Growth in Africa" *Finance and Development*, June, pp. 56–7.

Roland, G. 2000. *Transitions and Economics: Politics, Markets and Firms.* Cambridge, MA: MIT Press.

Roll, Richard and John R. Talbott. 2003. "Political Freedom, Economic Liberty and Prosperity" *Journal of Democracy*, vol. 14, no. 3, July, pp. 75–89.

Romer, Paul M. 1986. "Increasing Returns and Long-Run Growth" *Journal of Political Economy*, no. 94, pp. 1002–37.

Roodman, David. 2006. "Creditor Initiatives in the 1980s and 1990s" in Chris Jochnick and Fraser Preston, eds, *Sovereign Debt at the Crossroads: Challenges and Proposals for Resolving the Third World Debt Crisis*. New York: Oxford University Press, pp. 13–34.

Root, Hilton. 2005. *Capital and Collusion: The Political Logic of Global Economic Development*. Princeton, NJ: Princeton University Press.

Ros, Jamie. 2000. *Development Theory and the Economics of Growth*. Ann Arbor: University of Michigan Press.

Rosecrance, Richard. 1999. *The Rise of the Virtual State*. New York: Basic Books.

Rosen, George. 1985. *Western Economists and Eastern Societies: Agents of Change in South Asia, 1950–1970*. Baltimore, MD: Johns Hopkins University Press.

Rosenberg, Nathan and L.E. Birdzell. 1986. *How the West Grew Rich: The Economic Transformation of the Industrial World*. New York: Basic Books.

Rosenstein-Rodan. Paul. 1961. "International Aid for Underdeveloped Countries" *Review of Economics and Statistics*, vol. 42, no. 2, pp. 107–38.

Rostow, Walt. 1960. *The Stages of Economic Growth: A Noncommunist Manifesto*. London: Cambridge University Press (3rd edition published in 1990).

Rotberg, Robert, ed. 2003. *When States Fail: Causes and Consequences*. Princeton, NJ: Princeton University Press.

——. 2004. "Strengthening Governance" *The Washington Quarterly*, vol. 28, no. 1, Winter, pp. 71–81.

Rubin, Robert. 1998. "Strengthening the Architecture of the International Financial System" public statement delivered at the Brookings Institution, 14 April. Also published in *Treasury News* (14 April 1998).

Runge, Ford C., Benjamin Senauer, Philip G. Pardey, and Mark W. Rosegrant. 2003. *Ending Hunger in Our Lifetime*. Baltimore, MD: Johns Hopkins University Press.

Sachs, Jeffrey. 1986. "Managing the LDC Debt Crisis" *Brookings Papers on Economic Activity*, no. 2, pp. 397–431.

——. 1989. "The Debt Overhang of Developing Countries" in Guillermo Calvo, Ronald Findlay, Pentti Kouri and Jorge Braga de Macedo, eds, *Debt Stabilization and Development: Essays in Memory of Carlos Diaz-Alejandro*. Oxford: Blackwell, pp. 80–102.

——. 2001. "Natural Resources and Economic Development: The Curse of Natural Resources" *European Economic Review*, vol. 45, pp. 827–38.

——. 2002. "Resolving the Debt-Crisis of Low-Income Countries" *Brookings Papers on Economic Activity*, Spring, pp. 257–87.

——. 2003. "Spring Broke: Trade Negotiators Gone Wild" *The New Republic*, 29 September, pp. 12–13.

——. 2005. *The End of Poverty: Economic Possibilities of Our Time*. New York: Penguin.

——. 2005a. "The Development Challenge" *Foreign Affairs*, vol. 84, no. 2, March/April, pp. 78–90.

Sachs, Jeffrey and Andrew Warner. 1995. "Economic Reform and the Process of Global Integration" *Brookings Papers on Economic Activity*, no. 1, pp. 1–118.

——. 1997. "Sources of Slow Growth in African Economies" *Journal of African Economies*, vol. 6, pp. 335–76.

Sachs, Jeffrey, John W. McArthur, Guido Schmidt-Traub, Margaret Kruk, Chandrika Bahadur, Michael Faye, and Gordon McCord. 2004. "Ending Africa's Poverty Trap" *Brookings Papers on Economic Activity*, no. 1, pp. 117–240.

Sainath, P. 1996. *Everybody Loves a Good Drought: Stories from India's Poorest Districts.* New Delhi: Penguin.

Sala-i-Martin, Xavier. 2002. *The World Distribution of Income (Estimated from Individual Country Distribution).* NBER Working Paper no. 8933. Cambridge, MA: National Bureau of Economic Research.

Schedler, Andreas. 2001. "Measuring Democratic Consolidation" *Studies in Comparative International Development,* vol. 36, no. 1, pp. 56–76.

Scholte, Jan Aart. 2000. *Globalization: A Critical Introduction.* New York: St Martin's Press.

Schott, Jeffrey J. ed. 2000. *The WTO after Seattle.* Washington, DC: Institute for International Economics.

———. 2003. *Reflections on the Doha Ministerial.* Washington, DC: Institute for International Economics.

———. 2004. *Reviving the Doha Round.* Washington, DC: Institute for International Economics.

———. 2006. *Completing the Doha Round,* Policy Briefs in International Economics no. PBO6–7, October. Washington, DC: Institute for International Economics.

Schultz, Theodore W. 1964. *Transforming Traditional Agriculture.* New Haven, CT: Yale University Press.

Schumpeter, Joseph.1950. *Capitalism, Socialism and Democracy.* 3rd edition. New York: Harper and Row.

Scoones, Ian. 2006. *Science, Agriculture and the Politics of Policy: The Case of Biotechnology in India.* New Delhi: Orient Longman.

Scott, James. 1998. *Seeing like a State: How Certain Schemes to Improve the Human Condition have Failed.* New Haven, CT: Yale University Press.

Sen, Amartya. 1981. "Public Action and the Quality of Life in Developing Countries" *Oxford Bulletin of Economics and Statistics,* no. 43, pp. 367–74.

———. 1983. "Development: Which Way Now?" *Economic Journal,* vol. 93, December, pp. 745–62.

———. 1999. *Development as Freedom.* New York: Oxford University Press.

———. 2001. "Democracy as a Universal Value" in Larry Diamond and Marc F. Plattner, eds, *The Global Divergence of Democracies.* Baltimore, MD: Johns Hopkins University Press.

Sharma, Shalendra, D. 1999. *Development and Democracy in India.* Boulder: Lynne Rienner.

———. 2003. *The Asian Financial Crisis: Crisis, Reform and Recovery.* Manchester, UK: Manchester University Press.

———. 2003a. "Is India's Poverty Falling? The Debate Surrounding the 55th NSS Round" *Indian Journal of Social Development,* vol. 3, no. 1, June, pp. 33–43.

———. 2004. "The Promise of Monterrey: Meeting the Millennium Development Goals" *World Policy Journal,* vol. XXI, no. 3, Fall, pp. 51–66.

Shiva, Vandana. 1991. *The Violence of the Green Revolution: Third World Agriculture, Ecology and Politics.* London: Zed Press.

Shleifer, Andrei and Robert W. Vishny. 1993. "Corruption" *Quarterly Journal of Economics,* vol. 108, no. 3, August, pp. 599–618.

Shue, Vivienne. 1988. *The Reach of the State: Sketches of the Chinese Body Politic.* Stanford, CA: Stanford University Press.

Singer, Peter. 2002. *One World: The Ethics of Globalization.* New Haven: Yale University Press.

Skocpol. Theda. 1979. *States and Social Revolutions: A Comparative Analysis of France, Russia and China*. New York: Cambridge University Press.

——. 1995. *Social Policy in the United States*. Princeton, NJ: Princeton University Press.

Slaughter, Anne-Marie. 2004. *A New World Order*. Princeton, NJ: Princeton University Press.

Solimano, Andres. Eduardo Aninat, and Nancy Birdsall, eds. 2000. *Distributive Justice and Economic Development: The Case of Chile and Developing Countries*. Ann Arbor: University of Michigan Press.

Solnick, Steve. 2002. "Federalism and State-Building" in Andrew Reynolds, ed., *The Architecture of Democracy: Constitutional Design, Conflict Management and Democracy*. New York: Oxford University Press.

Solow, Robert M. 1956. "A Contribution to the Theory of Economic Growth" *Quarterly Journal of Economics*, no. 70, pp. 65–94.

——. 1957. "Technical Change and the Aggregate Production Function" *Review of Economics and Statistics*, vol. 39, pp. 312–20.

Soros, George. 1998. *The Crisis of Global Capitalism*. New York: Public Affairs Press.

Stasavage, D. 2005. "Democracy and Education Spending in Africa" *American Journal of Political Science*, vol. 49, no. 3, pp. 343–58.

Stein, Ernesto. Mariano Tommasi, Koldo Echebarria, Eduardo Lora and Mark Payne. 2006. *The Politics of Policies: Economic and Social Progress in Latin America, 2006 Report*. Cambridge, MA: Harvard University Press.

Stern, Nicholas. 2002. *A Strategy for Development*. Washington, DC: World Bank.

——. 2006. *The Stern Review on the Economics of Climate Change*, online at www.hm-treasury.gov.uk/Independent_Reviews/stern_review_economics_climate_change/stern-review_index.cfm.

Stern, Nicholas. Jean-Jacques Dethier, and F. Halsey Rogers. 2005. *Growth and Empowerment: Making Development Happen*. Cambridge, MA: MIT Press.

Stewart, Frances. 1985. *Basic Needs in Developing Countries*. Baltimore, MD: Johns Hopkins University Press.

Stiglitz, Joseph. 2002. *Globalization and Its Discontents*. New York: W.W. Norton.

——. 2002a "Overseas Aid is Money Well Spent" *Financial Times*, 14 April.

Stiglitz, Joseph and Andrew Charlton. 2006. *Fair Trade for All: How Trade Can Promote Development*. New York: Oxford University Press.

Stotsky, Janet. 2006. *Gender Budgeting*. IMF Working Paper no. 06/232, available at www.imf.org.

Strange, Susan. 1996. *The Retreat of the State: The Diffusion of Power in the World Economy*. New York: Cambridge University Press.

Streeten, Paul. 1986. *First Things First: Meeting Basic Human Needs*. Baltimore, MD: Johns Hopkins University Press.

Subramanian, Arvind. 2003. *Financing of Losses from Preference Erosion*, WT/TF/COH/14. Geneva: World Trade Organization.

Summers, Robert and Alan Heston. 1991. "The Penn World Table (Mark 5): An Expanded Set of International Comparisons, 1950–1988" *Quarterly Journal of Economics*, vol. 106, pp. 327–68.

Sundberg, Mark and Alan Gelb. 2006. "Making Aid Work" *Finance and Development*, vol. 43, no. 4, December, pp. 14–17.

Sutherland, Peter. 2005. "Correcting Misperceptions" *Foreign Affairs*, December; WTO Special Electronic Edition, available at www.foreignaffairs.org.

Svensson, Jakob. 1999. "Aid, Growth and Democracy" *Economics and Politics*, vol. 11, no. 3, September, pp. 275–97.

——. 2000. "Foreign Aid and Rent-Seeking" *Journal of International Economics*, vol. 51, no. 2, pp. 437–67.

Tanzi, Vito. 2000. "On Fiscal Federalism: Issues to Worry About," paper presented at the IMF Conference on Fiscal Decentralization, 20 November, Washington, DC: IMF.

Tarasofsky, Richard and Alice Palmer. 2006. "The WTO in Crisis: Lessons Learned from the Doha Negotiations on the Environment" *International Affairs*, vol. 82, no. 5, pp. 899–915.

Tarp, Finn, ed. 2000. *Foreign Aid and Development: Lessons Learnt and Directions for the Future*. London: Routledge.

Tendler, Judith. 1975. *Inside Foreign Aid*. Baltimore, MD: Johns Hopkins University Press.

——. 1997. *Good Government in the Tropics*. Baltimore, MD: Johns Hopkins University Press.

Ter-Minassian, Teresa, ed. 1997. *Fiscal Federalism in Theory and Practice: A Collection of Essays*. Washington, DC: International Monetary Fund.

Tignor, Robert. 2005. *W. Arthur Lewis and the Birth of Development Economics*. Princeton, NJ: Princeton University Press.

Tilly, Charles. 1975. *The Formation of Nation States in Western Europe*. Princeton, NJ: Princeton University Press.

——. 2006. *Democracy*. New York: Cambridge University Press.

Timmer, Peter C. 1997. *How Well Do the Poor Connect to the Growth Process?* CAER 11 Discussion Paper No. 17. Cambridge, MA: Harvard Institute for International Development, December.

Tisch, Sarah and Michael Wallace. 1994. *Dilemmas of Development Assistance: The What, Why and Who of Foreign Aid*. Boulder, CO: Westview Press.

de Tocqueville, Alexis. 1966. *Democracy in America*. edited by J.P. Mayer and Max Lerner. New York: Harper and Row.

Tokarick, Stephen. 2003. *Measuring the Impact of Distortions in Agricultural Trade in Partial and General Equilibrium*. IMF Working Paper no. 03/110. Washington, DC: IMF.

—— 2006. *Trade Issues in the Doha Round: Dispelling Some Misconceptions*. IMF Policy Discussion Paper PDP/06/04, August. Washington, DC: IMF.

Tornell, Aaron, Frank Westermann, and Lorenza Martinez. 2004. *The Positive Link between Financial Liberalization Growth and Crises*. NBER Working Paper no. 10293. Cambridge, MA: National Bureau of Economic Research.

Torstensson, Johan. 1994. "Property Rights and Economic Growth: An Empirical Study" *Kyklos*, vol. 47, no. 2, pp. 231–47.

Transparency International. 2004. *Global Corruption Report 2004*. London: Pluto Press.

Tsebelis, George. 1990. "Elite Interaction and Constitution Building in Consociational Societies" *Journal of Theoretical Politics*, vol. 2, no. 1, pp. 5–29.

UN Millennium Project. 2005. *Investing in Development: A Practical Plan to Achieve the Millennium Development Goals*, Report to the UN Secretary-General (the Sachs Report). New York: United Nations.

UNDP (United Nations Development Program). 2003. *Human Development Report 2003*. New York: Oxford University Press.

—— 2005. *Human Development Report 2005*. New York: Oxford University Press.

USAID (United States Agency for International Development). 1991. *Democracy and Governance.* Washington, DC: USAID.

Van de Walle, Nicolas. 2001. *African Economies and the Politics of Permanent Crisis, 1979–1999.* New York: Cambridge University Press.

Van Wijnbergen, Sweder. 1984. "The Dutch Disease: A Disease after All" *Economic Journal,* vol. 94, March, pp. 41–55.

Victor, David G. and C. Ford Runge. 2002. "Farming the Genetic Frontier" *Foreign Affairs,* vol. 81, no. 3, May/June, pp. 107–21.

Vreeland, James Raymond. 2003. *The IMF and Economic Development.* New York: Cambridge University Press.

Wade, Robert. 1987. *Village Republics: Economic Conditions for Collective Action in South India.* New York: Cambridge University Press.

—— 1990. *Governing the Market: Economic Theory and the Role of Government in East Asian Industrialization.* Princeton, NJ: Princeton University Press.

Wallach, Lori. 2000. *WTO: 5 Years of Reason to Resist Corporate Globalization.* New York: Seven Stories Press.

——. 2004. *Whose Trade Organization?* New York: New Press.

Wallach, Lori and Michelle Sforza. 1999. *Whose Trade Organization? Corporate Globalization and the Erosion of Democracy.* Washington, DC: Public Citizen.

Watkins, Kevin. 2002. *Cultivating Poverty: The Impact of US Cotton Subsidies on Africa.* Oxfam Briefing Paper no. 30. London: Oxfam.

——. 2003. "Farm Fallacies that Hurt the Poor" *Development Outreach,* July, Washington, DC: World Bank, pp. 1–6.

Weingast, Barry. 1995. "The Economic Role of Political Institutions: Market-Preserving Federalism and Economic Development" *Journal of Law, Economics and Organization,* vol. 11, no. 1, pp. 1–31.

Weiss, John and Heather Montgomery. 2005. "Great Expectations: Microfinance and Poverty Reduction in Asia and Latin America" *Oxford Development Studies,* vol. 33, nos. 3 and 4, September–December, pp. 391–416.

Weiss, Linda, 1998. *The Myth of the Powerless State.* Ithaca, NY: Cornell University Press.

——. ed. 2003. *States in the Global Economy: Bringing Democratic Institutions Back In.* New York: Cambridge University Press.

Weiss, Thomas, Tatiana Carayannis, Louis Emmerij, and Richard Jolly, eds. 2005. *UN Voices: The Struggle for Development and Social Justice.* Bloomington: Indiana University Press.

Weyland, Kurt. 2002. *The Politics of Market Reform in Fragile Democracies: Argentina, Brazil, Peru and Venezuela.* Princeton: Princeton University Press.

——. 2004. "Neoliberalism and Democracy in Latin America: A Mixed Record" *Latin American Politics and Society,* vol. 39, no. 3, pp. 143–49.

Wibbels, Erik. 2004. "Decentralization, Democracy and Market Reform." in Alfred P. Montero and David J. Samuels, eds. *Decentralization and Democracy in Latin America.* Notre Dame, IN: University of Notre Dame Press, pp. 203–34.

Williamson, John. 1993. "Democracy and the 'Washington Consensus'" *World Development,* vol. 21, no. 8, pp. 1329–36.

——. 1994. *The Political Economy of Policy Reform.* Washington, DC: Institute of International Economics.

——. 2005. *Curbing the Boom–Bust Cycle: Stabilizing Capital Flows to Emerging Markets.* Washington, DC: Institute of International Economics.

Williamson, Oliver. 1985. *The Economic Institutions of Capitalism: Firms, Markets, Relational Contracting.* New York: Cambridge University Press.

Winham, Gilbert R. 1986. *International Trade and the Tokyo Round Negotiations.* Princeton, NJ: Princeton University Press.

Winters, Alan. 2004. "Trade Liberalization and Economic Performance: An Overview" *Economic Journal*, vol. 114, February, pp. 4–21.

Winters, Alan and Thomas Hertel, eds. 2005. *Poverty and the WTO: Impacts of the Doha Development Agenda.* London: Palgrave Macmillan.

Winters, Alan, Neil McCulloch and Andrew Mack. 2004. "Trade Liberalization and Poverty: The Evidence so Far" *Journal of Economic Literature*, vol. XLII, March, pp. 72–115.

Winters, Jeffrey. 2002. "Criminal Debt" in Jonathan Pincus and Jeffrey Winters, eds, *Reinventing the World Bank*, Ithaca, NY: Cornell University Press.

Wolf, Martin. 2005. *Why Globalization Works.* New Haven, CT: Yale University Press.

Wolfensohn, James. 2005. *Voice of the World's Poor: Selected Speeches and Writings of World Bank President James D. Wolfensohn, 1995–2005.* Washington, DC: World Bank.

Wood, Robert. 1986. *From Marshall Plan to Debt Crisis: Foreign Aid and Development Choices in the World Economy.* Berkeley: University of California Press.

World Bank. 1990–99. *Global Commodity Markets.* Washington, DC: World Bank available at www.worldbank.org/prospects/gcmonline/index.htm and www.worldbank.org/prospects/gcmonline/index.htmn

——. 1998. *Assessing Aid: What Works, What Doesn't, and Why.* New York: Oxford University Press.

——. 2000. *Reforming Public Institutions and Strengthening Governance*, Washington, DC: World Bank.

——. 2001. *Finance for Growth: Policy Choices in a Volatile World.* Washington, DC: World Bank.

——. 2002. *Globalization, Growth and Poverty: Building an Inclusive World Economy.* New York: Oxford University Press.

——. 2002a. *Global Development Finance 2002.* Washington, DC: World Bank.

——. 2002b. *World Development Report 2002: Building Institutions for Markets.* New York: Oxford University Press.

——. 2002c. *A Case for Aid: Building a Consensus for Development Assistance.* Washington, DC: World Bank.

——. 2003. *Global Economic Prospects and the Developing Countries.* Washington, DC: World Bank.

——. 2003a. *Sustainable Development in a Dynamic World: Transforming Institutions, Growth and Quality of Life.* New York: Oxford University Press.

——. 2003b. "Market Access: Agricultural Policy Reform and Developing Countries", *Trade Notes*, no. 6, 10 September.

——. 2003c. *World Development Report 2004: Making Services Work for Poor People.* New York: Oxford University Press.

——. 2003d. *Global Economic Prospects: Realizing the Development Promise of the Doha Agenda 2004.* Washington, DC: World Bank.

——. 2004. *Global Monitoring Report 2004: Policies and Actions for Achieving the Millennium Development Goals (MDGs) and Related Outcomes.* Background Paper, 16 April. Washington, DC: World Bank.

——. 2004a. *Partnerships in Development: Progress in the Fight Against Poverty.* Washington, DC: World Bank.

——. 2004b. *Global Development Finance 2004.* Washington, DC: World Bank.

——. 2004c. *Global Economic Prospects 2004: Realizing the Development Promise of the Doha Agenda.* Washington, DC: World Bank.

——. 2004d. *World Development Report 2005: A Better Investment Climate for Everyone.* New York: Oxford University Press.

——. 2004e. *Directions in Development: Agriculture and Poverty Reduction.* Washington, DC: World Bank.

——. 2005. *Global Monitoring Report 2005: Millennium Development Goals: From Consensus to Momentum.* Washington, DC: World Bank.

——. 2005a. *Meeting the Challenge of Africa's Development: A World Bank Group Action Plan, Africa Region.* Washington, DC: World Bank.

——. 2005b. *Doing Business in 2005: Removing Obstacles to Growth.* New York: Oxford University Press.

——. 2005c. *Building Effective States, Forging Engaged Societies.* Report of the World Bank Task Force on Capacity Development in Africa, September, Washington, DC: World Bank.

——. 2006. *World Development Report: 2006.* New York: Oxford University Press.

——. 2006a. *Global Monitoring Report 2005: Strengthening Mutual Accountability – Aid, Trade and Governance.* Washington, DC: World Bank.

WTO (World Trade Organization). 2004. *The Future of the WTO: Addressing the Institutional Challenges in the New Millennium*, Report by the Consultative Board to the Director-General Supachai Panitchpakdi, Geneva: World Trade Organization.

Yergin, Daniel and Joseph Stanislaw. *The Commanding Heights: The Battle Between Government and the Marketplace that is Remaking the Modern World.* New York: Simon and Schuster.

Young, Alwyn. 1995. "The Tyranny of Numbers: Confronting the Statistical Realities of the East Asian Growth Experience" *Quarterly Journal of Economics*, vol. 110, pp. 641–80.

Yunus, Muhammad. 1999. *Banker to the Poor: Micro-Lending and the Battle Against World Poverty.* New York: Public Affairs.

Zakaria, Fareed. 2003. *The Future of Freedom: Illiberal Democracy at Home and Abroad.* New York: W.W. Norton.

——. 2004. "Islam, Democracy and Constitutional Liberalism" *Political Science Quarterly*, vol. 119, no. 1, Spring, pp. 1–20.

Index

*Globalization, Growth and Poverty:
Building an Inclusive World Economy*
19
GM foods 65–66
goals (MDGs) *see* MDGs (Millennium
Development Goals)
governance, good: characteristics of 35; and
decentralization 48–53; and democracy
38–48; and economic performance 25–26;
and foreign aid 112–114; and institutions
37–38; report recommendations 35–37;
and studies 34–35
Grameen Bank 28
grants 117–118, 133
green fertilizers 59
green revolution 56 *see also*
"second-generation green revolution"
GSP (Generalized System of Preferences)
see Generalized System of Preferences
(GSP)
Gulati, Ashok 91

Halperin *et al.* 40
Hanson, Gordon 20
Hathaway, D. 85
health care 13–14, 112, 129
health interventions 109
Heavily Indebted Poor Countries (HIPC)
Initiative *see* HIPC Initiative
Henry, Peter Blair 121–122, 139
Hertz, Noreena 133
Hewson, Paul (Bono) 107, 119, 136
high-income countries 144n6
HIPC Initiative 120, 121, 122–134
HIV/AIDS 6, 77, 106, 115, 130
Hong Kong: Ministerial Conference
(WTO) 95–98, 100–101
Hufbauer, Gary Clyde 96, 97
human capital: investment in 12–14; and
social services 27
Human Development Report 2003 35
Huntington, Samuel 51

IDA (Independent Development Agency)
114, 120
IFF (International Finance Facility) *see*
International Finance Facility (IFF)
"illiberal" democracies 42–43
IMF (International Monetary Fund) 7, 30
IMF–World Bank Financial Sector
Assessment Program 93
Import-Substitution Industrialization (ISI)
see ISI (Import-Substitution
Industrialization)

income distribution 68
Independent Development Agency (IDA)
see IDA (Independent Development
Agency)
India: agricultural liberalization 100;
biotechnology 68; debts 52; and
democracy 43; Doha Round 73, 75, 98;
economic growth and poverty reduction
11–12, 20, 56–57; education 13;
foodgrain output 61; and global markets
19; green revolution 67–68;
infrastructure 59; intellectual property
rights 69–70; MDGs 140; poverty 26
Indonesia 20, 29, 44, 45, 136
inequality 26
infrastructure, rural 57–59
Ingco, M. 85
institutions 24–25, 30, 37–38, 43–44
intellectual property rights 69–70
International Conference on Financing for
Development (Monterrey 2002) 7, 102,
140
International Finance Facility (IFF) 137,
139
International Monetary Fund (IMF) *see*
IMF (International Monetary Fund)
international trade 14–15, 17–19
interventionism 26–28
investment: in agriculture 57–61; in human
capital 12–14 *see also* FDI (Foreign
Direct Investment)
irrigation 59–60
ISI (Import-Substitution Industrialization)
57

Jackson, Robert 45
Japan: agricultural subsidies 31, 73, 78, 79,
82, 84–85; aid 102; Biosafety Protocol
70; Doha Round 75; IFF 137;
"Singapore issues" 76, 80; tariffs 86
Jensen, Michael 89
Jubilee 2000 petition 119
Jubilee Research 130–131, 136
"July Framework Agreement" 95, 97–98

Kanbur, Ravi 26
Kay, John 17
Keohane, Robert 30
"Keynesian consensus" 2
Kohli, Atul 39
Kraay, Aart 12, 18
Krueger, Anne 19
Krugman, Paul 23, 121
Kurtz, Marcus 41

For Product Safety Concerns and Information please contact our EU
representative GPSR@taylorandfrancis.com
Taylor & Francis Verlag GmbH, Kaufingerstraße 24, 80331 München, Germany

www.ingramcontent.com/pod-product-compliance
Ingram Content Group UK Ltd.
Pitfield, Milton Keynes, MK11 3LW, UK
UKHW021612240425
457818UK00018B/525